PROMINENT SISTERS

PROMINENT SISTERS

*Mary Lamb, Dorothy Wordsworth,
and Sarah Disraeli*

Michael Polowetzky

 **Westport, Connecticut**
London

Library of Congress Cataloging-in-Publication Data

Polowetzky, Michael.
    Prominent sisters : Mary Lamb, Dorothy Wordsworth, and Sarah
Disraeli / Michael Polowetzky.
        p.   cm.
    Includes bibliographical references and index.
    ISBN 0–275–95716–0 (alk. paper)
    1. Women authors, English—19th century—Biography.   2. English
literature—19th century—History and criticism.   3. Women and
literature—Great Britain—History—19th century.   4. Authors,
English—19th century—Family relationships.   5. Authorship—
Collaboration—History—19th century.   6. Brothers and sisters—
Great Britain—Biography.   7. Lamb, Mary, 1764–1847—Biography.
8. Wordsworth, Dorothy, 1771–1855—Biography.   9. Disraeli, Sarah,
1802–1859—Biography.   10. Influence (Literary, artistic, etc.)
11. Women—Great Britain—Biography.   I. Title.
PR119.P65   1996
820.9′9287′09034—dc20   96–21316
[B]

British Library Cataloguing in Publication Data is available.

Library of Congress Catalog Card Number: 96–21316
ISBN: 0–275–95716–0

First published in 1996

Praeger Publishers, 88 Post Road West, Westport, CT 06881
An imprint of Greenwood Publishing Group, Inc.

Printed in the United States of America

The paper used in this book complies with the
Permanent Paper Standard issued by the National
Information Standards Organization (Z39.48–1984).

10 9 8 7 6 5 4 3 2

To my mother
Karrie Polowetzky

Contents

Preface

In *A Room of One's Own*, Virginia Woolf recounts the life of Shakespeare's sister, a woman who, though possessing considerable talents of her own, was doomed because of the cultural prejudices of her time to die unknown, "buried at some cross-roads where the omnibus now stops outside Elephant and Castle."[1] Shakespeare, of course, had no sister; Woolf's tale was an allegory contained in a speech she delivered in 1928 to the young, aspiring female students of Cambridge University—that mighty symbol of male dominance that only in recent decades had consented to open its doors to women. Yet like so many fictional characters, the Bard's forgotten sister has counterparts in history, women of great intelligence and ability who frequently go underappreciated today because of the wider attention given to their more famous brothers. Three such figures lived during the nineteenth century, within fifty years of Woolf's birth in 1882, and were surely known to her. Although not as tragic as the tale of Shakespeare's legendary sister, their true stories are of considerable interest, not only in themselves, but also in the added dimension they bring to the brothers' careers and in the additional historical information they contribute to contemporary British culture as a whole.

The first of these three women is Mary Lamb, sister of Charles Lamb, the famous theater critic, letter writer, essayist, and a friend or associate of nearly all the major authors and poets of his generation. Charles Lamb's correspondence might easily be regarded as a chronicle of early nineteenth-century British Romanticism. Although historians have long recognized that his sister played a prominent role in her brother's life—as hostess of his celebrated Wednesday soirées, companion, and inspiration for several of his best-known works—they generally do not consider her as an important historical figure in her own right. This book, however, will demonstrate that far from being simply a passive observer of others' deeds, Mary Lamb was in fact an active, influential, and widely respected member of the literary community of her time.

The second woman whose life this book examines is Dorothy Wordsworth, sister of the great poet William Wordsworth. Unlike Mary Lamb's, her name is well known today. Her diary, the *Grasmere Journal* provides twentieth century readers with one of the finest and most intimate portrayals of the leaders of the Romantic period. Immortalized by her brother in such poems as *Tintern Abbey* and *The Preludes*, Dorothy Wordsworth has long been revered as one of this artistic and intellectual movement's most compelling emblems. Yet despite this renown, certain prominent aspects of her personality are still generally overlooked. As the following chapters will show, Dorothy Wordsworth was more than a manifestation of noble principles. She was also a perceptive social commentator and a pioneer in the field that would one day become known as sociology.

The final person discussed is Sarah Disraeli, sister of Benjamin Disraeli, prime minister, novelist, proto-Zionist, and founder of the modern British Conservative Party. Of the three women in this book, it is she whose fate comes closest to that of the character in Woolf's work. Both Mary Lamb and Dorothy Wordsworth were able to gain the recognition and respect of many of their peers, but the difficult circumstances of Sarah Disraeli's life forced her to lead a much more secluded existence. Her gifts known only to a small circle of intimates, she went largely ignored by her contemporaries and even today is usually remembered only as a shadowy figure. A closer examination, however, will prove that her life is far more interesting and historically important than traditionally supposed.

As does Shakespeare's fictional sister, the real Mary Lamb, Dorothy Wordsworth, and Sarah Disraeli possess a historic significance reaching beyond their own unique experiences. Through their pains and joys, failures and successes, these three exceptional individuals offer a vivid illustration of the conflict British women had to wage for personal and intellectual fulfillment during what historians have traditionally portrayed as the nation's most prosperous and glorious age.

The reader should be aware of the choices the author has made in regard to the spelling and grammar of quotations. Standardized rules of spelling and grammar were only beginning to gain popular acceptance during the period encompassed in this book. Many writers continued to employ their own styles well into the nineteenth century. Therefore all quotations appear exactly in the fashion they were originally constructed and have not been altered for today's audience.

The reader should also appreciate the value of currency transactions mentioned in these accounts. The British pound sterling during the late eighteenth and early nineteenth centuries was equivalent to between seven and eight United States dollars. However, during a period when an average farm laborer might expect to earn sixpence a week, a city worker, six shillings, and an annual salary of one-hundred-and-fifty pounds was considered solidly middle class, the currency's actual buying power was many times greater than today.

NOTE

1. Virginia Woolf, *A Room of One's Own*, London: Hogarth Press, 1928, 67.

Acknowledgments

I would like to thank the following for their assistance in writing this book: the trustees of the E. V. Lucas estate for allowing me to quote from the late scholar's great collection *The Complete Letters of Charles and Mary Lamb* (Methuen: 1935); Oxford University Press for permission to make use of extracts from *The Letters of William and Dorothy Wordsworth*, edited by Ernest de Selincourt (Oxford: 1967-88); and Toronto University Press for enabling me to borrow passages from their ongoing project, *The Disraeli Letters* (Toronto: 1982-92).

Part One

MARY LAMB

Chapter One

Brother and Sister

Wednesday evenings were always important to the members of London's literary community during the early decades of the nineteenth century. For it was at this time that the famous essayist and drama critic Charles Lamb invited many of them to his home to dine and to discuss the significant events of the day. Among his regular guests, first in the Inns of Court and then later at Covent Garden, were the poets William Wordsworth, Samuel Taylor Coleridge, and Percy Bysshe Shelley; the future poet laureate and historian Robert Southey; the journalists Leigh Hunt and Thomas De Quincey; and the publisher John Murray, the literary executor of the exiled Byron. At these gatherings, a visitor once remarked, one "might find those who had thought most deeply, felt most keenly, and were destined to produce the most lasting influences on the literature and manners of the age."[1] These evenings brought Lamb great renown. But he was always quick to remind his admirers that their shows of respect must go equally to his sister, Mary, for there were few aspects of his life he did not share with her.

Mary Anne Lamb was born on 3 December 1763 at No. 2 Crown Office Row, London, in the heart of that complex of legal chambers, research libraries, lecture halls, and residential flats known as the Temple.[2] It was in and around this area of the city that she and her younger brother were to spend much of their lives. Forever surrounded by vivid reminders of their nation's history and cultural accomplishments, it is perhaps not surprising they dedicated their lives to the disciplines they chose. Like nearby Gray's and Lincoln's Inn, the Temple, as its name suggests, was originally constructed during the Middle Ages as a home for religious orders, in this case for the Knights Templars of St. John of Jerusalem. Only after Henry VIII broke with Rome in 1533 was it was transformed into a legal center. At the western end of Crown Office Row was Middle Temple Lane, whose residents at the time of Mary's birth included the writers James Boswell,

Dr. Samuel Johnson, and Oliver Goldsmith, as well as the great legal theorist William Blackstone. It was at nearby Middle Temple Hall in 1602 that William Shakespeare personally directed the opening performance of *Twelfth Night* for Elizabeth I. Behind the meetinghouse was the flower garden where, according to tradition, the leaders of Lancaster and York chose their emblems for the War of the Roses. North of Crown Office Row is Inner Temple Hall, the place in which Thomas Norton and Robert Sackville's *Gorboduc*, the oldest-known blank-verse play in the English language, was first performed in 1561. In *The Sailor's Uncle*, Mary tells of the little girl who is taught the alphabet from the gravestones in the ancient cemetery near her house. The story was certainly at least partly inspired by the medieval Tansfield Church the author saw as a child from her bedroom window.

Like so many other residents of eighteenth-century London, Mary's parents were of rural origin, having migrated to the capital in search of better-paying jobs. Her father, John Lamb, was born in about 1721 in Lincolnshire, where some members of his family still live today.[3] After leaving home, he served for a period as a footman in Bath before settling in London. His wife, Elizabeth Field, was born around 1737 in Hertfordshire, where her mother was the housekeeper for William Plumer, the local member of Parliament and owner of a large and prosperous estate near Widford.[4] The precise date on which the Lambs relocated to London is not known, but church records do indicate they married there in 1761. No portraits of them survive, but many people who knew John and Elizabeth commented that the couple possessed almost exact likenesses to the famous dramatic performers of Drury Lane, David Garrick and Mrs. Siddons.

Soon after arriving in London, Mary's parents experienced the good fortune of meeting the distinguished barrister and Whig member of Parliament the Hon. Samuel Salt, who became their benefactor. John Lamb served as Salt's valet, scribe, and general assistant, while his wife took on the duty of housekeeper. During this period, property owners of Salt's high social status lived on only the ground and first floors of their houses; the upper levels were either rented out or occupied by the servants. Therefore, besides earning salaries they could never have obtained in the country, the Lambs enjoyed free board in a very prestigious section of the capital.

John and Elizabeth Lamb had seven children, only three of whom survived to adulthood. The eldest, also named John, was born on 5 June 1762. Purported to be his parents' favorite, he nonetheless remains a rather shadowy historical figure. In later years he owned Sir Peter Lely's painting of Milton, which today hangs in the National Portrait Gallery, and wrote a philosophical treatise, *Humanity to Animals*, which is now lost. He also attended a few of the Wednesday evening dinners. John Lamb, Jr., appears to have been a self-absorbed personality, and his refusal to come to his sister's assistance during the crisis of 1796 indicates he and his siblings were never close. Charles, the future author, was born on 10 February 1775.[5] Although twelve years separated him from Mary, the brother and sister were always very close. From early childhood Charles liked to take long walks with Mary about the historic Temple and discuss books and the events of the day. Elizabeth Lamb's many duties as housekeeper must have led her to appoint her daughter as surrogate mother for her youngest son.

Samuel Salt must have been very satisfied with his assistant and his housekeeper, because he paid for their two sons' higher education. At the age of seven, after attending grammar school for a couple of years at William Bird's Academy in Fetter's Lane, Holborn, Charles was enrolled in July 1782 at Christ's Hospital on Newgate Street, through Salt's influence.[6] Known popularly as the Bluecoat School because of the color of the students' uniforms, this highly prestigious institution for the education of working class scholars had been founded in 1552 by Edward VI as a replacement for an even older Franciscan Gray Friars school established there in the thirteenth century. Such a distinction was it to attend Christ's Hospital that every year on Easter Sunday the students were presented with freshly minted silver coins by the Lord Mayor of London. Charles spent seven years at Christ's Hospital and later, as *Elia*, wrote one of his most famous essays about his time there. It was during his days at Christ's Hospital that he established friendships with two individuals destined to exercise a lasting influence on his adult life. The first was with Leigh Hunt, the future radical publisher, who would play a major role in Charles's journalistic career. A figure who proved of even more significance, however, was Samuel Taylor Coleridge. Although he was two years Charles's elder, Coleridge's brilliant and forceful personality quickly acquired a place second only to Mary's in his affections. Coleridge probably inherited his ability to charm from his eccentric father, John Coleridge, the vicar of Ottery St. Mary's in Devonshire, who, despite delivering his sermons in ancient Greek, always won the admiration of his purely English-speaking parishioners.

Like students at all the great British Public Schools before the second half of the nineteenth century, those at Christ's Hospital were instructed in Greek and Latin and little else. A knowledge of classical Athens and Rome was viewed by educators as superior to an understanding of one's own era. Although Charles was praised by his teachers for his early endeavors at English-language poetry, he appears not to have mastered the ancient tongues very well and was generally regarded as only an average student. Nonetheless, by having gained admittance to Christ's Hospital, this son of Midland laborers was almost assured success in Britain's ever more powerful middle class.

Mary's education was much less involved. Her only formal instruction was restricted to William Bird's Academy as a child. "It was in fact a humble day-school," her brother recalled, "at which reading and writing were taught to us boys in the morning, and the same slender erudition to the girls, our sisters in the evening."[7] While Charles was expected to become a scholar and to make a name for himself in the world, as a girl, Mary was supposed to use her hands in order to provide money for her family. Her parents decided she would be a needlewoman, and after she left grammar school she was apprenticed to a professional sewer of mantua-cloth, a fabric then in great demand. Good eyesight was of prime importance in this profession, and Mary was forbidden to read anything except the large-type family bible—and then for only half an hour a day. From early childhood she had exhibited a great interest in learning; however, if she was to continue her studies, the mores of the day obliged Mary to follow a less traditional path than her brother.

The Lambs' patron took an interest in Mary, and despite the strict prohibitions her parents set on her reading, she was allowed to spend as much time as she wanted in Samuel Salt's library. "This was indeed a precious discovery," the fictional Margaret Green remembers in Mary's story *The Young Mahometan*: "I looked round on the books with the greatest delight. I thought I would read them every one. I now forsook all my favorite haunts, and passed all my time here. I took down one book, then another."[8]

In this private athenaeum, she studied history, ancient languages, and literature. She was introduced to the works of Milton, Swift, Cowper, Dante, and Sallust. Like all self-taught people, Mary must have developed certain prejudices and misconceptions that a more formal education would have steered her away from, but she was also introduced to a wider range of subject matter than was available at many of the most prestigious Public Schools.

Besides book learning, Mary had a love for drama, a passion acquired long before she collaborated with her brother in writing *Tales of Shakespear*. John and Elizabeth Lamb were probably not pleased with their daughter's frequent expeditions to their employer's library, but they do not appear to have objected to her attending the theater with them. In about 1773, when Mary was nine, she attended a production of *The Mourning Bride* by William Congreve, at Drury Lane. "There is nothing so charming in the world as going to a play," says Emily Barton in Mary's story *Visit to the Cousins*:

I shall never forget how delighted I was at the first sight of the house. My little friend and I were placed together in front, while our mammas retired to the back part of the box to chat by themselves, for they had been so kind as to come early that I might look about me before the performance began. . . . Frederica had been very often at a play. She was very useful in telling me what every thing was. She made me observe how the common people were coming bustling down the benches in the galleries, as if they were afraid they should lose their places. She told me what a crowd these poor people had to go through, before they got into the house. Then she shewed me how leisurely they all came into the pit, and looked about them, before they took their seats. She gave me a charming description of the king and queen at the play, and shewed me where they sate, and told me how the princess dressed. It was a pretty sight to see the remnants of the candles lighted; and so it was to see the musicians come up from under the stage. I admired the music very much, and I asked if that was the play. Frederica laughed at my ignorance, and then she told me, when the play began, the green curtain would draw up to the sound of the music, and I should hear a lady dressed in black say,

"Music hath charms to soothe a savage breast. . . ."[9]

Mary's parents probably considered the theater as little more than light entertainment, a pleasant and undemanding means of filling the hours of one of their periodic vacation days. But from her story, written over thirty years after the event, one easily sees how Mary was captured by the stage's magic from her first sight of it.

Although in the 1770s, quite elderly, Mary's maternal grandmother was still the housekeeper of the Plumer estate at Blakesware, in Hertfordshire. Constantly consumed with their work for Samuel Salt, John and Elizabeth Lamb frequently used the estate as a place to send their children in order to get them out of their way. When not taking care of her brother or practicing her needlework, Mary was regularly sent to Blakesware for extended trips. Around 1774 or 1775, not long before the birth of her brother, she stayed there for almost a year. This in itself proved an educational opportunity for a London child: a chance to learn to appreciate that a wide world existed outside the cramped and narrow streets of the capital. Recalling her first visit to Hertfordshire when she was about ten, Mary writes in *The Farm House*:

I had never in all my life been out of London, no, nor had I even seen a bit of green grass, except in Draper's garden, which was near my Papa's house in Broad-Street; nor had I ever rode in a carriage before that happy birthday.[10]

Blakesware was a large provincial residence built during the seventeenth century, offering an enquiring young mind many lessons and much time for reflection. Mary spent long hours wandering through its vast corridors. "The heads of the twelve Caesars were hung around the hall," she wrote in *The Young Mahometan*:

Every day I mounted on the chairs to look at them, and to read the inscriptions underneath till I became perfectly familiar with their names and features. . . . Hogarths were below the Caesars: I was very fond of looking at them, and endeavoring to make out their meaning. . . . An old broken battledore and some shuttlecocks with most of the feathers missing, were on a marble slab in one corner of the hall in one corner of the hall, which constantly reminded me that there had once been younger inhabitants here than the old lady and her gray headed servants. In another corner stood a marble figure of a satyr: every day I laid my hand on his shoulder to feel how cold he was. . . . This hall opened into a room full of family portraits. They were all in the dresses of former times: some were old men and women, and some were children. I used to long to have a fairy's power to call the children down from their frames and play with them. One little girl in particular who lay by the side of a glass door which opened into the garden, I often invited to walk there with me, but she still kept her station—one arm around a little lamb's neck, and in her hand a large bunch of flowers.[11]

As was the case when she was granted entry into Samuel Salt's library and when she was exposed to the magic of the theater, Mary was presented with yet another opportunity to obtain an education that her sex and social background would almost surely have otherwise denied her.

The year 1789 was a crucial moment in the history of the world. It also proved to be a crucial turning point in the lives of the Lamb family. In October, during the same month in which the citizens of Paris marched on the palace at Versailles and brought Louis XVI and Marie Antoinette as captives back to Paris, Samuel Salt died. The man who had been such a benefactor, not only materially but intellectually as well, was now gone. In recognition of their long years of tireless and faithful service, he bequeathed John and Elizabeth Lamb an annual legacy of one hundred pounds. This was quite impressive by eighteenth-century standards. Combined with their regular salaries, it would normally have assured the Lambs' initiation as solid members of the British middle class. But, unfortunately, this was not to be.

Both John and Elizabeth Lamb were now in their late sixties and in poor health. Samuel Salt's heirs showed no interest in keeping them on, and their former clerk and housekeeper were soon forced to leave the Temple and retire to a much smaller apartment at No. 7 Little Queen Street (now Kingsway), Holborn; a Roman Catholic church now stands on the spot. At about the same time, Elizabeth's sister, Sarah—"Aunt Hetty," also out of work and in poor health—moved in and needed to be supported. The family had held out great hopes for Charles; but without Samuel Salt's financial assistance, it was now impossible for him to remain any longer at Christ's Hospital. He departed without receiving a diploma and, along with his brother John, went to look for work. The two finally obtained permanent employment as clerks at the East India Tea Company, that political octopus that, until the Sepoy Mutiny in 1857, exercised almost unquestioned control over Britain's great Asiatic domain. As was the practice of the day, however, the two boys first had to go through a two-year internship before they started to receive a salary. Under these straitened conditions, it now fell to Mary, so often ignored in the past, to serve as the family's principal economic provider.

Mary, who was twenty-seven in 1789, was now an experienced needlewoman. She had even taken on her own apprentice to assist her with her mantua-cloth trade. Detailed records from this period are unavailable, but it appears that over the next seven years Mary was successful in fulfilling the task her family entrusted to her. Unfortunately, these years were also marked by steadily growing emotional strain, especially in her relations with her mother. Elizabeth Lamb was embittered by her family's economic decline and loss of social status and took out her frustration on her daughter. She had never exhibited the slightest affection for Mary, even when Mary was a child. Now, when Mary needed her mother's help and sympathy most, Elizabeth criticized her unrelentingly, blaming her for all her troubles, real and imagined. John Lamb, ever more ill and now approaching senility, was unable to intervene. The situation at home became explosive.

While Mary was pursuing her mantua-cloth trade, Charles Lamb was making his way in another section of the business world. Upon his leaving Christ's

Hospital, the family had initially entertained hopes that their son might be apprenticed to one of Samuel Salt's colleagues and one day rise to become a barrister. Unfortunately, the stutter from which Charles suffered his entire life quickly precluded a career in the Inns of Court. During the age before the typewriter and the copying machine, service as a clerk at a large institution like the Tea Company generally consisted of long, monotonous hours of filling columns in ledger books and reproducing official documents by hand. In 1791, after finally finishing his internship, Charles was given a salary of forty pounds a year. This increased in incremental amounts, so that by the time of his retirement, in 1825, he was earning seven hundred and thirty. Tedious as his job was, though, it did not prevent him from making his first tentative steps into the literary arena. It was at this same time, after all, that Charles renewed his relations with Samuel Taylor Coleridge.

The last several years had been quite hectic for Coleridge, leaving him little time for writing. After graduating from Christ's Hospital as an acknowledged scholar of Classics, he entered Jesus College, Cambridge, in 1791. He soon found the curriculum much too easy for him and spent most of his time idling and building up debt. In 1793, he suddenly left Cambridge without receiving a degree in order to volunteer in the Fifteenth Light Royal Dragoons. Unable to sit a horse well, however, he was quickly delegated to the canteen. Luckily, a year later his family succeeded in buying his release from the military, and he headed back to school. At Oxford, Coleridge met Robert Southey. The French Revolution was still very popular among students, and the two decided to leave Britain and found a utopian society in North America built along the line of France. Unfortunately, their scheme failed to materialize because of lack of financial support and the leaders' inability to attract sufficient followers. Coleridge did, however, develop a liking for one of the female members of his group, Sarah Fricker, and at his family's suggestion wed her. While not fated to be the happiest of marriages, this union did compel Coleridge finally to settle down and devote himself again to literature.

After a separation of several years, Charles and Coleridge started meeting again, often at a tavern in Smithfield, near the Tower of London. Although recent years had spared them little time to write, their interest in taking up the profession was just as keen. The two began by discussing poetry and soon composed pieces of their own. In the middle of 1794, each contributed works to the *Morning Post*. In the following year, they published a collection of sonnets entitled *Poems on Various Subjects*. It was a commercial success and in 1796 went into a second edition. In 1797, the authors produced a new collection, *Sonnets from Various Authors*.

Although no correspondence between Mary and Charles survives from this period, he clearly received a great deal of encouragement from his sister. The dedication to this second work reads:

Charles Lamb of the India House
to
Mary Anne Lamb, the author's best friend and sister[12]

The years during which Charles launched his literary career were not without their pain. In 1795, the same year he was introduced to William Wordsworth, he developed a romantic attachment to a woman from Blakeware named Ann Simmons and soon decided to marry her. Little is known about the affair except that Charles's parents were opposed and, despite their son's constant pleading, refused to give their blessing. Perhaps they already knew that evidence existed of some medical weakness in the Lamb family and did not want it perpetuated in another generation. By June, Charles could stand the situation no longer and suffered some kind of mental collapse that required his confinement in the Hoxton Asylum. Fortunately, he was released the following January.[13] Although plagued for the rest of his life by periodic bouts of violent depression and heavy drinking, Charles never again exhibited evidence of dementia. It is difficult to diagnose the precise condition from which he suffered. His relatives did all they could to hush the incident up, and no written data about it exists. Possibly he was a manic-depressive. However, the historian should not base his conclusions too firmly on psychological conjectures about a person dead for over one hundred and fifty years.

Although no details are available today concerning Charles's release from Hoxton Asylum in January 1796, it is safe to conclude he considered himself very lucky. During the eighteenth century, many persons judged to be mentally unstable were fated to spend the rest of their lives within the walls of an institution. Society generally looked upon mental illness as something shameful, as the inevitable result of moral decay. No one, it was insisted, could fall victim to this malady unless he and his relatives were consumed with venereal disease or practiced unmentionable perversions. If the Lambs had been a socially ambitious brood with political aspirations, rather than members of the working class, they might easily have chosen to have their stricken member locked away permanently in the hope he would be forgotten and thus not disgrace them. The concept of the mad genius—Mary Wollstonecraft Shelley's Dr. Frankenstein—was very popular among the followers of the incipient Romantic Movement, but Charles was surely glad he was not compelled to play the role.

The house to which Charles returned was not a happy one. His father and Aunt Hetty were now completely bedridden and needed constant attetion. His brother, John Jr., was also in poor health. Mary had to serve not only as the family's financial provider—a task requiring her to toil at her needlework from 9 a.m. to 11 p.m. six days a week—but as its nurse, as well. As for her mother, she continued her unremitting verbal attacks, pelting her daughter all day long with stinging insults. By September, Mary was showing signs she could not tolerate the situation much longer. While she previously had succeeded in ignoring her mother's abuse, she now began to respond with bitter words of her own. Friends started to whisper to Charles that his sister was becoming unstable and that he should consult a physician.

Suddenly, at the end of the month, Charles delivered a startling letter to Coleridge:

Charles Lamb to Samuel Taylor Coleridge
September 27, 1797

My dearest friend,

White or some of my friends or the public papers by this time may have informed you of the terrible calamities that have fallen on our family. . . . (September 22). . . . My poor dear dearest sister in a fit of insanity has been the death of her own mother. I was at hand only time enough to snatch the knife out of grasp. She is at present in a mad house, from whence I fear she must be removed to an hospital. God has preserved to me my senses,—I eat and drink and sleep, and have my judgement I believe very sound. My poor father was slightly wounded, and I am left to take care of him and my aunt. Mr. Norris of the Bluecoat school has been very kind to us, and we have no other friend, but thank God I am very calm and composed, and able to do the best that remains to do. Write,—as religious a letter as possible—but no mention of what is gone and done with—with me the former things are passed away, and I have something more to do than to feel—

God almighty
I have us all in
his keeping—[14]

The reports by the press the day before, however, were even more specific about what transpired:

The London Morning Chronicle
September 26, 1796

On Friday afternoon the Coroner and a respectable Jury sat on the body of a Lady in the neighborhood of Holborn, who died in consequence of a wound from her daughter the preceding day. It appeared by the evidence adduced, that while the family were preparing for dinner, the young lady seized a case knife laying on the table, and in a menacing manner pursued a little girl, her apprentice, round the room; on the eager calls of her helpless infirm mother to forbear, she renounced her first object, and with loud shrieks approached her parent.

The child by her cries quickly brought up the landlord of the house, but too late—the dreadful scene represented to him the mother lifeless, pierced to the heart, on a chair, her daughter yet wildly standing over her with the fatal knife, and the venerable old man, her father, weeping by her side, himself bleeding at the forehead from the effects of a severe blow he received from one of the forks she had been madly hurling about the room.

For a few days prior to this the family had observed some symptoms of insanity in her, which had so much increased on the Wednesday (September 21) evening, that her brother early the next morning went in quest of Dr. Pitcairn—had that gentleman been met with, the fatal catastrophe had, in all probability, been

prevented. . . . It has been stated in some of the morning papers, that she has an insane brother also in confinement—this is without foundation.
The Jury of course brought in their verdict, *Lunacy*.[15]

Mary was taken off in manacles to Islington Asylum. While the jury's verdict of lunacy rather than manslaughter had spared her from a sure death on the scaffold, it seemed likely she would never look upon the outside world again. The illness her brother Charles had suffered from the year before seemed like nothing now; although it had been painful, he had recovered and returned to his career. The illness that came upon his sister would trouble her for the rest of her life.

Luckily, Mary had not been sent to Bethlehem Hospital—Bedlam—that nightmare mental institution made famous in the etchings of *The Rake's Progress* by Hogarth. Here, she might have lived out her days chained to the wall, naked, subject to rape and daily beatings. It would be expensive to keep her at the smaller and more comfortable place where she was held instead, but Charles estimated the cost could be met:

Charles Lamb to Samuel Taylor Coleridge
October 3, 1796

My Aunt is recover'd and as well as ever, and highly pleased at thoughts of going . . . (to the country) . . . has generously given up the interest of her little money which was formerly paid my Father for her board wholy and soley to my Sister's use. Reckoning this we have, Daddy and I, for our two selves and an old maid servant to look after him, when I am out, which will be necessary, 170 or 180 pounds (rather) a year, out of which we can spare 50 or 60 at least for Mary, while she stays at Islington, where she must and shall stay during her father's life for his and her comfort. I know John [Jr.] will make speeches about it, but she shall not go to a hospital. The good Lady of the mad house, and her daughter, an elegant sweet and well behaved young Lady, love her and are taken with her amazingly, and I know from her own mouth she loves them, and longs to be with them.[16]

Charles was deeply affected by the degree of calmness and resignation with which his sister displayed herself after the tragic event:

Charles Lamb to Samuel Taylor Coleridge
October 17, 1796

Mary continues serene and cheerful. . . . I have not the letter beside me but will quote from memory what she wrote—"I have no bad terrifying dreams. At midnight when I happen to awake, the nurse sleeping by my the side of me, with the noise of the poor mad people around me, I have no fear. The spirit of my mother seems to descend, and smile upon me, and bid me live to enjoy the life and reason which the Almighty has given me—I shall see her again in heaven; she will then understand me better. . . ." Poor Mary, my Mother indeed *never understood* her right. Never could believe how much *she* loved her—but met her caresses, her protestations of filial affection, too frequently with coldness and repulse.[17]

Over the following months Mary's condition improved, and although still subject to periodic delusions, she never again posed a real physical threat to those around her. By the spring of 1797, she could safely be liberated from her original place of confinement and, under supervision, be allowed to reside in a more normal environment. The crime she committed was never discussed in her presence, and gradually knowledge of the terrible deed receded from her consciousness. Until her death fifty years later, in 1847, Mary mentions her mother's name only once in her correspondence. Elizabeth Lamb, Mary would insist to her friend Sarah Stoddart in a letter of 21 September 1803, "is always in my poor head and heart."[18]

Charles Lamb to Samuel Taylor Coleridge
April 7, 1797

By the way, Lloyd may have told you about my sister. I told him. If not, I have taken her out of her confinement, and taken a room for her at Hackney, and spend my Sundays, holidays, etc., with her. She boards herself. In one little half year's illness, and in such an illness of such a nature, and of such consequence! to get her out into the world again, with a prospect of her never being so ill again—this is to ranked not among the common blessings of Providence. May that merciful God make tender my heart, and make me as thankful, as in my distress I was earnest, in my prayers. Congratulate me on an ever-present and never-alienable friend like her.[19]

At the same time that Mary was recovering from her first bout with mental illness, her brother was experiencing a troubling episode in his own life—the temporary rupture in his relations with Samuel Taylor Coleridge. Since Charles first met Coleridge when they were children at Christ's Hospital, Coleridge had exercised the driving force in their friendship. Charles looked up to him, regarding him as his benefactor and intellectual leader. He constantly turned to Coleridge for suggestions about what to write and presented his finished works to him for editing. Whether or not Coleridge was conscious of his domination is hard to determine; he may simply have been one of those individuals who possess a psychological need to control those around them. However, in 1797, when Coleridge invited Charles to spend the summer with him and his wife at their home at Nether Stowey, in Somersetshire, he politely declined the offer.[20] Mary, he explained, had just suffered a relapse and been temporarily returned to the asylum, and he had to be near her. While this was true, Charles's first decision not immediately to obey his friend's command also symbolized the start of a major change in their relationship.

Recently, Charles had made the acquaintance of Charles Lloyd, a minor poet and the son of a Birmingham industrialist. Once a close associate of Coleridge,

Lloyd had lived with him and his wife for several months at Nether Stowey, in 1796. The exact reason that their friendship soured is still not clear; but it was certainly in part due to Coleridge's growing attachment to William Wordsworth, who as his artistic equal was a more stimulating intellectual companion. The embittered Lloyd retaliated by providing Lamb with information about Coleridge's private life that was far from complimentary. Coleridge should be admired for his great talent as a poet, Lamb now reasoned, but he need not be looked to as a moral guide.

In the spring of 1798, Lloyd again exhibited his anger with his former friend by publishing a novel entitled *Edmund Oliver*. Although technically fiction, the book was easily recognizable to followers of contemporary literature as a portrait of Coleridge. In it, Lloyd detailed Coleridge's poor military record; the fact that although married to Sarah Fricker, he was in love with a woman named Mary Evans; and, finally, his addiction to opium. Coleridge's most famous poem up to that time, *The Rime of the Ancient Mariner*, readers were told, was written while the author was under its influence. Coleridge was both enraged and embarrassed. He immediately called upon all his friends to denounce Lloyd publicly. He was surprised, therefore, when Charles refused to do so. With uncustomary assertiveness, Charles explained to Coleridge that the dispute had nothing to do with him. He pointed out as well that as Lloyd had just written a favorable review of his recent novel, *Rosamund Gray*, it would be ungrateful to criticize him now. It was up to Coleridge to settle the quarrel. Coleridge's precise reaction to this is not known, but in May 1798 the two friends abruptly broke off their correspondence.

In the end, Lloyd and the furor caused by *Edmund Oliver* really had little to do with the change in Charles's relations with Coleridge. Charles's actions were actually motivated by thoughts that had been germinating his mind for some time. He was maturing now; he was developing literary and artistic ideas all his own. He was becoming confident enough to make his own decisions concerning his career as a writer. He believed he could now survive without looking unquestioningly to someone else for all his inspiration. His friendship with Coleridge was an important part of his life; but for it to continue, Coleridge must understand that it must be established on an equal basis.

Coleridge accepted. After breaking off with Charles, he had spent much of the following eighteen months travelling in Germany with William and Dorothy Wordsworth. This gave him time for reflection; it helped him come to the realization that a deep and rewarding friendship dating back to childhood should not fall prey to vanity. Camaraderie need not be grounded on domination. When Coleridge returned to Nether Stowey at the end of 1799, his correspondence with Charles resumed. It would never be broken off again. In April of 1800, Charles and Mary—now living at home—invited Coleridge to visit them in London. He accepted and stayed for a month. Not long before his death in July 1834, Coleridge wrote on the margin of his poem *This Lime-Tree Bower*:

To
Ch. and Mary Lamb
Dear to my heart, dear as it were my heart[21]

In April 1799, John Lamb died at the age of seventy-eight. A few days later Mary was released from confinement and allowed to live with her brother in his new home at No. 36 Chapel Street, Pentonville.[22] In order to obtain Mary's release, Charles first had to swear to act as his sister's legal guardian and financial support for the rest of her life. Such a responsibility was bound to be very trying; however, Charles accepted the burden just in time. Only a year later, Parliament passed a law declaring persons guilty of committing crimes while of unsound mind eligible for release only at the king's pleasure. At thirty-six, Mary now entered upon the most productive part of her life, a period that would see her win the respect of much of the British literary community. But these years of achievement would not be without their pain. At least once every year she would suffer a relapse into insanity, episodes often lasting several weeks. The demon that possessed Mary was never totally to lose its grasp on her. Her mother's behavior may have been chiefly responsible for first bringing it to the surface, but it did not die with her. The tragedy of 1796 proved to be only the first manifestation of a disease that would afflict Mary until the day she died. These bouts of madness were first characterized by delusions and incoherent chatter, were followed by violence toward others, and ended with a collapse into a passive state. During a century when no effective medication existed, Mary's condition required her return to the asylum. Her brother's tireless love and tender care were a great source of consolation to her, but they also filled Mary with a terrible sense of guilt. In the eyes of many, Mary's illness had become the all-consuming force in the Lambs' existence:

The Memoirs of Barry Cornwall

Whenever the approach of her fits of insanity was announced, by some irritability or change of manner, Lamb would take her, under his arm, to Hoxton Asylum. It was very affecting to encounter the young brother and sister walking together (weeping together) on this painful errand; Mary herself, although sad, very conscious of the necessity for temporary separation from her only friend. They used to carry a strait jacket with them.[23]

**Samuel Taylor Coleridge to Sarah Fricker Coleridge
April 4, 1803**

I had purposed not to speak of Mary Lamb, but I had better write it than tell it. The Thursday before last she met at Rickman's at Mr. Babb, an old friend and admirer of her mother. The next day she *smiled* in an ominous way; on Sunday she told her brother that she was getting bad, with great agony. On Tuesday morning [29th March] she laid hold of me with violent agitation and talked wildly about George Dyer. I told Charles there was not a moment to lose; and I did not lose a moment, but went for a Hackney-coach and took her to the private house at Hugsden. She was quite calm and said it was the best to do. But she wept bitterly two or three times, yet all in a calm way. Charles is cut to the heart.[24]

Despite the pain and sorrow his sister's illnesses brought him, it was to her that Charles looked as his primary source of strength; it was to Mary that he turned for help and understanding. Unlike such figures as Wordsworth and Coleridge, who were able to find their true artistic voices early in their careers, Charles discovered his only through a long process of trial and error. The fame and prestige he was to possess as a theater critic and as the creator of *Elia* were achieved only after several much less successful attempts to locate himself in other domains of literature. Of his poetry, only *The Old Familiar Faces* and *Hester* are to be found in modern anthologies. His novel, *Rosamund Gray*, like so many of the romantic sagas of the period, is no longer read. His first drama, *John Woodvil* (1802), a tragedy, was turned down by Edmund Kean and never performed. His second, a satire, *Mr. H.* (1806), closed after only one performance. Throughout these disappointments, Mary stood by her brother, comforting and encouraging him. She told Charles he should not be discouraged; she assured him he really had talent as a writer. Charles took her words seriously, especially because Mary did not simply say things that would please him. She was not afraid to criticize his work when she believed it flawed or to insist on changes he did not always at first agree with. Mary stood beside him not only as his comforter but also as his adviser. Without her, Charles insisted to his friend Thomas Manning during one of his sister's confinements, "I totter and stagger with weakness, for nobody can supply her place to me."[25] Whatever worldly success he might attain, Charles believed, would be Mary's achievement as well.

Charles Lamb to Dorothy Wordsworth
June 14, 1805

I have every reason to suppose that this illness, like all her former ones, will be but temporary; but I cannot always feel so. Meantime she is dead to me, and I miss a prop. All my strength is gone, and I am like a fool, bereft of her co-operation. I dare not think, lest I shall think wrong; so used am I to look up to her in the least and biggest complexity.[26]

As they awaited what the new century would bring, Charles and Mary Lamb stood hand in hand.

Chapter Two

Triumph and Pain

As Mary left her place of confinement to reside with her brother, she did so with a determination to start a new life. She was keenly aware that illness would never be far away, but she was resolved it would not dominate her. If she had to experience pain, she would also know accomplishment. Charles was impressed by her courage and became convinced early on that she would succeed in her quest:

Charles Lamb to Samuel Taylor Coleridge
August 26, 1800

How do you like this little epigram? It is not my writing, nor had I any finger in it. If you concur with me in thinking it very elegant and very original, I shall be tempted to name the author to you. I will just hint it is almost or quite a first attempt.

Helen Repentant Too Late

1
High-born Helen!
Round your dwelling
These twenty years I've paced in vain:
Haughty beauty,
Your lover's duty
Has been to glory in his pain.
2
High-born Helen!
Proudly telling
Stories of your cold disdain;

I starve, I die:—
Now you comply,
And I no longer can complain.
3
These twenty years
I've liv'd on tears,
Dwelling for ever on a frown;
On sighs I've fed,
Your scorn my bread:
I perish now you kind are grown!
4
Can I, who loved
My Beloved
But for the "scorn was in her eye,"
Can I be moved
For my Beloved,
When she returns me "sigh for sigh?"
5
In stately pride,
By my bed-side,
High-born Helen's portrait's hung;
Deaf to my praise;
My mournful lays
Are nightly to the portrait sung.
6
To that I weep,
Nor ever sleep,
Complaining all night long to her!
Helen, grown old,
No longer cold,
Said, "You to all men I prefer.—"[27]

This poem, as was the case with so many of Mary's writings, was inspired by memories of Blakesware. As had his sister, Charles often spent long periods during his childhood at the Hertfordshire estate. As she had, too, he wandered through its corridors contemplating the musty paintings. During one of these sojourns, Charles's eyes fell upon one particular portrait, one of a beautiful and graceful lady. Fetching, yet at the same time aristocratic and unattainable, she was long the object of his boyish fascination. In presenting her brother with her first completed poem, it was fitting Mary offered him a reminder of a simpler, happier time in their lives.

In 1801, Charles and Mary Lamb moved back into the Temple, taking up residence at No. 16 Mitre Court Buildings. It was during their years here, that they inaugurated their famous Wednesday evening get-togethers, affairs that became the primary meeting place for London's literary greats. The fame of the Lambs' soirées was to a large degree a result of Charles's growing reputation as a theater critic. Since the age of ten, when Charles went with his sister to Drury

Lane to see Mrs. Siddons perform in Thomas Augustine Arne's *Artaxerxes*, he had been captivated by the theater.[28] Though his early efforts to become a playwright had proved unsuccessful, this did not dissuade him from taking on a different role in the dramatic world. Along with his colleague Leigh Hunt, Charles became one of the first two British theater critics actually to attend performances of the plays he reviewed. In a time when critics were traditionally little more than publicity agents—supplying newspaper readers with unstinting praise for one playwright or star and blanket condemnations of his or her rivals—Charles's articles in London's *Morning Chronicle* and *Morning Post* were seen as a true guide to the dramatic arts.

The hostess of No. 16 Mitre Court was also looked upon with growing admiration. For the followers of the new Romantic movement, writers who believed that beauty, virtue, and human dignity were best portrayed not in the rigid and artificial style of neoclassicism, but rather in the experiences of the real world, the predicament of a gifted woman struggling to express her talents while at the same time combatting a tragic and incurable illness, was very appealing:

The Memoir of Sir Thomas Noon Talfourd

Miss Lamb would have been remarkable for the sweetness of her disposition, the clearness of her understanding, and the gentle wisdom of all her acts and words, even if these qualities had not been presented in marvelous contrast with the distraction under which she suffered for weeks, literally months, in every year. There was no tinge of insanity discernible in her manner to the most observant eye; not even in those distressful periods when the premonitory symptoms had appraised her of its approach and she was making preparation for seclusion. In all its essential sweetness, her character was like her brother's; while by a temper more placid, a spirit of enjoyment more serene, she was enabled to guide him on the verge of the mysterious calamity, from the depths of which she rose so often unruffled to his side.[29]

Two individuals always invited to dinner on Wednesday evenings when they came to visit London were William and Dorothy Wordsworth. They had first been introduced to the Lambs by Coleridge in 1797 at Nether Stowey, but it was not until 1801, the year Charles and Mary moved to Mitre Court, that they became intimates. Since December 1799, Wordsworth and his sister had established their main place of residence at Dove Cottage, Town End, Grasmere, in Westmorelandshire. The majority of the foursome's intercourse was therefore by post, a correspondence that brought them great intellectual and emotional satisfaction. Like the Lamb-Coleridge letters, these missives too are of major cultural and historic consequence.

Mary was a great admirer of Wordsworth, who in 1799 had recently entered upon the most productive decade of his poetic career. They quickly became very good friends. But it was with his sister that Mary formed her deepest bond. At twenty-nine, a year older than her brother, Dorothy Wordsworth was a gifted woman in her own right. Her *Grasmere Journal*, with its vivid descriptions of nature and country life, was the direct inspiration for such poems by her brother as *The Daffodils*, *The Leech-Gatherer*, and *The Beggars*. Her accounts of nineteenth-century rural poverty and class relations also make Dorothy's *Journal* significant as a pioneering piece of social history. Unfortunately, most of the letters Dorothy wrote to Mary no longer exist. Those which survive, however, clearly demonstrate that the correspondents shared much in common; they illustrate how these two great ladies of the Romantic Age enjoyed a sincere and rewarding attachment to one another:

Mary Lamb to Dorothy Wordsworth
July 11, 1803

How pleasant your little house and orchard must be now. I almost wish I had never seen it. I am always wishing to be with you. I could sit upon that little bench in idleness day long. When you have a leisure hour, a letter from you, kind friend, will give me the greatest pleasure.[30]

In 1804 Mary mailed Dorothy Wordsworth her two latest poems. Both were contemplations inspired by works of art she had recently seen, the latter, a lithograph of Leonardo da Vinci's *Prudence and Modesty*, was currently hanging in Mary's brother's study:

Mary Lamb to Dorothy Wordsworth
June 2, 1804

1
Dialogue between a mother and child

Child. "O Lady, lay your costly robes aside,
(sings) No longer may you glory in your pride."
Mother. Wherefore to day art singing in mine ear
      Sad songs were made so long ago, my dear?
      This day I am to be a bride, you know.
      Why sing sad songs were made so long ago?
Child. "O Mother lay your costly robes aside,"
      For you may never be another's bride:
      That line I learnt not in the old sad song.
Mother. I pray thee, pretty one, now hold thy tongue;
      Play with the bride maids, and be glad, my boy,
      For thou shalt be a second father's joy,
Child. One father fondled me upon his knee:
      One father is enough alone for me

2

"The Lady Blanch"

That Lady Blanch, regardless of all her lovers' fears,
To the Urseline Convent hastens, and long the Abbess hears:
"O Blanch, my child, repent thee of the courtly life ye lead."
Blanch looked on a rose-bud, and little seem'd to heed;
On all her heart had whisper'd, and all the Nun had taught.
"I am worshipped by lovers, and brightly shines my fame,
"All Christendom resoundeth the noble Blanch's name;
"Nor shall I quickly wither like the rose-bud from the tree,
"My Queen-like graces shining when my beauty's gone from me.
"But when the sculptur'd marble is raised o'er my head,
"And the matchless Blanch lies lifeless among the noble dead,
"This saintly Lady Abbess has made me justly fear,
"It nothing will avail me that I were worshipt here."[31]

Dorothy Wordsworth wrote back, saying how much she enjoyed the poems.
She added that she had presented them to her brother, who also judged them to
be very good. Mary was delighted and quickly responded, thanking her friend for
her unsolicited kindness. Her letter also demonstrates that, besides literature,
Mary shared her confidante's interest in nature:

Mary Lamb to Dorothy Wordsworth
October 13, 1804

My brother and I have been this summer to Richmond; we had a lodging there for
a month, we passed the whole time there in wandering about & comparing the
views from the banks of the Thames with your mountain scenery, & tried, &
wished, to persuade ourselves that it was almost as beautiful. Charles was quite a
Mr. Clarkson in his admiration and his frequent exclamations, for though we had
often been at Richmond for a few hours we had no idea it was so beautiful a place
as we found it on a month's intimate acquaintance. Your very friendly invitations
have made us long to be with you, and we promise ourselves to spend the first
money my brother earns by writing certain books . . . in a journey to Grasmere.[32]

But before the time for the visit to Grasmere could be arranged, tragedy
struck. John Wordsworth, the inspiration for his brother's *The Happy Warrior*
(1806), was captain of the East Indiaman, *HMS Earl of Abergavenny*. At the end
of January 1805, as he was starting out on a voyage to China, he was drowned
along with nearly all the other two hundred members of his crew when his ship
was wrecked in a storm off Weymouth in the English Channel. As a clerk at the
East India Tea Company, Charles was privy to all the incoming dispatches and
was therefore one of the first persons to learn about the disaster. He quickly
wrote to the Wordsworths so that they could be informed of the tragic news by

a friend instead of by the newspapers. Consolingly he told them, ''We have done nothing but think of you, particularly Dorothy. . . . Mary writes this: as long as we remember we shall remember your Brother's noble person.''[33]

Coleridge at this moment was residing in Malta, where he had gone a year earlier, when Mary secured him the post of secretary to the local Judge Advocate, John Stoddart, brother of her friend Sarah. The moderate climate and steady work, she hoped, would give her friend the energy he needed to cure himself of his drug addiction.[34] Coleridge was therefore unable to be with the Wordsworths at this bitter time. Mary, however, was sure that he would return soon to comfort them:

Mary Lamb to Dorothy Wordsworth
February 5, 1805

Why is he wandering on the sea?
Coleridge should with Wordsworth be.
By slow degrees he'd steal away
Their woe and gently bring a ray
(So happily he'd time relief)
Of confort from their very grief
He'd tell them that their brother dead
When years have passed o'er their head,
Will be remembered with such holy,
true and perfect melancholy,
that even their brother John
Will be their heart's companion.
His voice they'll always hear, his face they'll always see,
There's might in life so sweet as such as many.[35]

Dorothy Wordsworth was very touched by Mary's display of concern. ''There is nobody in the world out of our home,'' she wrote to her friend, ''for whom I am more deeply interested.''[36] She promptly renewed her invitation for a visit to Grasmere during the summer. But in June, Mary suffered another relapse and once again had to be confined to the asylum. Although deeply important to both of them, the relationship between Mary Lamb and Dorothy Wordsworth was destined to remain primarily one of correspondence.

Despite the unhappiness that 1805 brought to Mary and those dear to her, the year also marked the beginning of a very productive period in her life. It was in that year that the publisher William Godwin contacted Charles, enquiring if he was interested in the idea of writing a children's book about the plays of Shakespeare. Charles, who was then preparing to publish the similarly styled book *The Adventures of Ulysses*, accepted and persuaded Godwin to allow Mary to co-author it. It was for this project that she was destined to be best remembered.

The idea of writing a children's version of the works of a famous literary figure was not entirely new. Books of this kind had already appeared on the poems of Virgil and Spenser; Godwin himself had produced one on Chaucer's *Canterbury Tales*. In fact, as recently as 1783, a French author named Perrin had actually published *Contes Amoraux, Amusant et l'Instructif á l'Usage de la Jeunesse Tirés de Tragédies de Shakespeare*.[37] However, several important features of the book Mary and Charles were planning to write would make it unique.

First, although the earlier books had been written with the expressed intention of supplying younger readers with a simplified alternative to the works of famous adult authors, the purpose of *Tales of Shakespear* was to excite children's interest in the stories. As Mary wrote in her preface:

What these Tales have been to you in childhood, that and much more it is my wish that the true plays of Shakespear may prove to you in older years—enrichers of the fancy, strengtheners of virtue, withdrawing from all selfish and mercenary thoughts, a lesson of all sweet and honorable thoughts and actions; to teach you courtesy, benignity, generosity, humility: for of examples, teaching these vocations, his pages are full.[38]

Second, Shakespeare was only now emerging from a long intellectual exile. The neo-classical taste of the Augustan Age had frowned on him; Addison judged his style unruly and his plots rather crude; Pope added his "improvements." For over a century, Shakespeare's plays occupied a very low standing in the British literary canon. While the Romantics of the nineteenth century were successfully resurrecting the Bard's reputation, the majority of Britons still worried about introducing his works to their children. Boys, they believed, should read them only after the "immoral" elements of the plays had first been expunged, and girls were too impressionable to see them at all. Mary and Charles rejected these prejudices and chose to let their young readers reach their own conclusions. Finally, and even more innovative, they intended their book to be read not only by boys but by girls as well.

The Lambs' work consisted of vignettes of twenty of Shakespeare's plays: fourteen comedies described by Mary and six tragedies recounted by Charles. As their letters from the period demonstrate, writing the book was a rewarding but sometimes a frustrating project:

Charles Lamb to Thomas Manning [39]
May 10, 1806

Mary says you saw her writing the other day, and she wishes you should know what they are. She is doing for Godwin's bookseller twenty of Shakespear[e]'s plays, to be made into Children's tales. Six are already done by her, to wit, "The Tempest," "Winter's Tale," "Midsummer Night," "Much Ado," "Two Gentlemen of Verona," and "Cymbeline." "The Merchant of Venice" is in forwardness.... I think it will be popular among the little people. Mary has done them capitally, I think you'd think.[40]

Mary Lamb to Sarah Stoddart
Beginning of June 1806

My *Tales* are to be published in separate story-books. I mean, in single stories, like the children's little shilling books. I cannot send you them in Manuscript, because they are all in Godwin's hands; but one will be published very soon and then you shall have it all in print. I go on very well, and have no doubt but I shall always be able to hit upon some such kind of job to keep going on. I think I shall get fifty pounds a year at the lowest calculation; but as I have not yet seen any of my own earning, for we do not expect to be paid till Christmas, I do not feel the good fortune, that has so unexpectedly befallen me, half so much as I ought to do. But another year, no doubt, I shall perceive it. Charles has written Macbeth, Othello, King Lear, and has begun Hamlet; you would like to see us, as we often sit, writing on one table (but not on one cushion) sitting like Hermia and Helena in the Midsummer's Night's Dream; or, rather like an old literary Darby and Joan: I taking snuff, and he groaning all the while, and saying he can make nothing of it, which he always says till he has finished, and then he finds out he has made something of it.[41]

Charles Lamb to William Wordsworth
June 26, 1806

Mary is just stuck fast in All's Well that Ends Well. She complains of having to set forth so many female characters in boy's clothes. She begins to think Shakespeare must have wanted Imagination. I to encourage her, for she often faints in the prosecution of her great work, flatter her with telling her how well such a play and such a play is done. But she is stuck fast and I have been obliged to promise to assist her. To do this it will be necessary to leave off Tobacco. But I had thoughts of doing that before, for I sometimes think it does not agree with me.[42]

Mary Lamb to Sarah Stoddart
July 6, 1806

I did not put this in the post, hoping to be able to write a less dull letter to you this morning; but I have been prevented, so it shall go as it is. I am in good spirits just at this present time, for Charles has been reading over the *Tale* I told you plagued me so much, and he thinks it one of the very best; it is All's Well that Ends Well. You must not mind the many wretchedly dull letters I have sent you; for, indeed, I cannot help it, my mind is so *dry* always after poring over my work all day. But it will soon be over.[43]

Most of the problems Mary and Charles complained of resulted from the difficulties they encountered in remaining faithful to the design they set for their book. In order to retain their young readers' interest, the authors decided that none of the *Tales* should exceed approximately five thousand words. This naturally required simplifying some of the plots, but doing so without substantially altering the original stories. Because of the complexity of many of

Shakespeare's comedies, most of this laborious work naturally fell to Mary. For example: in *Midsummer Night's Dream*, she omitted the scene in Act V in which Peter Quince and his troupe of actors put on "Pyramus and Thisbe"; in *Twelfth Night*, she eliminated Maria's criticisms of Sir Toby Belch and Sir Andrew Aguecheek in Act I; In *Taming of the Shrew*, Mary left out Bianca altogether and discussed only the battle between Katherine and Petrucchio. *As You Like It* now opened with the deposition of the rightful duke, not of Oliver's mistreatment of Orlando; while *The Merchant of Venice* started with a description of Shylock's hostility to Antonio, and not Antonio's friendships with Gratiano and Bassanio. *The Tempest* began with a portrait of the island and its strange animals instead of with an account of the storm. *The Comedy of Errors* proved so intricate, however, that Mary finally decided it could not be simplified without damaging the story as a whole. She therefore allowed this *Tale* to run a little longer than the rest.

The Lambs' desire to be assured that their book would be read by girls as well as boys eventually forced Mary to eliminate some of what most contemporary Britons still considered the "immoral" or "improper" qualities in Shakespeare's characters or plots. In her account of *All's Well That Ends Well*, for instance, she did not mention why Helena must keep secret the disease with which the king of France is suffering from a secret. In *The Comedy of Errors*, she converted the Courtesan into a lady of the court, and in *Much Ado about Nothing*, turned the Bastard into Don Pedro's half-brother. Mary also omitted the third act of *Cymbeline*, where Imogen is pursued by Cloten. After much consideration, she decided that no matter how many changes she made to *The Merry Wives of Windsor* with its irrepressible Falstaff, to *Troilus and Cressida* with its love triangle, and to the farcical *Love's Labor's Lost*, they would never satisfy the average British parent. The plays were therefore left out of the book.

Finally, the custom of the period required that children's books, especially those intended for girls, conclude either happily or with the triumph of justice; an implication was not considered enough. The Comedy of Errors originally ends with Adriana's reconciliation with her husband, Antipholus of Ephesus: in her version, Mary goes on to declare that the heroine never feels jealous again. In *Measure for Measure*, Isabella now not only becomes Duchess of Vienna, she also becomes a model for young ladies.

Despite the alterations convention forced Mary to make in her original text, *Tales of Shakespear* has remained a classic for nearly two hundred years. As her preface strenuously reminds young readers, her book is an introduction to, not a replacement for, the real plays. However, even in the edited form in which they finally appeared, the *Tales* are memorable. Neither crib notes, stuffy nineteenth-century morality stories, nor pieces of childish fantasy, they are a collection of fresh, entertaining, often humorous narratives that are still readable today. While making sure her stories are appealing to young readers, the author always takes her audience seriously, never talking down to them, and whenever possible introduces them to the vocabulary and literary style of Shakespeare's own time.

In *Midsummer Night's Dream*, for instance, Mary writes:

There was a law in the city of Athens, which gave to its citizens the power of compelling their daughters to marry whomsoever they pleased; for upon a daughter's refusing to marry the man her father had chosen to be her husband, the father was empowered by this law to cause her to be put to death; but as fathers do not often desire the death of their own daughters, even though they do happen to prove a little refractory, this law was seldom or never put in execution, though perhaps the young ladies of that city were not infrequently threatened by their parents with the terror of it.[44]

Work on the manuscript was completed by the fall of 1806, and the publication date was set for the beginning of 1807. The graphic artist William Mulready was hired to provide an illustration for each story. Judging it more profitable, Godwin decided to have the *Tales* printed in two large volumes rather than in twenty smaller ones, as planned earlier. Soon afterwards, however, he called for another change as well, this time one concerning the *Tales* authorship.

Like his daughter and his son-in-law, Mary and Percy Bysshe Shelley, William Godwin was a radical. He was famous as an anarchist, a freethinker, and a supporter of birth control. Among his friends he counted Thomas Paine, the international revolutionary. But like all publishers, he also wanted a profit. He therefore insisted on Mary Lamb's name being dropped from the title page of the new book. The precise words Godwin used are not known, but he clearly led the Lambs to understand that the average British parent would never purchase it if he or she was aware the work was coauthored by someone with a mental illness. Charles reluctantly agreed to the deletion, and his sister felt she had no alternative but to give her consent as well. No edition of *Tales of Shakespear* appeared bearing Mary's name until the second half of the nineteenth century, even after it was generally known she was the principle author.

The omission of Mary's name from the title page of her most famous book is a good illustration of the degree of sexism that existed in nineteenth-century British society. The same customers whom the publisher viewed as potential purchasers of his latest offering did not object to buying the poetry of the mentally disturbed William Cowper or to going to church on Sundays and singing the hymns of Christopher Smart, someone who, unlike Mary Lamb, had been confined to the infamous Bedlam. They also judged it perfectly acceptable to introduce these writers' works to their children. Of course, Cowper and Smart were men. At least since the time of Thomas Chatterton—Wordsworth's "Sleepless Soul"—the "mad" poet had been generally viewed as a romantic and sympathetic figure. His poignant writings and tragic life, so it was believed, would have an edifying effect on children. To women in a similar situation, like Mary, the majority of Britons were not so charitable. Intellectually limited, irrational, cowardly, unfaithful, women could exercise a negative effect on society even in the best of circumstances; in the worst, they could threaten its very existence. Authorship and other intrusions by them into the public arena should therefore be held to the absolute minimum. Thus, though Mary would be asking for criticism by writing a book even when she was completely well, doing so in her present condition would provoke a scandal, not to mention a financial disaster for her publisher. If books written by healthy female authors were considered of only limited benefit for children, those by "mad" women were seen as positively dangerous.

The book was at last published in January 1807 under the title *Tales of Shakespear. Designed for the use of young persons. By Charles Lamb and embellished with copper-plates.* It was an instant success. Such was the advertising, that the first edition was nearly completely sold out on the first day. A second edition was quickly printed, and a third after that. From distant China, Charles's friend Thomas Manning wrote off for a copy. The *Tales* were to serve as the chief introduction to Shakespeare for children around the world for well over a century. Translated into many languages, including Russian and Japanese, the *Tales* remain in print to this very day. Although Godwin did all he could to keep the general public in ignorance as to the authorship, the Lambs made no attempt to conceal it from their many friends in the literary community. Each Wednesday evening, Coleridge, Leigh Hunt, the Wordsworths, and other guests covered Mary with praise. She had written, declared Hunt, "a brilliant little book." But still more was to come. Already, in a letter to Thomas Manning on 5 December 1806, a month before the *Tales* were even published, Charles informed his friend, "Mary has begun a new work."[45]

In 1807, the Lambs began writing another children's book, this time intended specifically for girls. *Mrs. Leicester's School* as it was eventually entitled, was even more Mary's product than was *Tales of Shakespear*. Unfortunately, the historian is provided with very few letters revealing Mary's thoughts during this book's composition. After Charles's letter to Wordsworth on January 29, no further letter by him is available until sometime in June, and none with a verifiable date until December 29. One reason for this silence may be the fact that besides his share of *Mrs. Leicester*, Charles was also occupied with writing a major book of literary criticism, *Specimens of the English Dramatic Poets Who Lived about the Time of Shakespeare*. A far more significant reason, however, is that Mary, for whom no letters from 1807 exist before October, again suffered a major relapse, this time while vacationing with her brother at Thomas Clarkson's home at Bury St. Edmunds, and was once more confined to Hoxton Asylum:[46]

Charles Lamb to Thomas Clarkson
June (?), 1807

We got there about half past eight; and now 'tis all over, I have great satisfaction that she is among people who have been used to her. In all probability a few months or even weeks will restore her (her last illness confined her ten weeks) but if she does recover I shall be very careful how I take her so far from home again. I am so fatigued, for she talked in the most wretched desponding way conceivable, particularly in the last three stages, she talked all the way,—so that you can't expect me to say much, or even to express myself as I should do in thanks for your kindnesses. My sister will acknowledge them when she can.—[47]

For months, Mary was too ill to correspond with anyone. When she was finally released, either later that summer or during the early fall, she evidently decided to place her letter-writing aside temporarily and devote all her energy to the more important task of fashioning her next book.

In *Mrs. Leicester's School, or the History of Several Young Ladies, Related by Themselves*, ten girls from varied backgrounds, away from home for the first time, are instructed by their teacher to recount the stories of their early lives and the events that brought them to Amwell School. Seven of these narratives are written by Mary; the other three, *The Witch Aunt*, *The First Going to Church*, and *The Sea Voyage*, by Charles. As no written accounts of Mary's own early life exist, her stories can be of significant biographical value. In *The Farm House*, for instance, the narrator describes her first visit to a country estate, one that is generally believed to be the Blakesware of Mary's childhood. *Visit to the Cousins* provides the historian with a detailed illustration of the late eighteenth-century London in which Mary grew up, as well as a vivid portrayal of her early fascination with the stage. However, a study of *Mrs. Leicester's School* discloses more about its author than details of her early life. It also provides a window into Mary's personality, revealing her innermost motivations, her view of the world, and finally, what she thought was her place in it.

Ann Withers, the narrator of *The Changeling*, begins her story by explaining that until recently she was addressed by a different name. Soon after Ann's birth, her mother, a servant and tenant on the estate of Sir Edward and Lady Lesley, was called upon to be the wet-nurse and nanny of their own newborn daughter. In the eighteenth and early nineteenth centuries, this would have almost certainly required her to abandon her own child. Unable to bear such a heavy blow, she secretly switches the children, Ann now growing up under her mother's eye as Harriot Lesley, heiress to the manor, and her employers' real daughter becoming a peasant. The Lesleys do not detect the difference and raise Ann as their own. All goes well at first: The little girl is loved and cherished by devoted parents, and she is surrounded by luxury and privilege. No one questions her identity; only a true patrician could possess such natural intelligence and ladylike graces. As is the case with all those with her social status, Ann is taught to do good works, and one day she befriends a village girl her own age. They become close and often romp in the fields together. Inevitably, the village girl divulges to her playmate that the two were exchanged just after birth. The true Harriot Lesley says she feels no animosity toward Ann. She explains that while she was at first angry at being displaced from her rightful position, she has grown to accept her new life. Ann now feels it is her duty to become Harriot's patron and has her frequently brought to the manor to be educated. Unfortunately, instead of simply having her friend well supported and keeping the truth about their origins concealed, Ann, who is a romantic and literary sort, decides to dramatize her story, modeling it after *Hamlet*'s play-within-a-play. Everyone, family and servants, is invited to watch. At the crucial moment in Ann's play, her real mother, like Claudius, is overwhelmed by guilt and reveals the hidden truth.

Ann's world is immediately turned upside down. The Lesleys, who until this very moment loved her deeply as their child, now with equal bitterness cast her out. The true Harriot, whom the Lesleys treated with condescension before, is now suddenly showered with affection. Once heiress to the manor, Ann soon finds herself a peasant in the village. But this is not the end of her troubles. Although an aristocrat, Harriot does not have any of Ann's ladylike qualities, and the Lesleys order Ann to teach them to her. In the home where Ann was once loved as the Lesleys' daughter, she now finds herself treated as their servant. Harriot, too, is no longer warm to Ann. Once restored to her high social position, she forgets their recent intimacy and snubs her former playmate as an inferior. Even Ann's real mother is cold, blaming her daughter for her own indiscretions. The story ends as Lady Lesley, happy with the improvements Ann has made in Harriot, rewards her by sending her to Amwell School.

The Changeling is of course more than simply a children's tale. In recounting the sad story of Ann Withers, whose fortune is determined not so much by her own character or actions as by the manner in which she is perceived by others, Mary is instructing her young readers about the evils of the British class system, a hierarchical order in which an individual's value is measured not by her gifts and accomplishments but rather by her social position at birth. Ann may be praised for her intelligence, grace, and talent, but in the end her society really respects her only because it believes her to be a member of the landed aristocracy. Once the truth about her origins is discovered—once she is found to be of the village and not the manor—this respect quickly evaporates. For most people in nineteenth-century Britain, ability counted for little when compared to social status. Ann even discovers that this applies to parental love. Despite their numerous shows of affection, Sir Edward and Lady Lesley really only care for her as long as they think Ann is one of their own class. Once they find that she is not, they immediately transfer their affections to someone else and look down on the child they long cherished. The class system, the author warns her readers, is not merely a product of the adult world; even Ann's playmate obeys it. Once restored to her proper social position, Harriot, once so friendly to Ann, quickly repudiates her. In all the works she wrote for children, Mary treated her audience as equals. She knew they were not too young to contemplate important questions of right and wrong. This story is no exception.

In writing *The Changeling*, Mary was also reflecting on her own dubious position in society. Despite her literary and social successes, she was keenly aware that, like Ann Withers, she lived among people whom most Britons would forever view as her superiors. Unlike Coleridge, the son of a minister, and William and Dorothy Wordsworth, the son and daughter of an attorney, Mary and her brother were the children of servants and the grandchildren of peasants. While their friends were landowners, the Lambs were compelled to work for their livings—Charles as a scrivener and Mary as a needlewoman. Mary never forgot that while many Londoners were impressed with her Wednesday evening gatherings, still more believed she had no right to hold them. An intruder, living in a world in which she did not belong, Mary too, was viewed as a "changeling."

The Young Mahometan is also about the British class system, although its conclusion is more optimistic than the previous story's. Margaret Green comes from a family of "distressed gentlefolk"—educated and refined middle—or even upper-class persons whom financial misadventure or bad luck has left in reduced circumstances. Following her father's bankruptcy, Margaret and her mother are forced to accept the only alternative open to people in their situation—taking up lodging with a relative—in this case, with the wealthy Mrs. Beresford, who lives on a great country estate. Anxious to regain her lost social status, Margaret's mother devotes herself entirely to being Mrs. Beresford's companion and has no time for or interest in caring for her daughter. "Every morning" Margaret tells the reader, "when she first saw me, she used to nod her head very kindly, and say, 'How do you do, little Margaret?' But I do not recollect she ever spoke to me during the remainder of the day. . . ."[48]

Left on her own, Margaret spends most of her time meandering through the vast halls of the manor—contemplating the antique paintings and statues, opening the doors to musty forgotten rooms, investigating the old library. During one of these expeditions, she discovers a book about the history of Islam. It is badly damaged, with many of the pages torn out. Enough remain, though, to excite Margaret's curiosity. The Arabs, she reads, are the descendants of Hagar and Ishmael, who were cast out of their home and left to wander in the wilderness. Margaret is instantly attracted to the story. After all, has she not been living the life of Hagar herself? She decides to convert to Islam, believing it to be a most noble faith.

Finally, Mrs. Beresford, who is frequently absent, takes an interest in Margaret and convinces her that she is mistaken in her new convictions. If she had been able to read the lost pages of the book, she would discover that Islam is in actuality a most violent and benighted institution, one she would certainly not want to have anything to do with. Margaret's concern for important subjects like culture and religion, however, persuade her patroness that she is a highly intelligent girl and that her mind has long been allowed to go to waste. She is no longer left to her aimless wandering; she is introduced to the company of proper young ladies, and eventually Mrs. Beresford sends her away to Amwell School to attain the education she deserves.

The consequences to Margaret Green of her fall in social status are not the same as those experienced by Ann Withers in *The Changeling*. Ironically, it is not until her family loses its position and she is left as Mrs. Beresford's poor relation that Margaret at last meets people who fully comprehend her intelligence and discernment. In the prejudiced eyes of the class system her recent misfortunes may have diminished her in importance, but to those capable of measuring a person's true value she retains the respect she deserves. Although she may never again be regarded as a member of the ruling social élite, the reader feels sure by the conclusion of the story that Margaret can look forward to a fulfilling life.

Blakesware is once more the scene of Mary's story. Mrs. Beresford is modeled after her maternal grandmother, who for fourteen years was mistress at Blakesware in all but name. The Plumer family abandoned their Hertfordshire estate in 1778, after William Plumer MP died, and did not return until 1792. As sole permanent occupant during this period, Mary's grandmother, although officially only the caretaker, enjoyed all the legal prerogatives of an eighteenth century landowner. To Mary, who spent long periods there as a child, her grandmother was clearly the unchallenged lady of the manor. (The manor house was eventually demolished, in 1822.) The uncaring mother is based on Mary's own. She leaves Margaret to wander the lonely halls, just as Elizabeth Field left her own daughter in real life. Another story of interest is *The Merchant's Daughter*. Here, Charlotte Wilmot, whose father was a rich merchant, suddenly discovers herself reduced to poverty and compelled to seek the assistance of her father's onetime clerk and his family, the Hardys. When she was wealthy, Charlotte treated them in a condescending and haughty manner, and she now naturally expects that her former servants will take their revenge upon her. Instead, she is treated with kindness and is made aware that individuals from the "lower" classes possess many noble qualities which her own "higher" order lacks. Once again, the author instructs her readers, wealth and position are not the best means to judge the worth of human beings.

Mrs. Leicester's School was completed in the autumn of 1808 and became available for sale in two volumes at the beginning of January 1809. Compared with today, when the time required for transforming a written manuscript into a printed book is at least one year, the same procedure during the early nineteenth century could be carried out in a matter of weeks. Godwin was once more the publisher and once again insisted that Mary's name not appear on the title page. The book's authorship remained anonymous until 1818, when it was included in the collected writings of Charles Lamb. Some conservative critics at the time did not approve of the book's theme, insisting that *Mrs. Leicester's School* did not provide its young readers with sufficient instruction in traditional ethics. "We should have been happy," one remarked,

had something like morals been deduced from such incidents as afford them; and indeed we have long since determined that no book intended for youth is deserving of praise which does not either explicitly promote virtue, general or particular.[49]

This, however, was definitely a minority opinion. Another critic quickly retorted that Mary's work was "something of a higher cast" and that it possessed "a deep humanity which cannot fail to nurture and to mellow the opening heart, to render its seriousness sweeter, and its joy deeper and more lasting.''[50]

In his private journal, Coleridge wrote:

It at once soothes and amuses me to think—nay, to know—that the time will come when this little volume of my dear and well-nigh oldest friend, Mary Lamb, will not only be enjoyed but acknowledged as a rich jewel in the treasury of our permanent English literature.[51]

Mrs. Leicester's School, Coleridge declared, ''will be ranked as highly as Wilkie's *Epics* and Lord Bolingbroke's *Philosophics*.'' It would even be compared with *Robinson Crusoe*.[52] The poet and stylist Alfred Savage Landor pronounced Mary's stories ''an exquisite delight.'' They were equal, he said to Scott's *Lady of Lammermoor*.[53] *Mrs. Leicester's School* enjoyed great success. When Coleridge made his observation in 1825, the book had just appeared in its ninth edition. Although not so famous today as *Tales of Shakespear*, it remained a classic piece of children's literature throughout the nineteenth century.

In 1808, as *Mrs. Leicester's School* was being completed, the Lambs moved across the street from No. 16 Mitre Court to No. 4 Inner Temple Lane. During their years here, Mary not only continued to hold her large gatherings on Wednesday evenings but also invited some of her neighbors over individually on other days of the week. One of those frequently asked over for a tête-à-tête was the famous diarist, man of letters, and foreign editor of the *London Times* Henry Crabb Robinson. On 11 December 1814, he recorded in his journal:

After reading at home from eight to ten I called on Miss Lamb and chatted with her. She was not unwell, but she had undergone great fatigue from writing an article about needlework for the new *Lady's British Magazine*. She spoke of writing as a most painful occupation, which only necessity could make her attempt. She has been learning Latin mainly to assist her in acquiring a correct style. Yet, while she speaks of inability to write, what grace and talent has she not manifested in ''Mrs. Leicester's School.''[54]

The years Mary lived on Inner Temple Lane were also very important for her brother. This period witnessed Charles's emergence as a dominant figure in British literary criticism. In 1808, he published *Specimens of the English Dramatic Poets Who Lived about the Time of Shakespeare*, a book that stimulated renewed interest in the long-neglected works of such late sixteenth- and early seventeenth-century British dramatists as Webster, Ford, Kyd, Beaumont, and Fletcher. Three years later, in 1811, he published *On the Tragedies of Shakespeare*. It was in this work that Charles expressed the general opinion of the Romantic movement that Shakespeare was first and foremost a poet. The greatness of his verse, Charles argued, often went unrecognized because the acting profession, as it had existed up to the nineteenth century, was incapable of bringing it to life.

Thanks to his close association with Leigh Hunt, Charles was also able to demonstrate his talents to the public as an essayist. In 1811, for instance, the same year as the appearance of *On the Tragedies of Shakespeare*, Charles published an influential critique, "On the Genius of Hogarth," in Hunt's *Reflector*. In 1813, he printed his semiautobiographical "Recollections of Christ's Hospital" in Hunt's other newspaper, *The Examiner*. It was this essay that would later constitute the foundation of Charles's most famous work, *The Essays of Elia*. Charles also became briefly involved in Hunt's left-of-center politics, in 1813 publishing an anonymous lampoon in *The Examiner* on the fat, reactionary, and morally degenerate heir to the throne—"The Prince of Whales." But after this item led to the newspaper's suppression and Hunt's arrest and imprisonment, Charles withdrew from further activism. He spoke bitterly of press censorship and government encroachment on basic human freedoms, and he frequently went with Mary to visit Hunt in Horsemonger Gaol. However, he concluded that his destiny lay in literature and that he did not have the fire in him to be a political militant.

In the middle of the following year, 1814, as Henry Crabb Robinson recorded in his journal, Mary was approached by the women's periodical *The Lady's British Magazine* and asked to contribute an article. She consented. Her piece, which she wrote under the pseudonym "Sempronia," appeared in the magazine's April 1815 edition, and deserves much more historical attention than it is usually allotted.

Unlike other women's publications of the day, which dealt almost exclusively with fashion and society news, *The Lady's British Magazine* was involved in promoting its readers' interest and participation in social and political issues. "Needlework," the article Mary wrote, was an analysis of the position British women held in contemporary society and what they could do for themselves to improve it.

Despite its highly circumscribed nature, Mary believed, the role a woman played in nineteenth-century British society was extremely important. While not generally seen as such, the influence she exercised as caretaker, nurturer, moral example, adviser, and raiser of children was arguably more critical to the maintenance of a prosperous and enlightened culture than that of a politician, industrialist, theologian, scientist, or academic. Unfortunately, because women, unlike men, did not choose their roles freely, because their positions had no visible monetary worth, and because they performed them in private rather than in the public arena, women's tremendous contribution to society was consistently disregarded. Despite demonstrating they were strong, inventive, and energetic, women were yet perceived as weak, stupid, and dependent. Denied respect, belittled from their earliest years, it was not surprising many women acquiesced to this view of themselves—rejecting the value of their labors and passively accepting a position inferior to men:

"They can do what they like," we say. Do not these words generally mean they have time to seek out whatever amusements suit their tastes? We dare not tell them we have no time to do this; for, if they should ask in what manner we dispose of our time, we should blush to enter upon a detail of the minutiae which compose the sum of a woman's daily employment. . . .[55]

. . . Many a lady who allows not herself one quarter of an hour's positive leisure during her working hours, considers her husband as the most industrious of men, if he steadily pursues his occupation till the hour of dinner, and will be perpetually lamenting her own idleness.[56]

Unquestionably, Mary concluded:

To the execution of employment, in which the faculties of the body or mind are called into busy action, there must be a consoling importance attached, which feminine duties (that generic term for all our duties) cannot aspire to.[57]

So long as women confined themselves strictly to their traditional roles, important as these might be, they would continue to be undervalued. Only when they demonstrated their abilities in disciplines generally considered as the preserve of men—art, academics, literature—would they finally acquire the societal recognition and self-respect they deserved. Well aware of the activities of such contemporaries as Jane Austen, Mary Shelley, Madame de Stael, and Fanny Burney, the author was confident that they would succeed.

One of the main obstacles preventing women from achieving more, Mary believed, was the custom, still widely practiced during the early nineteenth century, that they should hand-produce most of their family's clothing. "Needlework," as it was often called, was an extremely time-consuming task that left the practitioner with very little time for other pursuits. Most readers of *The Lady's British Magazine* were comfortably middle class and came from families that could well afford to purchase their clothing. Needlework for them was not really necessary. Mary exhorted them to give up this tedious chore and dedicate the time they saved to writing, reading, and other scholarly, supposedly "male" occupations.

But it was more than the intellectual growth of women from the middle class about which Mary was concerned:

To lighten the heavy burthen which many ladies impose upon themselves is one object which I have in view; but, I confess, my strongest motive is to excite attention towards the industrious sisterhood to which I once belonged.[58]

The former mantua-cloth maker was referring, of course, to the women of the working class—a segment of society whose progress was hindered not only by social convention, but also by poverty. Few of them could depend on a benefactor like Samuel Salt for assistance; before they were able to devote their time to scholarship, they first needed education and economic self-sufficiency. Achieving this double task, Mary insisted, was not as difficult as might at first appear. The multitude of heavy responsibilities entailed in homemaking demonstrated that the female sex was highly "mechanical," that it was capable of performing all the industrial trades currently performed by males. Once this was recognized, once poorer families came to see their daughters as potential economic assets, their education and independence would naturally soon follow:

The parents of female children who were known from their birth to be destined to maintain themselves through the whole course of their lives with like certainty as their sons are, would feel it a duty incumbent on themselves to strengthen their minds and even the bodily constitutions of their girls so circumstanced, by an education which without affronting the perceived habits of society, might enable them to follow some occupation now considered above the capacity or too robust for the constitutions of their sex. Plenty of resources would then lie open for single women to obtain an independent livelihood when every parent would be upon the alert to encroach upon some employment . . . for such of their daughters as could then be exactly in the same predicament as their sons are now.[59]

Because "Needlework" was published only weeks after Napoleon's escape from Elba, during a period when most Britons were bolstering themselves for the possible outbreak of a vast new European war, it received very little attention. Even now, the article is traditionally regarded as a minor piece of Mary's writings, much overshadowed by *Tales of Shakespear* and *Mrs. Leicester's School*. Despite this, however, it boldly stands out today as one of the earliest expositions in British literature of what would later be called feminism—the doctrine advocating equal political and social rights for women. Almost as significant, in a culture so dominated by the class system, "Needlework" is remarkable for its ability to advocate its position with a total freedom from this prejudice. Although Mary may always be remembered chiefly as a writer of fiction, her historical importance can definitely be found in other areas as well.

In 1817, the Lambs at last moved out of the Inns of Court, settling in a larger apartment at No. 20-21 Bow Street, Covent Garden. Mary was saddened at leaving her birthplace. "Here we are," she wrote dejectedly to Dorothy Wordsworth,

transported from our native soil. I thought we never could have been torn up from the Temple. Indeed it was an ugly wrench, but like a tooth now it is out and I am easy. We never can strike root so deep in any other ground. This, where we are, is a light bit of gardener's mold, and if they take us up from it, it will cost no blood and groans like mandrakes pull'd up.[60]

As time passed, however, Mary grew accustomed to her new surroundings. The spot was convenient for Charles's work, as the neighborhood's famous theater was now within a walk of only about five minutes; those friends who had visited them on Wednesday nights when Mary and Charles lived in the Temple continued to attend when they were asked to come here. The move also proved beneficial to the Lambs' growing interest in rare first editions. Next door, at No. 19 Bow Street, was a large bookstore, which over the next few years helped Charles and Mary add considerably to their collection. Among the works they purchased there were a first folio of the plays of Beaumont and Fletcher and a special individual printing of Shakespeare's *Hamlet*. It also was in this store that they discovered one of the few remaining copies of Izaak Walton's 1653 classic, *The Compleat Angler*.

In 1818, the same bookstore was selling *The Works of Charles Lamb*. This five-volume set, dedicated to Coleridge and again published by Godwin, brought together all the author's writings—essays, poems, novels, short stories, plays, literary criticism—going back to the late 1790s. It was very successful, doing much to spread Charles's name beyond the journalistic and theatergoing circles of London and awakening interest in his writing among the nation's readers as a whole. The inclusion of *Tales of Shakespear* and *Mrs. Leicester's School*, which had until now always appeared under a pseudonym, confirmed the general public's longheld suspicion that Charles was connected with them. But once more there was no mention of his sister.

Beginning in the early 1820s, the Lambs found themselves performing a function they never expected to discharge—parenthood. For Mary, matrimony had never been a serious possibility. The tragedy of 1796 and her lifelong bouts with dementia forever eliminated any chance of it. Yet even if a proposal were ever made to her, Mary long ago had made up her mind to reject it. "I am glad I am an old maid," she wrote her friend Sarah Stoddart, now Mrs. William Hazlitt, in 1810; "for, you see, there is nothing but misfortunes in the married state."[61] As Mary saw it, in the early nineteenth century, this most august of institutions generally offered women little more than submission to the will of their husbands. Also, during a period when on the average only one of five offspring survived to adulthood, Mary, with her great affection for children, saw marriage as a very mournful experience. For his part, Charles proposed in 1819 to the famous Covent Garden actress Fanny Kelly, but was politely turned down by her on the same day.[62] Following this rebuff, the idea of either of the Lambs starting a family seemed very unlikely.

In recent years, however, Mary and Charles had become familiar during their trips to the country with an Italian expatriot named Charles Isola, who served as the Esquire Bedell—or director of security, for Cambridge University. His daughter Emma was a charming, highly intelligent little girl, for whom Mary and Charles quickly developed a fond attachment. Her father, who was a widower, did not earn a high salary; and when he suddenly died in 1821, it was evident Emma would be unable to take care of herself. Mary and Charles quickly decided to get permission from her temporary guardian, a Miss Humphreys, to allow the girl to visit them for extended periods of time in London. Although literary friendships with people like the Wordsworths and Leigh Hunt were always entertaining and intellectually stimulating, a child clearly fulfilled an emotional yearning these relationships could never satisfy. The Lambs' letters and other writings illustrate their feelings vividly:

Charles Lamb to Miss Humphreys
January 9, 1821

Emma is a very naughty girl, and has broken three cups, one plate and a slop-bason with mere giddiness. She is looking over me, which is impertinent. But if you can spare her longer than her holidays, we shall be happy to keep her, in hopes of her amendment. Will you, dear Miss Humph. permit Emma to stay a week or so beyond the holidays. She is studying algebra &. the languages. I teach her *dancing*.[63]

In 1823, Mary and Charles legally adopted Emma. Because they did not earn enough money to send her to a prestigious school, they decided to educate her at home themselves. Emma quickly demonstrated a great ability in history and literature, but she found Latin, which Mary taught her along with Coleridge's daughter Sara, much more difficult. Her teacher did not want her to become discouraged:

To Emma learning Latin
Droop not, dear Emma, dry those falling tears,
And call up smiles into thy pallid face,
Pallid and care-worn with thy arduous race:
In few brief months thou hast done the work of years.
To young beginnings natural are these fears,
A right good scholar shalt thou one day be,
And that no distant one; when even she,
Who now to thee a star far off appears,
That more rare Latinist, the Northern Maid-
The Language-loving Sarah, of the Lake-
Shall hail thee Sister Latinist. This will make
Thy friends, who now afford thee careful aid,
A recompense most rich for all their pains,
Counting thy requisitions their best gains.[64]

Mary's hopes proved correct. Emma Isola became an excellent student of the classics. She gave Mary and Charles great satisfaction. When she grew up and married the publisher Edward Moxon, she became the leader of her own intellectual circle, hostessing among others Wordsworth, William Gladstone, Alfred Lord Tennyson, and Henry Hallam. Emma's stepparents were very proud of her, but also sad to see her leave them.

When Charles Lamb's collected writings appeared in 1818, most readers of the day assumed the work represented a memorial to an already completed career. He was then forty-three, after all, and had certainly produced enough to allow him to now sit back and rest on his reputation. Few realized that his most fruitful years were yet to come.

In the following year, Leigh Hunt, now released from prison, introduced Charles to John Scott, the editor of *The London Magazine*. Scott, who had been very impressed by Charles's 1813 semi-autobiographical essay, "Recollections of Christ's Hospital," invited him to contribute similar pieces to his periodical. These compositions, which began to appear on a monthly basis in August 1820, were to overshadow anything Charles had ever written previously and would assure him a permanent place in the history of British literature.

British essay-writers at this time still followed in the tradition of Addison: Their works were short and succinct and expressed with precise diction; they dealt with elevated topics—justice, mercy, beauty, kingship—and were directed almost exclusively to a small, highly educated readership. Finally, authors tried as hard as possible to withdraw from their treatises and to offer no revelations about themselves. The twenty-eight essays that Charles wrote for *The London Magazine* between 1820 and 1822 and published as a book in 1823 totally revolutionized this discipline—altering its style, augmenting its subject matter, and most important, expanding the audience that was expected to read it. As was the custom, Charles wrote under a pseudonym, signing himself "Elia"—the name of a long-retired business associate of Portuguese ancestry who, like Charles, had once been employed as a clerk at the British East India Tea Company; and it is as *The Elia Essays* that this work is remembered today.[65] Published in several editions in the United States, it was also responsible for the spread of the author's reputation abroad.

Like Montaigne before him, Charles employed the essay form in order to write both an autobiography and a social history of his time. He accomplished this not by the traditional method of recounting major experiences and contemporary events but rather through an intimate analysis of his thoughts and a series of anecdotes on seemingly minor but revealing subjects. The effectiveness of this personal narrative technique is demonstrated amply in such pieces as "The South-Sea House," "Oxford in the Vacation," "Dream Children," "Christ's Hospital Five and Thirty Years Ago," "The Old Benchers at the Inner Temple," and "Mrs. Battle's Opinions on Whist." While sometimes accused of demanding of current readers a historical knowledge of the era in which they were composed, *The Elia Essays* are nevertheless generally accepted today as an extremely important contribution to British nineteenth-century British prose. Besides being written in a more flowing and expansive manner than any other essays of the period, they are dedicated not to arcane, philosophical themes, but rather to aspects of ordinary life—work, affection, happiness, family. This and their strongly nostalgic flavor made Charles's new style of writing especially popular with the general British reading public, who until then had found their lives overlooked by major authors.

"The streets of London," Hazlitt wrote enthusiastically of *The Elia Essays*, "are his faery land, teeming with wonder, with life and interest to his retrospective glance, as it did to the eager eye of childhood; he has contrived to weave its tritest traditions into a bright and endless romance."[66]

"British literature," declared the great Lamb scholar E. V. Lucas,

has nothing that in its way is better than *Elia*'s best. The blend of sanity, sweet reasonableness, tender fancy, high imagination, sympathetic understanding of human nature, now wistful, now frolicsome, with literary skill of unsurpassed delicacy, makes *Elia* unique.[67]

Describing the *Essays* in *A Room of One's Own* (1929), Virginia Woolf spoke of "that wild flash of imagination, that lightning crack of genius in the middle of them which leaves them flawed and imperfect, but starred with poetry."[68]

The Elia Essays also shed an interesting light on the closely interwoven lives of the author and his sister. "Poor Lamb!" Coleridge confessed to Godwin in June 1800, "how cruelly afflictions crowd upon him."[69] He was not the only individual to express such feelings. Despite her literary successes and high social visibility, Mary was forever haunted by the specter of insanity. In 1822, at Amiens, while on a vacation in France, she had suddenly collapsed into horrible ravings and had to be rushed back to London in restraints.[70] Though never discussing openly, many privately conjectured about the sufferings Mary's condition must be inflicting on her brother. To obtain her release from Hoxton Asylum in 1799, after all, Charles had been forced to accept total legal and financial responsibility for her. As charming as she might often appear, people whispered, Mary must be a terrible burden. Surely, the fact that in his mid-forties Charles still lacked a family of his own must be due to the strain of his sister's illness. After all, what lady would agree to marry the famous critic if she knew she would be obliged to share her home with such a sister-in-law. However, as Charles's essays demonstrate, his relationship with Mary was far from the smothering, oppressive affair so many outsiders imagined.

Hardships there undoubtedly were, but Charles accepted them; he knew he would never find anyone else who offered him the same camaraderie as Mary. She was not only his sister, she was his soul mate. "Bridget Elia," he explained to his readers in "Mackery End,"

has been my housekeeper for many a year. I have obligations to Bridget, extending beyond the period of memory. We house together, old bachelor and maid, in a set of double singleness; with much tolerable comfort, upon the whole, that I, for one, find in myself no sort of disposition to go out upon the mountains, with the rash king's offspring, to bewail my celibacy.[71]

"Her education in youth," the author continued,

was not much attended to; and she happily missed that grain of garniture, which passeth by the name of accomplishment. She was tumbled early by accident or design, into a spacious closet of good English reading, without much selection or prohibition, browsed at will upon fair and wholesome pasturage. Had I twenty girls, they should be brought up exactly in this fashion.[72]

"We agree pretty well in our tastes and habits," Charles said of their relationship,

—yet so, as "with a deference." We are generally in harmony, with occasional bickerings—as it should be among near relatives. . . . We are both great readers in different directions. While I am hanging over (for the thousandeth time) some passage in old Burton, or one of his strange contemporaries, she is abstracted in some modern tale, or adventure, whereof our common reading-table is daily fed with assiduously fresh supplies.[73]

In spite of the public attention brought to him by his Wednesday evening dinners and the success of his literary career, Charles was by nature a very private individual. He was shy, afflicted with a bad speech impediment, and liable to long bouts of depression. Although engaging and expansive in the company of his small circle of intimate friends like Coleridge, Leigh Hunt, and the Wordsworths, he felt extremely uncomfortable in large groups. While skillful at elaborate discussions of important intellectual subjects, he was not gifted at what is today called small talk. As for marriage, it was his reticent disposition, not his sister's medical condition, that presumably dissuaded most women from considering him a prospective husband. Given these circumstances, it seems only natural that when searching for a companion, Charles would turn to Mary. Like the fictional Bridget of "Mackery End," Mary shared her brother's literary and artistic interests, his enjoyment of scholarly discourse, his friendships, and most significant, his desire for a quiet, peaceful existence. Mary's intellectual fellowship and emotional support were very important for Charles as he began to experience increasing periods of loneliness and depression. "Charles was drunk last night," Mary remarked to Sarah Hazlitt, "and drunk the night before."[74] Who, Charles now reasoned, would be able to appreciate another's sufferings better than his sister? Much was said of Mary's dependence on her brother, but very little of his reliance upon her. In a letter to Hazlitt, he referred to her as *Epistemon*, a figure in Greek mythology who is the manifestation of wisdom and prudence.[75]

In 1825, Charles retired after thirty-three years' service as a scrivener at the British East India Tea Company. Release from that seemingly interminable period of dreary, poorly paid, and largely unrecognized labor came as a great relief. He felt at first as if he were one of the Hebrews after completing the flight from Egypt. The year 1825 would also mark, however, the end of the Wednesday evening dinners. Many of the Lambs' friends now had their permanent residences outside of London and could attend only periodically. In 1822, Leigh Hunt left Britain altogether and joined the Shelleys and Lord Byron in Italy. Also, the duration of Mary's bouts of mental illness was increasing. Charles wondered if they were exacerbated by the many duties she had to fulfill as a hostess. Lastly, his own experiences with depression sometimes made these occasions difficult. For these reasons, he decided the famous dinners should come to an end. It was sad, but after volunteering their home as the principal meeting place of literary London for over two decades, the Lambs could safely say they deserved a rest. It was now time for someone else to take the lead.

In an attempt to find a more restful atmosphere, the Lambs soon moved to Enfield, several miles northeast of London. Today absorbed into the sprawl of the capital's greater metropolitan area, Enfield was at the time a small country town bordering a forest filled with wild deer, badgers, and rabbits. Life here was especially attractive to Mary and Charles, because while it offered them the peace of the countryside, it was also close enough to London that they could easily visit their old haunts.

At first, the move seemed the answer to all their problems, bringing as it did feelings of freedom and relaxation. Liberated from the East India Company and able now to devote all his time to literary pursuits, Charles was very happy. Mary's physical and mental condition started to improve as well:

Charles Lamb to William Wordsworth
April 4, 1825

I can sit at home in rain or shine without a restless impulse for walkings. I am daily steadying, and shall soon find it as natural to be my own master, as it has been irksome to have had a master. Mary wakes every morning with an obscure feeling that some good has happened to us.

Leigh Hunt and Montgomery[76] after their releasements describe the shock of their emancipation much as I feel mine. But it hurt their frames. I eat, drink, and sleep as sound as ever. I lay no anxious schemes for going hither and thither, but takes things as they occur. Yesterday I excursioned 20 miles, today I write a few letters. Pleasuring was for fugitive play days, mine are fugitive only in the sense that life is fugitive. Freedom and life co-exist. . . .[77]

Charles Lamb to Robert Southey
August 19, 1825

We got your little book but last night, being at Enfield, to which place we came about a month since, and are having quiet holydays. Mary walks her twelve miles day some days, and I my twenty on others. Tis all holidays with me now, you know. The change works admirably.[78]

Charles received a yearly pension of four hundred-and-forty-one pounds, not a tremendous amount, but certainly enough for him and Mary to live quite comfortably in a small town.[79] They were able to possess a home of their own (now Lamb Cottage) and to continue expanding their library, which now included first editions of Pope, Chaucer, Bunyan, Milton, Dryden, Evelyn, and Fielding, as well as early translations of Greek and Latin classics such as Chapman's *Iliad*. Best of all, Emma was with them. Their stepdaughter's eager intelligence and loving personality were a constant source of happiness for them.

Unfortunately, this situation did not last; the move to Enfield brought only a temporary amelioration of Mary's condition. Attacks of madness would now last not days, but weeks or months. She made several attempts over the next few years to write again, but each time the strain on her mind was too great, and she would break down. On a number of occasions, she had to be returned to the asylum. Early nineteenth-century medicine being as primitive as it was, there was no treatment available to halt her steady decline. By 1832, Mary's once-sharp mind possessed no more than six months each year of unclouded reason.

In the following spring, Charles decided to move again, this time to Edmonton, another small town outside of London, several miles to the east. Here, he hoped, there might be more facilities nearby to care for Mary:

Charles Lamb to William Wordsworth
End of May 1833

Mary is ill again. Her illnesses encroach yearly. The last was three months, followed by two of depression most dreadful. I look back upon her earlier attacks with longing. Nice little duration of six weeks or so, followed by complete restoration—shocking as they were to me then. In short, half her life she is dead to me, and the other half is made anxious with fears and lookings forward to the next shock. With such prospects, it seem'd to me necessary that she should no longer live with me, and be fluttered with continual removals, so I am come to live with her, at a Mr. Walden's and his wife, who take in patients, and have arranged to lodge us only. They had the care of her before. I see little of her; alas! I too often hear her. Sunt lachryhmae rerum—and you and I must bear it.[80]

These were not the words of a man who, as many in society believed, was enslaved to his sister by a heavy chain of obligation. Rather, they were words of love. Despite the great burden her sufferings brought upon him, Charles would never leave the person who did more than anyone else to help him attain the place in history he achieved.

In the same letter, Charles announced to Wordsworth Emma's engagement to his young associate, Edward Moxon.[81] A rising figure in the publishing profession, he recently brought out Charles's latest collection of articles, *The Last Essays of Elia*. In later years, Moxon was also to be the original publisher of many of the works of Shelley, Robert Browning, and Alfred Lord Tennyson. During recent months he and Emma had become very intimate friends and had now decided to marry. Charles was saddened to see Emma leave him. She was, as he wrote Wordsworth, "my old and true walking companion, whose mirthful spirits were the 'youth of our house.'. . ."[82] At the same time, however, he believed it was a very good match and gave her his full approval. It would also be good for Emma to leave her ever more dreary home and start a life of her own. To help her decorate it, Charles gave his stepdaughter the family's painting of Milton, the one that hangs today in the National Portrait Gallery.

The wedding took place on 30 July 1833.[83] It proved to be a very happy occasion because Mary, who had been ill for much of the Spring, had recovered sufficiently to attend. When the ceremony concluded and the new couple was preparing to embark on their honeymoon, she composed a short note to them expressing her feelings.

Mary Lamb to Edward and Emma Moxon
July 30, 1833

Accept my sincere congratulations, and imagine more good wishes than my weak nerves will let me put into good set words. The dreary blank of *unanswered questions* which I ventured to ask in vain was cleared up on the wedding-day by Mrs. W. *taking* a glass of wine, and with a total change of countenance, begged leave to drink Mr. &. Mrs. Moxon's health. It restored me, from that moment: as if by an electric stroke: to the entire possession of my senses—I never felt so calm and quiet after a similar illness as I do now. I feel as if all tears were wiped from my eyes, and all care from my heart.[84]

Emma's wedding proved to be the last true joy in the double lives of Mary and Charles Lamb. With their stepdaughter's departure, they were now alone. Emma and her husband promised to visit, and they did so as much as possible; but the process of setting up a new home inevitably took up most of their attention. Not a great deal of information is available about the events of the following year, except that Mary once more declined in health, and Charles was disappointed by the overall reception of *The Last Essays of Elia*. Wordsworth, among others, was extremely impressed, especially with such pieces as "The Superannuated Man" and "Old-China," but the general reading public appears not to have appreciated it as much as it did the previous work. This concern was quickly overwhelmed, however, by the news that Coleridge had died on 25 July 1834. He was just short of sixty-two.[85]

The decade following Coleridge's return from Malta in 1806 had been the darkest in his life. These years witnessed his final separation from his wife, Sarah Fricker; the failure of a promising journalistic career; and most painful of all, his schism with the Wordsworths. In each case, the principal cause was the poet's growing drug abuse. Once a magnetic and vibrant personality, he had been transformed by his addiction into a paranoid, lethargic, and untrustworthy individual totally unable to manage his own affairs or to appreciate the needs and concerns of others. His condition had an equally destructive affect on his creative powers; except for periodic lecture tours and a modestly successful play at Drury Lane in 1813, Coleridge had ceased to be a writer. Finally, in April of 1816, after several abortive attempts and now deeply in debt, he at last sought a cure, moving into the home of the famous physician Dr. James Gillman of Highgate, where he remained for the last eighteen years of his life. The extent to which Gillman was able actually to break Coleridge's dependence on opium is uncertain; but his constant and devoted care did put it under control. In 1817, after so many wasted years, Coleridge published his great philosophical work, *Biographia Literaria.* He had at last regained a measure of his former self, and with it peace of mind. Beginning in 1824, the year before the Lambs moved out of London, Coleridge even inaugurated a literary evening of his own, at Gillman's Highgate house on Thursdays. Many of those who came were the members of a younger generation that had previously only known of their host during his decline, and these get-togethers played a major role in the poet's rediscovery.

Charles never really recovered from the loss of his friend. Coleridge had been his oldest and most intimate male companion. They had known each other for fifty years, since their days as Bluecoat Boys at Christ's Hospital. It had been to Coleridge that Charles first turned for consolation upon discovering his sister's madness; with Coleridge he first entered upon a career in literature. Their relationship was like a portrait of the Romantic Age: Even though it was sometimes scarred by bitterness and rivalry, both cherished it. For Charles, Coleridge held a place in his heart second only to Mary. The news of his friend's passing was a great shock to him. It sent him into another violent fit of depression. For months, he was seen walking alone about the streets of Edmonton muttering to himself and in tears. It was during one of these solitary odysseys, on December 22, that Charles stumbled and fell, badly striking his head. For some time he had been suffering from erysipelas, a streptococcal inflammation of the skin tissue. The blow allowed the illness to reach the bloodstream, infection set in, and the condition quickly worsened; on Christmas Day 1834, he died.[86] Charles was fifty-nine. He was buried in the cemetery near his home on Church Street (now the Lamb Museum), where his grave can be seen today. At Moxon's suggestion, Wordsworth was selected to write the epitaph. His memorial came to eighty-three lines, much too long to fit on the tombstone, but after some discussion, three of them were chosen:

Still, at the centre of his being lodged
A Soul by resignation sanctified:
O, he was good, if ever good man lived

Mary could not attend the funeral. She was still suffering from a fit of delusions that came over her a month earlier. Only several weeks later was she well enough to understand at least partially that Charles had died. Even then, though, she perceived it as a strange, shadowy event with which she was only vaguely connected. This was perhaps just as well. Writing in his journal after a visit with her on 11 January 1835, Henry Crabb Robinson recalled pensively:

She was neither violent nor unhappy; nor was she entirely without sense. She was, however, out of her mind, as the expression is; but she could combine ideas, although imperfectly. . . . She gave me her hand with great cordiality, and said, ". . . this is very kind, not merely good natured to come and see me in my affliction." . . . I have no doubt that if ever she be sensible of her brother's loss, it will overset her.[87]

Twelve years her brother's senior, Mary was now seventy-two. Suffering from the effects of advanced mental illness, few had expected her to survive

Charles. His friends long wondered how he would be able to handle such a heavy loss. Naturally assuming that no financial arrangements had been made for the event, they were now very concerned about how Mary could manage alone. Henry Crabb Robinson announced his intention of launching a fund-raising campaign for her benefit. In the end, this did not turn out to be necessary. Charles's will made provisions for the possibility that his sister would outlive him. He bequeathed Mary two thousand pounds in three-percent British East India Tea Company savings bonds. The interest provided her with a yearly income of one hundred-and-twenty pounds, enough to enable her to remain at home with the assistance of a nurse.[88]

Mary spent the last years of her life far away from the impassioned London literary scene she once played hostess for. Occasionally, she received visits from Hazlitt, Robinson, and other old friends, but most of her time was shared with her nurses, the James Sisters, the daughters of the Rector of Beguildry Parish in Shropshire. She was very close to them, having taught the girls French when they were children. In 1841, after one of them married and rumors arose that Mary was being neglected by her landlady, she was moved to a house at No. 41 Alpha Street, St. John's Wood. It still stands today. Here, she stayed with one of her two young companions, one now Mrs. Parsons, until her death.

From the little information available today, Mary appears to have been generally happy in her secluded existence. She still enjoyed lucid moments; sometimes she even went out for walks and wrote letters to friends:

Mary Lamb to Jane Norris
December 25, 1841

I long to shew you what a nice snug place I have got into—in the midst of a pleasant little garden. I have a room for myself and my old books on the ground floor, and a little bed room up two pairs of stairs. When you come to town, if you have not time to go to the Moxons, an omnibus from the Bell and Crown in Holborn would bring you to our door in a quarter of an hour. If your dear Mother does not venture so far, I will contrive to pop down to see her.[89]

Mary remained in close contact with Emma and the rest of her family:

Mary Lamb to Emma and Edward Moxon
October 3, 1842

My cold is quite well. I enclose a pleasant letter from Jane Norris—I have written a few lines to thank her for it. Can you write me a line to say how you are. I have not been out, except on a ride with Mrs. Talfourd, since I saw you, and I shall keep in the house as much as I can this winter.
Love to your husband & children & Mary.
Yours Ever,
M. Lamb[90]

This is the last letter written by Mary Lamb that is known to exist. She died peacefully in her bed on 20 May 1847, at the age of eighty-three.[91] Having survived not only her brother, but also Coleridge, Byron, Keats, Shelley, and Blake, she had outlived all the major figures of the British Romantic Age except the Wordsworths. Her passing almost symbolized the passing of an era.

Mary was buried next to her brother in Edmonton churchyard on May 28. The funeral was a small, solemn affair, most of those who might have attended having already preceded her to the grave. No one questioned why Dorothy Wordsworth was absent; she would not have understood what was happening anyway. Like her friend, she had long been rendered mentally incapacitated, in her case from arteriosclerosis. Among those who did attend the ceremony, only Edward Moxon and Henry Crabb Robinson could say they knew Mary intimately. And yet amid his sadness, the diarist noted, there was also a feeling of relief, if not exactly happiness. Liberated now from her many sufferings, Mary could once more join her brother. As they stood together in life, so now they could stand together in history.

NOTES: PART ONE

1. Percy Fitzgerald, ed. *The Life, Letters and Writings of Charles Lamb* (London: Constable, 1875), vol. 1, 78.

2. Edward V. Lucas, *The Life of Charles Lamb* (New York: Putnam's, 1905), vol. 1, 4.

3. Ibid.

4. Ibid.

5. Ibid., 1.

6. William Carew Hazlitt, *The Lambs* (London: Matthews, 1897), 16.

7. Lucas, *The Life*, 55-56.

8. Charles and Mary Lamb, *The Works of Charles and Mary Lamb*, ed. E. V. Lucas (London: Methuen, 1904), vol. 3, 306.

9. Ibid., 315-17.

10. Ibid., 283.

11. Ibid., 306-7.

12. Barry Cornwall (Bryan Waller Procter), *Charles Lamb: A Memoir* (London: Moxon, 1876), 33.

13. Hazlitt, *The Lambs*, xii.

14. Charles and Mary Lamb, *The Complete Letters of Charles and Mary Lamb*, ed. E. V. Lucas (London: Methuen, 1935), vol. 1, 39-40.

15. *London Morning Chronicle*, 26 September 1796.

16. Charles Lamb, *The Selected Letters of Charles Lamb*, ed. T. S. Matthews (New York: Farrar, Strauss and Cudahy), 1956, 13.

17. Lamb, *Complete Letters*, 47.

18. Ibid., 360.

19. Ibid., 103.

20. Lucas, *The Life*, 159.

21. Ibid., 129.

22. Lamb, *Complete Letters*, 155.

23. Lucas, *The Life*, 238. Barry Cornwall--penname of Bryan Waller Procter (1787-1874), dramatist, songwriter, frequent Wednesday-evening visitor, and father of the poet Adelaide Procter.

24. Samuel Taylor Coleridge, *Collected Letters of Samuel Taylor Coleridge*, ed. Leslie Griggs (Oxford: Clarendon, 1956), vol. 1, 497.

25. Lamb, *Complete Letters*, 189.

26. Ibid., 169.

27. Ibid., 209-10.

28. Alfred Ainger, *Charles Lamb*, (New York: Harpers, 1902), 23.

29. Sir Thomas Noon Talfourd, *Memoirs of Charles Lamb* (London: Gibbings, 1982), 223. Sir Thomas was an MP and a family acquaintance and the author of the first biography of Charles Lamb.

30. Lamb, *Complete Letters*, 354.

31. Ibid., 371.

32. Ibid., 379. Thomas Clarkson was a mutual friend and a well-known campaigner against the slave trade.

33. Lucas, *The Life*, 355.

34. Lamb, *Complete Letters*, 375.

35. Charles and Mary Lamb, *The Letters of Charles and Mary Lamb*, ed. Edwin Marrs, Jr. (Ithaca, NY: Cornell University Press, 1978), 166.

36. Lucas, *The Life*, 536.

37. Lamb, *Complete Letters*, vol. 2, 9.

38. Lamb, *The Works*, vol. 3, 4.

39. Thomas Manning, an orientalist, linguist, and longtime family friend, was about to start a career as a Protestant missionary in China. He would also travel to Tibet, becoming the first white man to reach Lhasa and meet the Dalai Lama.

40. Lamb, *Complete Letters*, vol. 2, 188.

41. Ibid., 10. Mary Stoddart, a close friend of Mary Lamb, was about to become the wife of the critic William Hazlitt.

42. Ibid., 14.

43. Ibid., 18.

44. Lamb, *The Works*, vol. 3, 11.

45. Lamb, *Complete Letters*, vol. 2, 29.

46. Ibid., 36.

47. Ibid., 36-37.

48. Lamb, *The Works*, vol. 3, 306.

49. Edmund Blunden, *Charles Lamb and his Contemporaries* (Cambridge: Cambridge University Press, 1933), 75.

50. Ibid.

51. Reginald L. Hine, *Charles Lamb and His Hertfordshire* (London: Dent, 1949), 135.

52. Ibid.

53. Malcolm Elwin, *Landor* (London: MacDonald, 1958), 355.

54. Henry Crabb Robinson, *Diary, Reminiscences, and Correspondence of Henry Crabb Robinson*, ed. T. S. Sadler (London: Macmillan, 1872), vol. 1. 189.

55. *Lady's British Magazine*, April 1815.

56. Ibid.

57. Ibid.

58. Ibid.

59. Ibid.

60. Lucas, *The Life*, 536-37.

61. Lamb, *Complete Letters*, vol. 2, 97.

62. Lucas, *The Life*, vol. 2, 19.

63. Lamb, *Complete Letters*, vol. 2, 290.

64. *Blackwood's Magazine*, June 1829.

65. Lamb, *Complete Letters*, vol. 2, 290.

66. Cornwall, *Charles Lamb*, 237.

67. Lucas, *The Life*, vol. 2, 61.

68. Virginia Woolf, *A Room of One's Own* London: Hogarth Press, 1929), 8.

69. Lamb, *Complete Letters*, vol. 1, 588.

70. Mary Wollstonecraft Shelley, *The Letters of Mary Wollstonecraft Shelley*, ed. B. Bennett (Baltimore: Johns Hopkins, 1980), vol. 1, 373.

71. Charles Lamb, *The Essays of Elia* (London: Methuen, 1902), 158.

72. Ibid., 159.

73. Ibid. Robert Burton (1577-1640) was an Oxford scholar and author of the highly influential *Anatomy of Melancholy* (1621).

74. Lamb, *Complete Letters*, vol. 2, 97.

75. Ibid., 102.

76. James Montgomery (1771-1854) was a Scottish poet and journalist, best remembered today for his hymn, *Hail to the Lord's Annointed*. In 1796, he was imprisoned for writing articles opposing Britain's war on Revolutionary France.

77. Lamb, *Selected Letters*, 197.

78. Ibid., 198.

79. Hazlitt, *The Lambs*, 52

80. Lamb, *Selected Letters*, 276.

81. Ibid.

82. Ibid.

83. Lamb, *Complete Letters*, vol. 3, 380.

84. Ibid.

85. Lucas, *The Life*, vol. 2, 417.

86. Ibid., 396.

87. Robinson, *Diary*, vol. 2, 155.

88. Hazlitt, *The Lambs*, 52.

89. Lucas, *The Life*, vol. 2, 402. Jane Norris was a longtime family friend. Her grandfather had been librarian of the Inner Temple at the same time John Lamb was assistant to Samuel Salt.

90. Lamb, *Complete Letters*, vol. 3, 380.

91. Lucas, *The Life*, vol. 2, 400.

Part Two

DOROTHY WORDSWORTH

Chapter Three

A Pensive Young Lady

Unlike her brother William, Dorothy Wordsworth appears today in no authentic portrait. Keats, who visited her at Rydal Mount in 1818, claimed to have seen one; but if he did, that likeness was lost long ago. The most famous written description of her is probably found in a letter that Samuel Taylor Coleridge mailed to his publisher, Joseph Cottle, on 3 July 1797:

> Wordsworth and his exquisite sister are with me,—She is a woman indeed!—in mind, I mean, & heart—for her person is such, that if you expected to see a pretty woman, you would think her ordinary—if you expected to see an ordinary woman, you would think her pretty!—But her manners are simple, ardent, impressive—
>
> In every motion her most innocent soul
> Outbeams so brightly, that who would say,
> Guilt was a thing impossible in her.[1]

As compelling as Coleridge's memorable passage is, it unfortunately does no more than Keats to supply the twentieth-century historian with verifiable details about its subject's image. Yet if her physical characteristics may never be known precisely, there is no doubt that the actions of her eventful life and the ideals which motivated them make the personality of Dorothy Wordsworth stand out as one of the truest portraits of the British Romantic Age.

Dorothy was born on Christmas Day of 1771, the third child and only daughter of John Wordsworth and Ann Cookson.[2] Unlike Mary Lamb, who was born in the historic Middle Temple district of the City of London, Dorothy spent her earliest years in the unremarkable little West Country town of Cockermouth, Cumberlandshire, a few miles inland from the Irish Sea. In a period so dominated by the class system, however, this lack of a historic birthplace was more than made up for by the Wordsworth family's superior position in society. While Mary's father was a scribe and valet, Dorothy's was a solicitor. In such a capacity, he exercised the multiple positions of bailiff, recorder for the borough, and official coroner. Sir James Lowther (later the first Earl of Lonsdale), the largest landholder in the county, also employed him as his business and legal agent. In the eighteenth century, such a situation was not viewed as a conflict of interest; and as a spokesman of both the law and property, John Wordsworth was able to attain for himself and his family a position of great prestige in their community. This status assured that his daughter, even during her days of economic distress, was always referred to as a *lady*.

Dorothy and William—born the previous year on 7 April 1770—won a place in history, but all five of the Wordsworth children were successful in their own way. Richard, the eldest, born in 1768, followed his father into the law; John, born in 1772, rose to be a sea captain for the British East India Tea Company; and the youngest, Christopher, born in 1774, became Master of St. John's College, Cambridge. Except for attendance at Cockermouth's local grammar school, run by Mrs. Birkett, however, the brothers and their sister spent most of their childhood and adolescence living apart. In 1777, when Dorothy was six, her mother, Ann Wordsworth, developed a case of consumption while visiting friends in London. Such an ailment was incurable in the unhygienic conditions the majority of Britons lived in at the time, and by the middle of the following year she was clearly dying. For all his professional attainments, Dorothy's father was unable to handle the situation. While the premature loss of a spouse was a not uncommon occurrence at this time and was usually taken in stride, John Wordsworth, who possessed a very strong emotional attachment to his wife, was thrown into terrible grief at the prospect of being forced to live on without her. Ann decided that her husband would not have the strength to raise the children on his own, and so, just before her death in late 1778, she had them dispatched to the supervision of boarding schools or various relatives.[3]

Dorothy was sent to Halifax, Yorkshire, to live with her aunt Elizabeth Threlkeld, soon Mrs. William Rawson.[4] The nine years she lived there were important in shaping her intellectual interests and public concerns as an adult. Aunt Rawson, as she was affectionately called, was a member of a newly formed theological group called the Unitarians. As such, she was a champion of free inquiry and the individual's personal search for knowledge and was a fierce opponent of dogmatism, both religious and secular. Most often, Dorothy Wordsworth is remembered as her brother's faithful helper, as a loyal disciple striving ceaselessly for the accomplishment of her leader's aspirations. The fact that her endeavors were actually motivated by talents and convictions all her own is true in large part because of the upbringing she received in Halifax.

Aunt Rawson, who at this time was already raising the children of her widowed older brother, had no offspring of her own. Her decision to take on the task of caring for her niece as well was prompted not only by the wish to ease the worries of the dying Ann Wordsworth, but also by a desire to attain some of the maternal satisfactions that had been denied her. She put all her energy into raising Dorothy as her own daughter and, inspired by her progressive worldview, gave the girl an intellectually stimulating education. While the curriculum of conventional British female education at the time centered around making its students attractive to prospective husbands—dancing, singing, watercoloring, etiquette—Aunt Rawson was interested in nurturing her charge's scholarly attributes. Quickly perceiving that Dorothy was a clever child, her aunt insisted she familiarize herself with the writings of her country's major creative authors. Among others, she had Dorothy read the works of Pope, Shakespeare (a rare experience for girls at the time), Milton, Dryden, Chaucer, and Richardson. She was introduced as well to classical poets like Homer and Virgil. But besides reading the works of others, Dorothy was also called upon to write essays and stories of her own. Such classroom compositions would have great significance later on. They awakened in her an intuitive literary talent, one that would propel Dorothy as an adult into the roles of early sociologist and chronicler of British Romantic literature.

Besides an interest in academic and artistic subjects, Aunt Rawson also imparted to her niece a sense of duty and selflessness. It was very easy, Dorothy was often told, for a member of the relatively sheltered middle class to ignore the hard and often painful existence of Britain's workers, to believe that their condition was somehow divinely ordained. Dorothy must not surrender to this prejudice; she must respect those not so lucky as herself and do what she could to improve their lot. She should also do all she could to help people who were ill or unable to care for themselves properly. Dorothy's abiding sympathy for the lower classes is vividly displayed throughout the pages of the *Grasmere Journal*, and her desire to assist the ill is demonstrated in the many months she gave to nursing the self-destructive Coleridge.

The years Dorothy spent in Halifax were very happy. She was admired throughout the community for her intelligence, cultured mind, and public spirit. Many neighborhood parents considered her as a living example for their own children to emulate. In later decades, she would look back upon this period in her life as a lost idyll. It was in Halifax, too, that Dorothy developed her first important friendship. Jane Pollard, who lived nearby, was a girl of about her own age and had many of the same interests. The two adolescents spent nearly all their free time together and, when separated, wrote each other long letters. This correspondence, which continued for a number of years after Dorothy departed from Halifax, is valuable as the earliest written record of her intellectual evolution.

Dorothy Wordsworth to Jane Pollard
August 6-7, 1787

I am also mu[ch] obliged to you for your l[i]t[terar]y intelligence. I do not
[remember] having heard of the conversations of Emily. I ha[ve] a very pretty
little collection of Books from my Brothers [ ] which they have given me. I will
give you a catalog[ue]. I have the *Iliad*, the Odyssey [?] works, Fielding's works,
Hayley's poems, Gil Blas (in French), Gregory's *Legacy to his Daughter*, and my
Brother Ric[hard] intends sending me Shakespeare's Plays and the *Spect* [*ator*].
I have also Milton's Works, Dr. Goldsmith's poems, [and] other trifling things.
. . .[5]

In 1787, Dorothy's pleasant sojourn in Halifax came to an end, and she was
forced to move in with her maternal uncle Christopher Crackanthorpe and her
grandparents, Mr. and Mrs. William Cookson, in the town of Penrith,
Cumberlandshire.[6] Two years earlier, in 1785, her father had died, never having
fully recovered from the loss of his wife. After his death, it was discovered that
he had previously loaned the Earl of Lonsdale five thousand pounds, quite a
considerable sum for the time, a sum that the Earl now refused to pay back. Such
was the legal system of the time that there was no way of compelling him to do
so. While the unfortunate affair had not totally wiped out the Wordsworth
family's savings, leaving Dorothy and her brothers impoverished, it had severely
restricted their future prospects. Those of the brothers who wished to do so could
still attend college, for instance, but there would be little left afterward to assist
them in launching their careers. As for their sister, barred as she was from both
higher education and a profession, Uncle Kit and the Cooksons, now the
children's official guardians, decided that under these reduced circumstances the
best thing for her was to stop wasting her time reading novels and writing essays
and to devote herself to learning the domestic chores necessary if she were ever
to obtain a husband to support her. They therefore ordered Aunt Rawson to send
her to reside with them.

The period Dorothy spent in Penrith could hardly be described as cheerful.
Strong supporters of the Church of England and, ironically, supporters of the
Earl of Lonsdale in the Wordsworths' legal dispute, Dorothy's guardians had
always looked upon the Unitarian Aunt Rawson with suspicion; from the
beginning, they opened a campaign to cleanse their ward of the "wild spirit" she
had been "infected" with in Halifax. They forbade her to read many of the
literary works she had come to love over the years. They were particularly
hostile to the poetry of Robert Burns, who they claimed was a "very wild
individual." They insisted that intellectual pursuits in general were really beyond
the purview of a *proper young lady* or middle-class housewife. When Dorothy,
who had been taught to think for herself, did not quietly give in to their
demands, she was locked in her room or forbidden to leave the house. Not a day
passed without a reprimand.

Aunt Rawson was not the only person Uncle Kit and the Crackanthorpes feared would exercise a corrupting influence on young Dorothy. Soon after she arrived at Penrith, her brother William arrived for a visit. In spite of their close historical association, in 1787 brother and sister had not seen each other since their mother's death.[7] During the intervening nine years, while Dorothy was in Halifax, William had attended Public School at Hawkshead. Just graduated, he was now on his way to enroll at St. John's College, Cambridge. His visit lasted three weeks, and he and Dorothy enjoyed a wonderful time together, becoming reacquainted and discovering the many intellectual interests they had in common. Without asking their grandparents' permission, the two often went on long walks under the stars during which they discussed their plans for the future. These strolls would form the basis of William's first important poetic work, *An Evening Walk*. Unfortunately, the guardians soon found out about these clandestine excursions quickly. Considering them questionable, they ordered William to depart quickly. But their triumph was to be of brief duration. Although abruptly severed, it was not long before the bond that now existed between brother and sister would manifest itself again.

Seeing that she could no longer openly resist the plans her relatives had for her, Dorothy continued her intellectual pursuits in secret. "I think I hear you saying," she wrote to Jane Pollard:

"how will [you] have time to read all these things?" I am determined to re[ad] a great deal now both in French and English. My Gandmr sits in the shop in the afternoons and by working par[ticularly] hard for one hour I think I may read the next, withou[t] [be]ing discovered, and I rise pretty early in the morning so [I hope] in time to have perused them all.[8]

Not all of Dorothy's experiences in Penrith were negative, however, for it was during her stay there that she became acquainted with the four Hutchinson sisters, descendants of a Cromwellian general. Two of them, Mary and Sara, were to play lasting roles in her life.[9] Like Dorothy and her brothers, they were orphans and lived under financially distressed conditions. Their mother died in 1783 while giving birth to her tenth child, and their father, an unsuccessful importer, died two years later after going bankrupt. Since that time, the sisters had lived at Penrith under the care of their aunt, Elizabeth Monkhouse. Dorothy developed an almost instant friendship with them and spent nearly all her free time with her new companions. William was introduced to the sisters during his visit and was particularly attracted to Mary Hutchinson, who was the same age as himself. Her surviving correspondence clearly indicates that Dorothy was conscious of the attraction and even at this early moment contemplated some future relationship between Mary and her brother. What exactly the nature of that relationship would be, however, Dorothy was not as yet sure.

Dorothy's ordeal at Penrith came to an end quicker than she expected; only two years after her arrival, she was delivered. In 1788, her other uncle, the Reverend Dr. William Cookson, the pastor of the joint parishes of St. Peter and

St. Mary in Forncett, Norfolkshire, came for a visit. In spite of the less than complimentary observations he received from his hosts concerning her, the Reverend Cookson was quite taken with his niece. For his part, he found Dorothy highly intelligent and gifted. He even went so far as to ask if she could come to live with him. Her relatives said that they would consider the proposition. Soon after Christmas, Dorothy's grandfather died. A few months later, in early 1789, Uncle Kit married and lost much of his interest in reforming his rebellious ward. In declining health herself and feeling that she would never be able to oversee Dorothy on her own, her grandmother agreed to the Reverend Cookson's request.[10]

Life in Forncett was a great relief from the rigid and depressing atmosphere of Penrith. Dorothy could once more read the books she wanted and discuss the important issues of the day. She also began to study Latin and Italian. Most of all, she was grateful for the new respect she received. Soon after her arrival, the Reverend Cookson told her that he wished to establish one of the rooms in his rectory as a grammar school for the children of the local laborers and asked Dorothy to be its teacher. She consented.

Dorothy Wordsworth to Jane Pollard
January 25-26, 1790

I have nine scholars, I had at first ten but I dismissed one and during the winter I did not think it prudent to supply her place. Our hours in winter are, on Sunday mornings from nine till church time: at noon from half past one till three: and at night from four till half past 5: those who live near us come to me every Wednesday and Saturday morning.

I only instruct them in reading and spelling and they get off prayers hymns and catechisms. I have one very bright scholar, some very tolerable, and one or two very bad. We distribute rewards such as books, caps, aprons &. We intend in a little time to have a school upon a more extensive plan—so that this of mine is only a temporary thing.[11]

Dorothy appears to have been a very good teacher. One of the children, she told Jane Pollard,

[who] came to me six months on Sundays and a very few times a part of that time in the week days is able to read excellently well in the testament [,] can repeat catechism and a part of an explanation of it; five or six hymns, the Lord's prayer, the creed and a morning and evening prayer; she can read the church prayer book as well as I could desire and did not know a letter when she came to me—[12]

Dorothy's teaching won her much respect from the parents of the community, who often greeted her with compliments when they passed on the street. The Reverend Cookson was a good friend of William Wilberforce, the two having met as students at Cambridge. When the great abolitionist visited Forncett in the spring of 1790 and was introduced to Dorothy and told about her activities, he was impressed. Before leaving, he gave her ten guineas with which to expand the school.[13]

Unfortunately, Dorothy's pedagogical career was soon brought to a sudden end. Early in the following year, 1791, an epidemic of smallpox broke out in Norfolkshire; to reduce the risk that it might infect the children, she ordered the school temporarily closed. She anxiously looked forward to reopening it as soon as the plague had passed. When it did abate, however, not enough of her former students returned to making reopening practical.[14] Yet the experience had not been a total failure. Through it, Dorothy learned she was abundantly capable of living her life in a manner true to Aunt Rawson's call for responsibility and assistance to others.

Dorothy's spirits were raised further by a visit she soon received from her brother, who was traveling on his way to France. Three years had now passed since their evening strolls in Penrith. William was taking his junior year off, in order to investigate the dramatic events taking place on the Continent. Like Coleridge, he discovered life at Cambridge to be less than stimulating. Despite its cultural prestige and historic associations, the university at this time was at a very low point in its existence as an educational institution. Most of its students never attended lectures, preferring instead to hunt and frequent social clubs; the majority of its faculty were of an inferior caliber, and a general sense of indolence pervaded the medieval quadrangles. William completed his various examinations without much effort and was confident he could easily take a year off and still graduate at the usual time. The Reverend Cookson agreed, but reminded his nephew that because of his lack of financial resources, it would be more difficult for him to find gainful employment afterward. As a solution, he recommended that William take holy orders, promising to pay for his training and to obtain a curacy for him.[15] Many young men would have eagerly accepted the proposal; during the eighteenth century, the Church of England was a traditional means of support for indigent scholars—in recent years, the great chemist Joseph Priestley and the political economist Thomas Malthus. But William had other plans; the ideals fueling his youthful vision of the world could never find fulfillment as an instrument of a dominant religion. Judging it rash openly to spurn his uncle's offer of assistance, however, he said he could not give a definitive answer until his return from France. The Reverend Cookson agreed to wait, but advised William it would do him no harm to start learning some Hebrew and Arabic in the meantime.

While William had yet to return from France, the Reverend Cookson, who had recently married, was promoted to the position of Canon of Windsor.[16] He, his wife, and their niece moved into a residence not far from the great Norman citadel that served as the British monarch's country residence. Dorothy frequently saw George III strolling with members of the royal family. The monarch was an amiable man who enjoyed conversing with the local inhabitants and their children.

Dorothy Wordsworth to Jane Pollard
October 16, 1792

The King stopped to talk with my Uncle and Aunt, and to play with the children, who though not acquainted with the new-fangled Doctrine of Liberty and Equality, thought a King's Stick and his Family at Windsor as fair Game as any other man's, and that princesses were not better than mere Cousin Dollys. . . . I say it is impossible to see them [the Royal Family] at *Windsor* without loving them, because at Windsor they are unattended by Pomp or State, and they seem so desirous to please that nothing but Ill-nature or Envy can help being pleased. The King's good Temper shews itself in no instance so much as in his affection for children. He was quite delighted with Christopher and Mary. Mary he considers as a great Beauty and desired the Duke of York to come from one side of the Terrace to the other to look at her. The first time she appeared before him she had an unbecoming and rather a shabby hat on. We had, then got her a new one. "Ah" says he, "Mary that's a *pretty* hat!"[17]

Dorothy did not possess the same affection for the king's languid elder sons. The Prince of Wales (later George IV) and the Duke of Clarence (later William IV) exhibited none of their father's interest in communing with the local inhabitants. Their future subjects could only catch fleeting glimpses of them as they passed by at a distance—on their way out for shooting in the morning, or returning to the castle in the evening with their hangers-on after an afternoon at the nearby race course. While George III's friendliness sometimes made Dorothy momentarily forget the vast gulf between throne and cottage, his sons' behavior quickly disabused her of her illusions. She began to feel bitter. How much longer, she now asked herself as the princes galloped by, could these representatives of the privileged few continue to maintain an existence totally encapsulated from the political and social transformations taking place just across the Channel?

Before the end of the year, William returned, having been an eyewitness of these memorable events. He was full of enthusiasm. Together with a Cambridge friend, Robert Jones, he had spent the last year touring France, Switzerland, and northern Italy. France he found by far the most interesting. The Revolution was still in its progressive phase. Since the fall of the Bastille two years earlier, the once absolute Louis XVI had steadily surrendered to the popular calls for an elected legislative assembly, the establishment of a constitution, the separation of church and state, and large-scale land redistribution, all with a relatively minor amount of bloodshed. These triumphs by democracy over feudalism bolstered the aspirations of liberals throughout Europe, who now anxiously looked forward to developments in France sweeping across the Continent in a great wave of enlightened reform. William was a fervent supporter of this cause. He described himself as "a patriot of the world" (*Preludes XI*). While staying in the city of Blois, he met a French officer, Captain Michel Beaupuy, who convinced him to take an active part in current events. Regrettably, shortage of funds compelled him to return home, but William insisted that he would go back to France as soon as possible in order to join the Girondins, the center-left party of Brissot and Mme. Roland, which was at this moment holding the helm of the Revolution. Sadly, forces beyond William's control were about to overpower him and dramatically alter his plans for the future.

William's graduation from St. John's College, Cambridge, hastened the moment when he would be required to respond to his uncle's proposal that he take up holy orders. His interest in joining the church no stronger than before, William again asked for additional time to consider the matter. Yet as relieved as he was when the Reverend Cookson again agreed to his request, he knew that eventually he would have to give an answer. Then, in late 1792, the issue was abruptly taken out of his hands. In the account he had given of his adventures in France, William had failed to mention Annette Vallon, the daughter of an Orleans surgeon whom he met and fell in love with. News now arrived that she had recently given birth to a daughter and that he was the father.[18] The Reverend Cookson, so helpful, so open-minded on all other matters, proved himself to be quite a traditionalist when it came to the issue of sexual misconduct. Whatever his private political or intellectual beliefs, he declared, a cleric was supposed to present himself as a moral example to his community. No man who behaved in William's reckless manner could ever be deemed worthy of holding office in the Church of England. With this, he angrily withdrew his offer of assistance and banished William from the house, telling him he now had to survive on his own. While his nephew must have been thankful at being spared the dreary existence of an obscure provincial vicar, he must have regretted that his deliverance had had to be purchased at the cost of exile from his family, especially his sister. Only a few months later, war broke out between London and Paris, making it impossible for William to return to France. A decade would pass before he could see Annette Vallon and their daughter again, and his inability to support them was to fill him with guilt for the rest of his life.

After recovering from the initial pain of his banishment, William soon realized that the event might actually have been propitious. While a social outcast, he was now no longer dependent on his uncle's patronage and was thus free to fulfill his desire to become an author. His first two published collections of poetry, however, both appearing at the end of January 1793, were trashed by the press. An Evening Walk was condemned as juvenile and overemotional by critics not yet prepared to accept the Romantic movement.[19] Descriptive Sketches, a work praising the reforms on the Continent and condemning the social inequalities at home in Britain, was denounced as incendiary, coming as it did only weeks after the beheading of Louis XVI. If fame was to be his, William learned, it would not come without a struggle.

William's struggle would be not only with the established literary order but also with his own emotions. It was not until this latter contest was won that he was truly able to emerge as a poet. The year 1793 also marked the outbreak of the Reign of Terror. The French Revolution, which William had recently seen as so noble and pure, now appeared to have degenerated into a mindless bloodbath. Rather than ushering in a glorious age of hope and liberty for the world, he felt, it was forsaking all its original ideals. Already unhappy because of the hostile reception given to his writings, this turn of events in France left William further disheartened. It was while in this vulnerable state of mind that he met Godwin. The future publisher of Mary Lamb's *Tales of Shakespear* was an anarchist, opposed to all organized governments, even the one created by the best reforms of the French Revolution. The only just society, he argued, was a Quaker-like community of rational individuals, making their decisions totally unconstrained by pressure from politicians. Seeking an answer to his seeming failure as a writer and a place to direct his progressive social beliefs after his disillusionment with the French Revolution, William temporarily fell under the influence of Godwin. This relationship lasted only a year, William finding the publisher's doctrine very shallow. But when it ended, William was no less troubled in spirit; he had now twice given himself to a cause that had failed to fulfill his expectations. He wondered if his wish to be a poet, too, were a piece of bad judgment.

Like the Reverend Cookson, Dorothy too was shocked on first learning that William had fathered an illegitimate child. Yet unlike their uncle's, Dorothy's anger does not appear to have lasted long. The remorse William showed for his actions greatly affected her; the memory of the love and concern he had shown her during her bleak years at Penrith remained one of Dorothy's dearest memories. Her inherent generosity of spirit quickly triumphed over her initial loyalty to accepted social conduct. Within a short time, brother and sister were reconciled. Although now separate, she and William remained in constant contact by letter. She discussed his future. She admitted that some of the criticisms made of William's poetry were correct. Parts of *An Evening Walk* and *Sketches* were indeed somewhat oversentimentalized. But whatever "blemishes" there were on these, his first works, they could not disguise a great natural talent, one that, given time and experience, was sure to make itself apparent. She urged William to labor on. Her brother read Dorothy's letters avidly, and her reassurances were important in helping him start to regain his confidence.[20]

Despite bitter setbacks, it becomes clear that as early as 1793 Dorothy already felt sure enough of the future to envision a day when she and William could set up a home together. No longer financially dependent on their relatives, they would be able to devote themselves entirely to their literary callings. If Dorothy ever seriously considered a traditional arranged marriage to someone she must "love, honor and obey," she had rejected it by now. Like Mary Lamb, she knew that no such husband, however open-minded and benevolent he might be, could ever provide the companionship offered by her brilliant brother. Writing to her friend in Halifax, she described what her "little parsonage" would look like:

Dorothy Wordsworth to Jane Pollard
February 16, 1793

When I think of Winter I hasten to furnish our little Parlour, I close the Shutters, set out the Tea-table, brighten the Fire. When our Refreshment is ended I produce our Work, and William brings his book to our Table and contributes at once to our Instruction and amusement, and at Intervals we lay aside the Book and each hazard our observations upon what has been read without the fear of Ridicule or Censure. We talk over past days, we do not sigh for any Pleasures beyond our humble Habitation "The central point of all our joys."[21]

Two more years would pass before Dorothy and her brother could take the first step toward establishing a home of their own. By 1794, William was hard at work on his next piece of poetry, *Incident on Salisbury Plain*. However, in the eighteenth century, few outside the aristocracy and landed gentry were wealthy enough to devote their full time to literature. Exceptions like Alexander Pope were only able to do so after first winning the favor of a noble patron. Lacking such a figure, William therefore went in search of a profession to support himself. He first tried his hand as an independent journalist, publishing articles like *Letter to Bishop Landaff*, an editorial condemning the government's suspension of habeas corpus. Interesting as it was, however, this occupation did not provide the money he needed. He then experimented as a playwright, but his drama was rejected by Drury Lane. Dorothy supplied him with encouraging words from Halifax, where she had returned to live with Aunt Rawson in February 1794. But with little money of her own and barred from the business world because of her sex, she could at the moment provide no real practical assistance.

As was the case with nearly all the aspiring writers of his time, William eventually received the financial aid he sought from the traditional sources. In 1795, he was bequeathed nine hundred pounds in interest-bearing bonds.[22] Raiseley Calvert, a friend whom William had come to know while attending St. John's with his brother, came from a wealthy merchant family in Bristol. During the early 1790s he developed a case of consumption, and William spent a great deal of time nursing him. In search of a healthy environment they embarked on an expedition to the mountains of Wales and were even seriously considering sailing to Portugal when Calvert died, in early 1795. Calvert showed his gratitude for William's concern by remembering him in his will. Soon afterwards, another friend, Basil Montagu, natural son of the fourth Earl of Sandwich, and a widower, asked the Wordsworths to tutor his young son. The money he offered to pay, when combined with the interest from Calvert's bonds, would provide William and Dorothy with an annual income of one hundred and eighty pounds—not a fortune, but certainly enough for two unmarried people to survive on their own.[23] Finally, a third wealthy Bristol acquaintance, John Pinney, whose late father's residence at Racedown Lodge, Dorsetshire, had long been lying empty, provided them with a place to live. The Wordsworths moved in on 26 September 1795.[24]

Racedown was a quiet community, at first glance no different from a great many other small towns in rural southern England. However, it was also the place where the Wordsworths really began to emerge as historic figures. Looking back upon his days there with his sister, William reflected, "She, in the midst of all, preserved me still/A Poet, made me seek beneath that name,/ And that alone, my office upon earth" (*Preludes XI*). Today's reader might ask to what extent these words, written years after the event, were truth and to what degree they were nostalgia. Yet even if memory somewhat exaggerated her deeds, it is apparent that the companionship William received from his confident and determined sister played a crucial role in releasing him from his remaining doubts about his future. At Racedown, William became certain he would become a poet. Here too, the Wordsworths founded a triumvirate, one that would not only permanently affect the lives of each of its three members but also influence the whole course of nineteenth-century English literature.

About forty miles away in the neighboring county of Somersetshire was Nether Stowey, the residence of Samuel Taylor Coleridge. He and the Wordsworths appear to have already corresponded with each other intermittently for about two years. In 1796, Coleridge read *Incident on Salisbury Plain*, declaring to Joseph Cottle that the author was "the best poet of the age."[25] Some time in May 1797, he traveled to Racedown Lodge to make a visit unannounced. Dorothy recalled that he leaped over the garden wall and ran up to the door. Her attraction to him was immediate:

Dorothy Wordsworth to Mary Hutchinson
June 1797

You had a great loss in not seeing Coleridge. He is a wonderful man. His conversation teems with soul, mind, and spirit. Then he is so benevolent, so good tempered and cheerful, and, like William, interests himself so much about every little trifle. At first I thought him very plain, that is, for about three minutes: he is pale and thin, has a wide mouth, thick lips, and not very good teeth, longish loose-growing half-curling rough black hair. But if you hear him speak for five minutes you think more of them. His eye is large and full, not dark but grey; such an eye as would receive from a heavy soul the dullest expression; but it speaks every emotion of his animated mind; it has more of the "poet's eye in a fine frenzy rolling" than I ever witnessed. He has fine dark eyebrows, and an overhanging forehead.[26]

Dorothy asked Coleridge to come in. Not much time was wasted on formalities: "The first thing that was read after he came was William's new poem *The Ruined Cottage* with which he was much delighted; and after tea he repeated to us two acts and half of his tragedy *Osorio*."[27] And so the conversation continued almost without a break for twelve days. Upon finally departing, Coleridge invited the Wordsworths to make a return visit to Nether Stowey. This they did in early June, remaining with him for about ten days. "There is everything here," Dorothy wrote Mary Hutchinson, "sea, woods wild as fancy ever painted, brooks clear and pebbly as in Cumberland, villages so romantic. . . ."[28]

The Wordsworths were of course not the first to be captured by Coleridge's forceful and engaging personality. Charles Lamb, after all, had followed his star since their days as children together at Christ's Hospital. Cottle had promised to publish every verse Coleridge composed; Thomas Poole, the prosperous entrepreneur and landowner, volunteered to be his business agent; and Josiah Wedgewood, grandfather of Darwin and founder of the famous porcelain company, paid him an annuity simply to write. A Nonconformist lay preacher, Coleridge spoke to churches filled with parishioners waiting on his every word. During this early period, before his drug addiction and when he was entering upon his most productive literary phase, Coleridge commanded the admiration of nearly all those who came in contact with him.

Coleridge's relationship with the Wordsworths, however, was special. He understood from the beginning that he had found in them not only friends but also peers, individuals who would be not simply admirers but artistic and intellectual compatriots. Of Dorothy, he remarked to Cottle after that first visit, "Her formation various—her eye watchful in minutest observation of nature—and her taste a perfect electrometer—it bends, protrudes, and draws in, at subtlest beauties & most recondite faults."[29] Forty miles was a long distance for intimates to place between one another, Coleridge insisted, and in July he was able to persuade Dorothy and William to leave Racedown Lodge and move to Somersetshire. Thanks to Poole, who contributed the twenty-three pounds rent, the Wordsworths, taking Basil Montagu's son along with them, were able to take up residence at a pleasant and picturesque country estate named Alfoxden Park.[30]

Dorothy Wordsworth to Mary Hutchinson
August 14, 1797

The house is a large mansion, with furniture enough for a dozen families like ours. There is a very excellent garden, well stocked with vegetables and fruit. The garden is at the end of the house, and our favorite parlour, as at Racedown, looks that way. In front is a little court, with grass plot, gravel walk, and shrubs; the moss roses were in full beauty a month ago. . . . We are now only three miles from Nether Stowey, and not two miles from the sea.[31]

Coleridge came over for frequent visits, the friends entertaining each other with readings from their latest poetry. Coleridge was much impressed with William's newest work, *The Old Cumberland Beggar*. At other times, the three went on hiking expeditions. As an earlier generation of British poets had looked to the Greek and Roman ruins of southern Europe for a source of inspiration, so now these younger writers turned to the splendors of their own countryside for artistic stimulus:

Dorothy Wordsworth to Mary Hutchinson
November 1797

[From Porlock] we kept close to the shore about four miles. Our road lay through wood, rising almost perpendicularly from the sea, with views of the opposite mountains of Wales; thence we came by twilight to Lynmouth in Devonshire. The next morning we were guided to a valley at the top of one of those immense hills which open at each end to the sea, and is from its rocky appearance called the Valley of Stones. We mounted a cliff at the end of the valley, and looked from it immediately on to the sea.[32]

This letter recounts a historic journey. For it was as he gazed out upon the crashing waves that day, near the Valley of Stones, probably on November 13, that Coleridge conceived *The Rime of the Ancient Mariner*. Dorothy was not to be simply a chronicler of other peoples' deeds, however. While British Romanticism's admiration for nature is commonly perceived as being primarily the creation of her brother and Coleridge, Dorothy too played a major role in the establishment of this style of literature. Her *Grasmere Journal* is the best proof of this, but evidence can also be easily found in the considerable attention she gives to the natural world in her correspondence.

The *Grasmere Journal* is only one of several diaries Dorothy kept recording the events of her adult life. She wrote her first at Racedown Lodge, but unfortunately it has not survived. Her second, *The Alfoxden Journal*, was written between 20 January and 22 May 1798, ending not long before the Wordsworths were abruptly forced to vacate their home. The spring thaw came remarkably early that year, and as in her letters, Dorothy's natural surroundings are always close to her thoughts:

20 January: The green paths down the hill-side are channels for streams, The young wheat is streaked by silver lines of water running between the bridges, the sheep are gathered together on the slopes. After the wet dark days [of winter], the country seems more populous. It peoples itself in the sunbeams. The garden, mimic of spring, is gay with flowers.[33]

13 February: Walked with Coleridge through the wood. A mild and pleasant morning; the near prospect clear. The ridges of the hills fringed with wood, showing the sea through them like the white sky, and still beyond the clear horizon of the distant hills, horizon as it were in one undetermined line between sea and sky.[34]

The *Alfoxden Journal*, like the one written at Grasmere, is also important in helping the historian to determine the inauguration and completion dates of famous pieces of poetry:

23 March: Coleridge dined with us. He brought his ballad finished. Rime.[35]

20 April: William all the morning engaged in wearisome composition. Peter Bell begun.[36]

When he purchased the lease on Alfoxden Park, Poole had assured the owners of the property, the aristocratic Albyn family, that the Wordsworths were respectable, well-connected members of the middle class. But by the summer of 1798, the hiking, poetry-writing, and what many viewed as the generally bohemian existence Dorothy and William led convinced the landlords that their tenants were dangerous radicals. They therefore canceled the lease and ordered the Wordsworths to leave. Unable to find a new home immediately, they moved to Nether Stowey. While happy to give his friends lodging, Coleridge quickly revealed himself to be not in the best of health. He was depressed by his temporary break with Charles Lamb and indignant at the embarrassing stories about his private life appearing in Lloyd's recently published sensational *Edmund Oliver*. To ease his growing despondency, Coleridge had begun experimenting with opium. In order to take their minds off their current troubles, William suggested that the three go on a trip to Germany. Such an adventure would be expensive, however, and to finance it he and Coleridge decided to print a joint collection of their newest works.

While Coleridge remained at Nether Stowey, the Wordsworths went hiking in the mountainous region of eastern Wales. On 13 July 1798, they trekked for over fifty miles along the Wye river, resting for a brief time near the remains of a medieval cloister.[37] In this beautiful and isolated spot, a place yet untouched by the violent upheaval of the Industrial Revolution, William suddenly understood the true measure of the love and admiration he possessed for his sister. For him, her mind would always be "a mansion for all lovely forms. . ."; her memory "a dwelling-place for all sweet sounds and harmonies"; her "wild eyes" and "holier love" his inspiration. That night, while at an inn in Bristol, he put his thoughts to paper in one of the most famous and moving of all his poems, *Lines composed a few miles above Tintern Abbey*.

By the end of the summer, all of the twenty-three works planned for the new collection of poetry were completed. The volume was to be entitled *Lyrical Ballads, with a few other Poems*. Among William's contributions to this historic volume were *Tintern Abbey, Lines Left upon a Seat in a Yew-Tree, We are Seven, Simon Lee, The Thorn*, and *The Idiot Boy*. Coleridge's included *The Rime of the Ancient Mariner* (the only true ballad in the text), *Fears in Solitude, Frost at Midnight, France: An Ode*, and *The Nightingale*. William had intended to add a philosophical piece, *The Recluse*, but this was never finished and evolved in later years into *The Preludes*. *Lyrical Ballads* was scheduled to appear anonymously at the beginning of October. During this period, younger authors usually sold the rights to their books in advance and did not receive royalties. As Coleridge and the Wordsworths hoped, the amount they received was enough to pay for their trip, and in early September they boarded a ship at Yarmouth for Germany.[38]

The excursion began in Hamburg. As the son of a prominent cleric, Coleridge was invited to dine with several important figures in the Lutheran Church, thus enabling his companions to be introduced to the city's high society. As Dorothy's *Hamburgh Diary* demonstrates, though, not all their time was spent socializing. During the stay, one of the poems left out of the *Lyrical Ballads* was finished: "*October 1*: Coleridge carried 'Khan' MS.''[39] After leaving Hamburg, they preceded to Lübeck. From here, Coleridge went to spend the winter in Ratzeburg, and the Wordsworths journeyed to Goslar, near the Harz Mountains of Lower Saxony, two hundred miles to the south. Like many travelers spending nearly all their waking hours together, frictions may have arisen, and they judged it best to separate for a time.

News soon reached Dorothy and William about the reaction to the publication of *Lyrical Ballads*. The nation's most prestigious literary periodical, the *Edinburgh Review*, harshly criticized the collection; but as the standard-bearer of the artistic status quo, this Tory organ was hostile to all new authors. It would later attack the early poetry of Byron. Most of the other critics, however, were fairly positive in their opinions. While not altogether having the success he had hoped for, William was nonetheless encouraged by this initial public reception to what was soon to be called British Romantic literature. During the winter months he composed several additional poems, among them the *Lucy Gray* series, which he planned to contribute to a second, larger edition of the book.

Unfortunately, receiving the news from home about *Lyrical Ballads* turned out to be the only positive moment for Dorothy and William that winter. Most of the months the two spent at Goslar they found lonesome and depressing. The town was a small, isolated community without the institutions of higher education, theaters, or artistic circles found in university cities like Heidelberg, Bonn, and Leipzig. Many of the buildings were in an advanced state of decay, making it difficult to find adequate lodgings. Without the assistance of the multilingual Coleridge, Dorothy and William, who spoke only a few words of German, found it very difficult to communicate with their neighbors. Yet even if they had been totally fluent, the local residents they encountered, perpetually suspicious of foreigners, demonstrated very little interest in conversing with them. In April 1799, after the snows had melted away and the rough roads through the mountains had become usable again, the Wordsworths eagerly packed their belongings and departed for home.

Still lacking a permanent home after their eviction from Alfoxden Park, Dorothy and William went to stay with the Hutchinson sisters, who since their aunt's marriage had been living on their own in the town of Sockburn-upon-Tees, near Durham in Yorkshire.[40] It became clear from the moment of his arrival that William's early attraction for Mary Hutchinson had not diminished. The two spent long periods alone together strolling in the gardens or sitting in the library, deep in conversation. As she had at Penrith, Dorothy does not appear to have been disturbed by this development. Rather than perceiving Mary as a possible rival for her brother's affections, she believed that Mary's relationship with him was purely platonic. Their talks after all, usually concerned art, literature, and politics. Dorothy in fact believed that William could benefit from having another close intellectual female friend. Mary, she reasoned, would be her ally in motivating William to express his talents to the fullest.[41]

In June, Coleridge arrived on the scene, having returned from Germany a few months earlier independently of the Wordsworths. Back at Nether Stowey, he heard that William and Dorothy were gravely ill and came to Sockburn hoping he could help nurse them. He was much relieved to discover the news was only a rumor, and whatever disagreements may have come between the friends during their trip were quickly healed. Invited to stay on, Coleridge quickly became captivated with Mary Hutchinson's sister Sara, thus initiating a long, sad, and ultimately unresolved love affair. Coleridge's marriage to Sarah Fricker was not a happy one. The two were ill-suited and had entered into their match hastily after the collapse of Coleridge's utopian community and break with Mary Evans. His wife did not share her husband's avant-garde literary interests or liberal political beliefs, and his taste for adventure did not make him much of a family man. Intrigued with poetry, fiction, and all aspects of creative writing, Sara Hutchinson (of whom, like Dorothy, no portrait exists today) must have seemed a refreshing change to Coleridge; her admiration for him and her eagerness to help forward his career must have also salved his ego. The possibility of a companionship with such a lady was enticing, but their union unfortunately was not to be. Divorce, without special permission from Parliament, was not possible until 1857; and despite his general cultural iconoclasm, the Bard of Xanadu proved himself enough of a traditionalist to consider the prospect of leaving his wife for Sara Hutchinson unacceptable. Even after the Coleridges formally separated in 1806, the poet could still not countenance living openly with her. Their relationship was to inspire much verse, but also many tears.

These tragic events were still all far in the future, however, when in the second week of December 1799, the Wordsworths finally departed from Sockburn to return to their native West Country. Dorothy was especially happy. Now, at long last, after many years of hoping, she and her brother could possess a permanent home of their own.

Chapter Four

Grasmere and Beyond

Dove Cottage (also known as Town End), situated in the small and picturesque community of Grasmere, Westmorelandshire, where the Wordsworths settled on 20 December 1799, stood about twenty miles southeast of Cockermouth, their birthplace.[42] It was one of several small towns in a region dotted with lakes—among them, Lake Grasmere not far from the Wordsworth's front door, Windemere to the south, Rydal and Derwent to the north. Dorothy had visited the area once before, in April 1794, while traveling with William and Raisley Calvert. "I walked with my brother at my side," she had written to Jane Pollard at the time,

from Kendal to Grasmere, eighteen miles, and afterwards to Keswick, fifteen miles through the most delightful country that was ever seen. We are now at a farmhouse, about half a mile from Keswick. When I came, I intended to stay for only a few days; but the country is so delightful, and, above all, [I am] so full of enjoyment of my brother's company, that I have determined to stay a few weeks longer.[43]

Reflecting in later years, Dorothy would insist that the decision she and her brother made to return to this rural region of western England known as the Lake District was instrumental in the creation of some of the most famous British poetry of the nineteenth century.

The first six months of William's stay at Grasmere were not too productive, however. None of the early drafts of the poems he brought with him from Sockburn, like *Peter Bell*, were completed. He had high expectations for the second edition of *Lyrical Ballads*, which included such new pieces as *Nutting* and *She Dwelt among the Untrodden Ways*. He even sent an inscribed review copy to the leader of the Whigs, Charles James Fox. Yet when the collection appeared in early 1800, the critics, rather than increasing their estimation of it as William had anticipated, received his work with the very same assortment of middling evaluations they had given its predecessor. Though their comments had been encouraging to the first-time author in 1798, they were a disappointment now. It was not until 1815 that William's poetry would really begin to gain acceptance from the general public. Depressed and disappointed, he took several months to recover the energy he needed fully to continue his writing.

Dorothy, now twenty-nine, was much concerned with William's difficulties; and when he was absent on a trip to Yorkshire with his brother John, she decided to record some thoughts she hoped he might find useful for his poetry. "I resolved to write a journal of the time till W. and J. return," she wrote in its original entry of Wednesday, 14 May 1800, "and I set about keeping my resolve, because I will not quarrel with myself, and because I shall give Wm. pleasure by it when he comes home again."[44] She quickly found the recording of her daily life satisfying in itself and continued her diary long after Willliam's return, only stopping, abruptly, after her entry of Wednesday, 16 January 1803. Today, her chronicle is remembered as the *Grasmere Journal*.

The *Grasmere Journal* is Dorothy Wordsworth's most famous and most important piece of writing. Shorter than those of Samuel Pepys, John Evelyn, or her contemporary Henry Crabb Robinson, Dorothy's diary is of at least equal historical significance. It consists of an intimate and many-layered account of the lives, thoughts, and environment of some of the principal figures of the British Romantic Age and is also a pioneering work of sociology.

The *Grasmere Journal* has traditionally been utilized as a quarry for information on the personal life of William Wordsworth during what is generally considered his most artistically productive decade. Thanks to the detailed observations Dorothy makes of her brother, historians have acquired knowledge about such subjects as the poet's medical condition, reading tastes, work habits, social life, and leisure time. It is known today, for instance, that William was often in poor health, his writing being interrupted during these years by frequent and debilitating bouts of influenza, insomnia, toothache, boils, and headache. It is known, too, that like the Lambs, he was a great admirer of the then still underappreciated Shakespeare, although the plays he most read were the less-performed ones like *The Winter's Tale*, *Timon of Athens*, *Richard the Second*, and *As You Like It*. The diary also reveals that major poems from this period like *Michael* and *Ruth* were finished only after going through many drafts; that besides enjoying the company of his intellectual circle, William was on very good terms with his neighbors; and that he spent much of his leisure time taking long walks either alone or with his sister. Ironically, one purpose the *Grasmere Journal* has not often been used for is to examine the personality and literary importance of the woman who wrote it. When undertaken, such an inquiry demonstrates that rather than existing simply as her brother's chronicler, Dorothy Wordsworth had a life that was a fascinating story in itself. Her writings, for so long judged as merely ancillary to her brother's, are actually those of a distinct and talented individual.

Like all great diarists, Dorothy was able to write truthfully about her inner feelings, making her work memorable not only for the information it supplies on major historic figures but equally for the intimate picture the author presents of herself. She emerges not only as another name in the annals of British letters but as a warm and appealing human being, someone with many of the same hopes, fears, and aspirations as ourselves. From the moment of her arrival in Grasmere, we learn, Dorothy was happy with their home. She had always hoped that when she and William finally obtained a home of their own, it would be situated in a place whose natural surroundings matched the sensations of her heart. "It was very pleasant," she wrote as she looked out her window on Saturday, 26 December 1801,

Grasmere Lake a beautiful image of stillness, clear as glass, reflecting all things, the wind was up, and the waters sounding. The Lake of a rich purple, the fields a soft yellow, the island yellowish-green, the copses red-brown, the mountains purple. The Church and buildings, how quiet they were.[45]

As Dorothy's diary also reveals, her desire for a home of her own extended beyond her relations with her brother. Unmarried, having been sent away from her parents as a small child, having dwelt under the custody of various relatives as an adolescent, and having been evicted from one of the places she resided as an adult, Dorothy had always been a boarder, always subject to the pleasure of others for a roof over her head. By becoming mistress of Dove Cottage, she was able to gain a sense of security and independence previously denied her; the commonplace daily occurrences of a housekeeper's life now became for her as worthy of being recorded as the progress of Willliam's poetry or the visits they received from Coleridge:

Tuesday, 27 May 1800: I walked to Ambleside with letters—met the post before I reached Mr. Partridge's, one paper, only a letter for Coleridge. I expected a letter from Wm. It was a sweet morning, the ashes of the valley nearly in full leaf, but still to be distinguished, quite bare on the higher ground, I was warm in returning, and becoming cold with sitting in the house I had a bad headach—I went to bed after dinner, and lay still till after 5. Not well after tea. I worked in the garden, but did not walk further. A delightful evening before the sun set, but afterwards it grew colder—mended stockings etc.[46]

Friday, 22 August 1800: Very cold. Baking in the morning, gathered pea seeds and took up—lighted a fire upstairs. Walked as far as Rydale with John intending to have gone on to Ambleside, but we found the papers at Rydale—Wm. walking in the wood all the time. John and he went out after our return—I mended stockings. Wind very high shaking the corn.[47]

As in her earlier *Alfoxden Journal*, Dorothy filled her diary with many detailed observations about her environment. Like the male literary figures of the British Romantic movement, she too possessed a particular fascination with nature, sometimes regarding its various components as an almost singular entity she could personally relate to. "When we were in the woods behind Gowbarrow Park," she wrote in her entry of Thursday, 15 April 1802:

we saw a few daffodils close to the water-side. We fancied that the lake had floated the seeds ashore, and that the little colony had so sprung up. But as we went along there were more and yet more; and at last, under the boughs of the trees, we saw that there was a long belt of them along the shore, about the breadth of a country turnpike road. I never saw daffodils so beautiful. They grew among the mossy stones and about them; some rested their heads upon these stones as on a pillow for weariness; and the rest tossed and reeled and danced, and seemed as if they verily laughed with the wind, that blew upon them over the lake; they looked so gay, ever dancing, ever changing. This wind blew directly over the lake to them. There was here and there a little knot, a few stragglers a few yards higher up; but they were so few so as not to disturb the simplicity, unity, of that one busy highway.[48]

Dorothy began her journal with the hope the thoughts she recorded might prove of assistance to her brother in his writing, and that William made use of his sister's descriptive powers is quite apparent. The scene she witnessed that spring day is still vividly remembered in one of William's best-known set of verses, *The Daffodils*. That he was not present with her and actually wrote the poem two years later, in 1804, is but one example of how Dorothy frequently opened up her diary to him in future years.

Throughout the years they lived at Dove Cottage, Dorothy, as her diary demonstrates, played an important part in the final construction of William's writings:

Friday, 1 August 1800: In the morning I copied *The Brothers*. Coleridge and Wm. went down to the lake. They returned and, we all went together to Mary Point[49], where we sate in the breeze and the shade, and read Wm.'s poems. Altered *The Whirlblast* etc.[50]

Sunday, 18 April 1802: I lay in bed late, again a mild gray morning, with rising vapours. William wrote the poem on *The Robin and the Butterfly*. I went to drink at Luff's, but as we did not dine till 6 o'clock, it was late. It was mist and small rain all the way, but very pleasant. William met me at Rydale—Aggie accompanied me hither. We sate up late. He met me with the conclusion of the poem of the Robin. I read it to him in bed. We left out some lines.[51]

In a letter William wrote to Sara Hutchinson on 14 June 1802, Dorothy added in at the bottom:

When you happen to be displeased with what you suppose to be the tendency or moral of any poem which William writes, ask yourself whether you have hit upon the real tendency and true moral, and above all never think that he ever writes for no reason but merely because a thing happened—when you feel any poem of his to be tedious, ask yourself in what spirit it was written—whether merely to tell the tale and be through with it, or to illustrate a particular character or truth.[52]

Even when she was not providing William with specific ideas for poems, as in the case of *The Daffodils*, he found Dorothy's multiple roles as his secretary, proofreader, literary consultant, and test audience of invaluable assistance in perfecting his art. Like *The Glow-worm*, her constant presence was a source of great comfort encouragement and inspiration.

Early in 1800, Coleridge moved from Nether Stowey to the Lake District so he could once more be near his friends.[53] Although established at Greta Hall, in Keswick, a few miles away, he spent a great deal of his time with William and Dorothy at Dove Cottage. *The Grasmere Journal* is filled with entries about the renewed intimacy of the triumvirate. They went riding, took long walks around the lakes, and stayed up late discussing their poetry. Dorothy, much impressed with the progress of Coleridge's *Christabel*, believed that when completed it might prove to be his best. Yet, as her diary also reveals, Coleridge was no longer the forceful and charismatic figure who had jumped over the garden wall at Racedown in 1797. "I was melancholy, and could not talk," she wrote on Tuesday, 10 November 1801, after a visit to Keswick, "but at last I eased my heart by weeping—nervous blubbering, says William. It is not so! O! how many, many reasons I have to be anxious for him."[54]

Coleridge was now suffering from the painful symptoms of arthritis, stomach ulcers, and gout. As debilitating as they might be, however, these ailments are now generally viewed to have been psychosomatic—outward reactions to deep-seated personal problems. Coleridge's relations with his wife had not improved since his return from Germany, and there was already talk of a formal separation. This prospect brought him little relief, however, as he was yet unable to free himself from the conviction that it would be wrong to live openly with Sara Hutchinson. Instead, they met discreetly, either where they were not easily recognized or in the homes of friends. Coleridge traveled several times to Sockburn so he could go riding with Sara; the lovers spent much of November and December 1800 in furnished rooms in London and stayed over the Christmas holidays with the Wordsworths at Grasmere. During some of these visits, one or another of Coleridge's two sons was brought along to make the rendezvous appear more respectable. Dorothy, as her journal demonstrates, was thoroughly committed to Coleridge. She raised no objections to his and Sara Hutchinson's meeting at Dove Cottage and encouraged the couple to come as much as they wished. She made sure that Sara Hutchinson was present when Coleridge recited the newly completed *Part Two* of *Christabel*. But it proved far easier for Coleridge's friends to accept this relationship than for him. He loved his new companion but was also filled with guilt, believing himself to be a seducer. His unresolved feelings for Sara Hutchinson, when combined with his unhappy marriage and perceived physical ailments, left Coleridge in an ever more weakened condition. He was plagued with morbid fits of depression. "We received a letter from Coleridge," Dorothy wrote in her diary on Friday, 25 December 1801, "while we were at John Fisher's—a terrible night—little John brought the letter. Coleridge poorly but better—his letter made us uneasy about him. I was glad I was not by myself when I received it."[55]

"A heart-rending letter from Coleridge," she wrote again on Friday, 25 January 1802, "—we were sad as we could be"[56]

Unable to free himself from his deep and painful melancholy, Coleridge turned progressively to the blank sleep of opium, a substance then still legal in Britain. An experimenter since 1798, he had by 1802 become an addict. Though his drug abuse was to have an increasingly negative effect on his literary powers, it did not altogether destroy them. He still experienced periods of stunning creativity. On Wednesday, 21 April 1802, Coleridge recited to Dorothy the poem he had just written in honor of Sara Hutchinson, *Dejection: An Ode*.[57] "I was affected by them," Dorothy wrote of the verses, "and was on the whole, not being well, in miserable spirits." Despite these brief comments, this poem, which possesses the same power as *Tintern Abbey*, greatly impressed her. She immediately copied down all of its three hundred-and-forty-one lines, the only work by another writer she included in the *Grasmere Journal*.

Dorothy was not only a keen observer of her natural environment but also an astute commentator on her society. While Britain as a whole was now taking her first steps into the Industrial Revolution, large elements of the earlier agrarian culture still persisted, especially in regions like the Lake District. Isolated from the vibrant mainstream of nineteenth-century British society, these areas and much of their populations lived an existence whose economy and traditions had changed little since the time of the Tudors. For those members of the lower classes who did not migrate elsewhere, poverty was a way of life. Unemployment was perpetually high, and even those individuals lucky enough to be hired as field laborers could expect to earn no more than sixpence a week. Nearly everyone had at some time experienced being a beggar or vagabond. Dorothy was not the first writer to record the life of her country's rural poor; but unlike previous authors, she did so with a sympathy they frequently lacked. Instead of looking condescendingly upon the poor as social outcasts or mental inferiors, she portrayed them as persons whose undramatic lives, although often arduous and bitter, were nevertheless deserving of respect and understanding from her more privileged readership.

On Wednesday, 3 September 1800, Dorothy, William, and Coleridge watched the funeral of a local day laborer named John Dawson:

About 10 men and 4 women. Bread, cheese and ale. They talked sensibly and chearfully about common things. The dead person, 56 years old, buried by the parish. The coffin was neatly lettered and painted black, and covered with a decent cloth. They set the corpse down at the door; and, while we stood within the threshold, the men with their hats off sang with decent and solemn countenances a verse of a funeral psalm. The corpse was then borne down the hill, and they sang till they had passed the Town-End. I was affected

to tears while we stood in the house, the coffin lying before me. There were no near
kindred, no children. When we got out of the dark house the sun was shining, and the
prospect looked so divinely beautiful as I never saw it. It seemed more sacred than I had
ever seen it, and yet more allied to human life.[58]

"When Wm. and I returned from accompanying Jones,"[59] Dorothy wrote
in her journal on Friday, 3 October 1800, "we met an old man [bent over]
almost double."

He had on a coat, thrown over his shoulders, above his waistcoat and coat. Under this he
carried a bundle, and had an apron on and a night-cap. His face was interesting. He had
dark eyes and a long nose. John, who afterwards met him at Wytheburne, took him for
a Jew. He was of Scotch parents, but had been born in the army. He had a wife, and "a
good woman, and it pleased God to to bless us with ten children." All these were dead
but one of whom he had not heard for many years, a sailor. His trade was to gather
leeches, but now leeches are scarce, and he had not strength for it. He lived by begging,
and was making his way to Carlisle, where he should buy a few goodly books to sell. He
said leeches were very scarce, partly owing to this dry season, and were of slow growth.
Leeches were formerly of 2s. 6d. [per] 100; they are now 30 s. He had been hurt in
driving a cart, his leg broken, his body driven over, his skull fractured. He felt no pain
until he recovered from his first insensibility.[60]

"A woman came who was travelling with her husband," Dorothy wrote on
Friday, 27 November 1801,

He had been wounded and was going to live with her at Whitehaven. She had been at
Ambleside the night before, offered 4 d. at the Cock for bed—they sent her to one
Harrison's where she and her husband had slept upon the hearth and bought a penny
worth of chips for a fire. Her husband was gone before, very lame—"Aye" says she, "I
was once an officer's wife, I, as you see me now. My first husband married me at
Appleby; I had eighteen pounds a year for teaching school, and because I had no fortune
his father turned him out of doors. I have been in the West Indies. I lost the use of this
finger right before he died; he came to me and said he must bid farewell to his children
and me I had a muslin gown like yours—I seized hold of his coat as he went from me,
and slipped the joint of my finger. He was shot directly. I came to London and married
this man. He was a clerk to Judge Chambray, that man, that man that's going on the road
now. If he, Judge Chambray, had been at Kendal he would [have] given us a guinea or
two, and made nought of it, for he is very generous."[61]

"As we came up the White Moss," says Dorothy's entry of Tuesday, 22
December 1801,

we met an old man, who I saw was a beggar by his two bags hanging over his shoulder;
but, from a half laziness, half indifference, and a wanting to try him, if he would speak,
I let him pass. He said nothing, and my heart smote me. I turned back, and said, "You
are begging?" "Ay," says he. I gave him a halfpenny. William, judging from his
appearance, joined in. "I suppose you were a sailor?" "Ay," he replied, "I have been

57 years at sea, 12 of them aboard a man of war, under Sir Hugh Palmer." "Why have you not a pension?" "I have no pension, but I could have gotten into Greenwich Hospital, but all my officers are dead." He was 75 years of age, had a freshish colour in his cheeks, grey hair, a decent hat with a binding around the edge, the hat worn down and glossy, his shoes were small thin shoes low in the quarters, pretty good. They had belonged to a gentleman.[62]

"After dinner, a little before sunset," Dorothy recalled on Sunday, 14 February 1802,

I walked out about 20 yards above Glow-Worm Rock. I met a carman, a Highlander I suppose, with 4 carts, the first 3 belonging to himself, the last evidently to a man and his family who had joined company with him, and who I guessed to be potters. The carman was cheering his horses, and talking to a little lass about 10 years of age, who seemed to make him her companion. She ran to the wall, and took up a large stone to support the wheel of one of the carts, and ran on before with it in her arms to be ready for him. She was a beautiful creature, and there was something uncommonly impressive in the lightness and joyousness of her manner. Her business seemed to be all pleasure—pleasure in her own motions, and the man looked at her as if he too was pleased, and spoke to her in the same tone as he spoke to the horses. There was a wildness in her whole figure, not the wildness of a Mountain lass, but a Road lass, a traveller from her birth, who had wanted neither food nor clothes. Her mother followed the last cart with a lovely child, perhaps about a year old, at her back, and a good-looking girl, about 15 years old, walked beside her. All the children were like the mother. She had a very fresh complexion, but she was blown with fagging up the hill, with the steepness of the hill and the bairn that she carried. Her husband was helping the horse to drag up by pushing with his shoulder.[63]

The *Grasmere Journal* is filled with many similar portraits. Its intimate descriptions of that great majority of the population that lived beyond the walls of the manor house makes Dorothy's diary far more valuable for understanding the life of rural Britain than any other account of the time. By influencing such poems by her brother as *The Beggars, The Daffodils, Alice Fell*, and *The Leech-Gatherer*, it demonstrated to the poets of the Romantic Age that artistic inspiration could be found as much in the transient struggle of the common man as in the eternal glory of nature.

The cause for the *Grasmere Journal*'s abrupt termination after the entry of Sunday, 16 January 1803, becomes clear in light of an incident eight months earlier.[64] On Wednesday, 5 May 1802, William informed Dorothy that he and Mary Hutchinson had decided to get married.[65] The news cannot have come to Dorothy as a complete surprise; she had seen her brother's attachment to Mary grow steadily since the Wordsworths' arrival at Grasmere in December 1799; believing it was simply platonic, she even warmly encouraged the relationship. Her discovery that the couple's attraction for one another was actually romantic in origin does not at first seem to have visibly pained Dorothy. She must have realized her brother would inevitably marry one day, and the fact he chose someone as intelligent, warm, and dedicated as Mary Hutchison further helped her to accept the situation. Most important of all, both William and Mary insisted that Dorothy continue to live with them at Dove Cottage. Yet no matter how much of her former bond with William was retained, it could never be totally restored. Seeing that she would no longer be William's primary companion, Dorothy gradually began to conclude that her journal had lost its reason for being. The entries grew progressively shorter after the wedding in October and, after the new year, expired.

Yet before it closed, Dorothy's journal still had some notable events to record. The first involved the settlement of her family's long monetary dispute with the estate of the Earls of Lonsdale. After the first Earl died in early 1802, his successor announced on May 24 that he would repay all his father's debts to the Wordsworths, along with the accumulated interest. As a result, Dorothy received in several installments a sum that amounted to approximately five thousand pounds.[66] Finally independent, she could now remain at Grasmere as a desired guest, without fearing she was imposing a financial burden on her family. Another incident described in the later section of Dorothy's diary was the journey she took with William to France.

Before his marriage, William was determined to have a final meeting with Annette Vallon and to be introduced to the daughter he had never met. Even after twelve years of separation, he still felt tremendous guilt for having been unable to care for them. The eighteen-month cessation in hostilities brought about by the Treaty of Amiens permitted William at last to visit them and hopefully to obtain a reconciliation. He departed for France with Dorothy on Friday, July 29, by coach, stopping for two days in London. So long accustomed to quiet small towns, she was immensely affected by the activity, size, and majesty of what she considered the greatest metropolis in the world. Her words also offer the reader a striking image of how London appeared before the coal fires of the nineteenth century. "We mounted the Dover coach at Charing Cross," she wrote with awe in her diary on Sunday, 31 July 1802:

It was a beautiful morning. The City, St. Paul's, with the river and a multitude of boats, made a most beautiful sight as we crossed Westminster Bridge. The houses were not overhung by their cloud of smoke, and they were spread out endlessly, yet the sun shone so brightly, with such a fierce light, that there was even something like the purity of one of nature's own grand spectacles.[67]

That William was also swayed by the exquisite sight is well known, for he immortalized it in perhaps his most famous sonnet, *Lines Composed upon Westminster Bridge*. Less recognized today, however, is that, as in the case of *The Daffodils*, the words and phrases he employs in his celebration of the city's waters, domes, and sky possess a striking resemblance to his sister's journal entry.

On Monday, August 1, the Wordsworths crossed the Straits of Dover and landed at Calais where Annette Vallon and her daughter Caroline were waiting for them. Although Dorothy does not give any details, the reconciliation William long wished for was achieved; past bitterness was removed, and friendship was restored. The Wordsworths remained at Calais for three weeks. Almost every night William, Dorothy, Annette, and Caroline walked alone along the beaches laughing and telling stories. "The reflections in the water," wrote Dorothy, "were more beautiful than the sky itself, purple waves brighter than precious stones, for ever melting away upon the sands."[68] Yet by the end of the month, William decided it was time to leave. Napoleon had just engineered his election as Consul for Life, and relations between France and Britain were souring again, making another terrible war only a matter of time. Each time he caught sight of the White Cliffs of Dover and its lighthouse in the distance, William yearned for home. At last, on Sunday, August 29, he and his sister set sail for Britain, reaching land the next morning. "We both bathed," Dorothy wrote, "and sate upon the Dover Cliff, and looked upon France with many a melancholy and tender thought. We could see the shores almost as plain as if it were an English lake."[69]

They returned to London, where William finished two more sonnets, continued on to Windsor, where they made up with the Reverend Dr. Cookson, and were back at Grasmere on Friday, September 22. This was to be the last journey Dorothy would ever take with her brother alone.

On Monday, October 4, William and Mary were wed at the Hutchinson family home at Gallow Hill. Dorothy did not attend the service. She remained at home at Dove Cottage upstairs in her bedroom, while Sara Hutchinson prepared the meal for the reception. "I kept myself as quiet as I could," Dorothy recalled,

but when I saw the two men running up the walk, coming to tell us it was over, I could stand it no longer, and threw myself on the bed, where I lay in stillness, neither hearing or seeing anything till Sara came upstairs to me, and said, "They are coming." This forced me from the bed where I lay, and I moved, I know not how, straight forward, faster than my strength could carry me, till I met my beloved William, and fell upon his bosom. He and John Hutchinson led me to the house, and there I stayed to welcome my dear Mary. As soon as we had breakfasted we departed.[70]

Despite her easy intellectual acceptance of the change in her relationship with her brother, it proved much harder for Dorothy to acquiesce to it emotionally. By the close of the summer of 1803, however, she was recovered sufficiently to begin work on yet another diary, *Recollections of a Tour Made in Scotland*. Her family and friends were not in the best physical condition at this time. Plagued by psychosomatic illnesses and addicted to opium, Coleridge was now in very poor health; William had suffered several times over the last twelve months from influenza; and Mary, who recently delivered a son, had experienced a long and difficult labor. For Dorothy, as for most people of her day, the best method of regaining one's health lay in an extended trip; and so in August, she was able to convince her companions to go on a tour of Scotland.

The popular conception of pre-twentieth-century Scotland as a land of heroism and romance is essentially the creation of Sir Walter Scott. The Scotland that Dorothy, William, Mary, and Coleridge entered was much different from its fictional counterpart. Since 1745, when the English crushed the Second Jacobite Rebellion, the clans had become little more than ceremonial bodies, and the wearing of the tartan on public occasions had been outlawed. The General Enclosure Act of 1801 gave formal justification to the already long-established practice of landlords' closing off communal grazing areas to local farmers; and the destruction of villages to make room for textile mills became so notorious throughout Europe that it was later described by Karl Marx in *Das Kapital*. Despite being the birthplace of such figures as Scott, John Knox, James Boswell, Adam Smith, Robert Burns, and David Hume, the majority of the population was still illiterate; and large numbers, rarely exposed to English culture, continued to speak only their native Gaelic. Dorothy often commented in her journal about the sense of sadness that was never far from even the loveliest landscape.

One of the first places the travelers went to visit was Dumfries, the home of Robert Burns, whose verses the Crackanthorpes believed had provoked their granddaughter's *wildness*. It was not a happy place; the lyricist seemed nearly forgotten by the land he celebrated.

"Went to visit his grave," Dorothy wrote:

He lies at the corner of the churchyard, and his second son, Francis Wallace, beside him; there is no stone to mark the spot; but a hundred guineas have been collected, to be expended on some sort of monument.
All around—"There lies such-and-one."[71]

The party continued north to Glasgow and into the Highlands to Loch Lomond, passing through beautiful country but also through poverty-stricken villages consisting of broken-down shacks and huts, their inhabitants in tattered clothes, the children barefoot. Dorothy was much moved by the friendliness the people showed her. Few visitors ever came their way, and Dorothy's appearance was an event. Villagers, temporarily casting aside their troubles, were eager to make Dorothy and her fellow travelers welcome, enquiring how they could be of assistance and happily answering all the newcomers' questions. "At one of the clusters of houses," Dorothy remembered amusingly:

we parted with our companion, who had insisted on bearing my bundle while she stayed with us. I often tried to enter into conversation with her, and seeing a small tarn [lake] before us, was reminded of the pleasure of fishing and the manner of living here, and asked her what sort of food was eaten in that place; if they lived much upon fish; or had mutton from the hills; she looked earnestly at me, and shaking her head, replied, "Oh yes! eat fish—no papishes, eat everything."[72]

They were rowed around Loch Lomond and its opening in a ferryboat captained by a cheerful and voluble young girl. Yet despite her congenial spirits and the lake's famous associations and impressive vista, Dorothy found the experience rather melancholy:

The lake is magnificent; you see it . . . winding away behind a large woody island that looks like a promontory. The outlet of the lake [however] . . . is very insignificant. The bulk of the river is frittered away by small alder bushes, as I recollect,—I do not remember that it was reedy, but the ground had a swampy appearance; and here the vale spreads wide and shapeless, as if the river was born to no inheritance, had no sheltering cradle, no hills of its own.[73]

While the expedition helped to reinvigorate William's and Mary's constitutions, the physical exertions it required finally proved too much for Coleridge; a few days after reaching Loch Lomond, he decided to return to England. His rheumatism, Dorothy reported in a letter to Sara Hutchinson, prevented him from continuing. The roads were often so poor that the travelers were obliged to go on foot for many miles every day over rocky terrain. In the course of their journey, Dorothy reported to Sara that Coleridge "had performed miracles." Despite his pain, he "exhibited uncommon strength," walking farther than anyone would have expected. Between August 31 and September 2, he hiked forty-five miles from the lake to Glen Coe. Although he had to turn back now, his determined efforts convinced her that Coleridge was winning back his old vitality.

Dorothy, her brother, and Mary went on by themselves, soon coming upon the sanctuary of the hero Robert MacGregor—Rob Roy. "We went a considerable way further," Dorothy wrote,

and landed at Rob Roy's Caves, which are in fact no caves, but some fine rocks on the brink of the lake, in the crevices of which a man might hide himself cunningly enough; the water is very deep below them, and the hills above steep and covered with wood. The little Highland woman, who was in size about a match for our guide at Lanark, accompanied us hither. There was something very gracious in the manner of this woman; she could scarcely speak five words of English, yet she gave me, whenever I spoke to her, as many intelligible smiles as I had needed English words to answer me, and helped me over the rocks in the most obliging manner.[74]

Not far away was the weed-ridden cemetery where the Scottish Robin Hood was said to be buried. Dorothy and Willliam passed through the gates and eagerly searched about for his grave. Unfortunately, the inscriptions on the cracked and tumbled-down tombstones had all been washed bare by the effects of time and storm, and the precise resting place of the legendary hero was impossible to locate.

The tour was completed with a visit to Edinburgh and Roslin, where Dorothy was invited to dine at the home of Sir Walter Scott, who before the publication of *Waverly* in 1814 was not yet a nationally known figure. Worried about the eradication of traditional Highland culture, he was currently compiling a collection of local folk ballads, though some of his critics accused him of composing a few of them himself. Satisfied that she had now seen most of the country's important sites, Dorothy turned south again for England. The route she took led her through some of the areas once clustered with prosperous small farms, but now barren, victims of the brutal enclosure movement. One day as she gazed at this lonely yet once glorious land, she reflected:

One could not but think with some regret of the times when from the now depopulated Highlands forty or fifty thousand men might have been poured down for the defense of the country, under such leaders as the Marquess of Montrose or the brave man [Robert Bruce] who had so distinguished himself upon the ground where we were standing.[75]

By the beginning of October, Dorothy had returned to Dove Cottage. Some of the areas she visited in the north were quite nice, she wrote to Sara Hutchinson, but none, she believed, possessed the beauty of the Lake District. While the world portrayed in the *Grasmere Journal* was essentially a positive one, an environment where even poverty was not without its dignity, the land described in Dorothy's next diary is a somber place. Unlike Westmorelandshire, Scotland was one of the first parts of Great Britain to experience the violent social upheavals of the Industrial Revolution; here, nature and the common man, two of Dorothy's sacred ideals, were in full retreat. Many readers later commented on what they perceived as the often-pessimistic style with which the author wrote *A Tour Made in Scotland*, a style markedly different from the hopefulness that characterized her previous work. Yet given her political and philosophical beliefs, the conclusions she came to could have had no other tone.

Whatever its drawbacks, Dorothy hoped the trip to Scotland would rejuvenate her spirits after the loss of her special relationship with William and also usher in a new period of fulfillment. In fact, the coming decade was to be one of the bitterest periods in her entire life. Despite his valiant efforts when traveling through the Highlands, it soon became apparent that Coleridge was not recovering his former vigor. Once returned to Keswick, he reverted to his opium addiction. Under its influence, his quick, brilliant personality gave way to a blank lethargy, his literary creativity coming almost to a halt. Only a further extended trip, he was told, offered any chance of curing him; so in the following April, in 1804, financed by the ever-faithful Thomas Poole, Coleridge sailed for Malta.[76] His friends looked forward to seeing him again as the man they had once known.

In 1802, Dorothy's brother John sailed for the East as commander of the East Indiaman, *HMS Abergavenny*. When he was younger, John was often viewed as the family's problem child. As he exhibited neither the literary interests of his sister or of William, nor the academic calling of his brother Christopher nor his brother Richard's desire to pursue the law, relatives frequently expressed worry about whether he could ever support himself. Defying all their grim predictions, however, John made a very successful career for himself at sea, traveling all over the world as a ship's captain, delivering cargoes to such places as Jamaica, Barbados, Bombay, Madras, Calcutta, and Malacca. Dorothy was proud of him, and now in early 1805, as his ship was setting sail again, she looked forward to his returning with many fascinating stories about the mysterious, faraway empire of China. Then suddenly, on February 5 (the same month she completed copying out *The Prelude*), Dorothy received word from Charles Lamb, who as a clerk at the East India Tea Company's headquarters at Leadenhall Street in London was privy to all in-coming dispatches, that the *Abergavenny* had just been wrecked in a Channel storm off Weymouth.[77] Except for a handful of survivors, John and the entire crew were drowned; none of their bodies was ever recovered.

Dorothy was filled with grief. Yet her emotions were even further strained when she heard rumors that, rather than going down with his ship, Captain Wordsworth had deserted his crew and died trying to reach shore alone in a lifeboat. Not only had he lost his life, people whispered, he had lost his honor. Hearing of her distress, Lamb swiftly transmitted to Dorothy accounts from the survivors proving the rumors were false.[78] Not long afterward, she received a letter from his sister enclosing her famous poem of consolation. Dorothy would always be grateful to the Lambs for the support they showed her during this time of terrible anguish. Recently, she had been developing a close personal attachment to Mary Lamb, and her friend's action here guaranteed that tie for the rest of their lives.

Dorothy also found comfort from William's verses. John's spirit lived on as the inspiration for his brother's poem *The Happy Warrior*, one of the most popular of the nineteenth century. Many years later, Harriet Martineau would please Dorothy by telling her it was her favorite.[79] Thanks to her work and the companionship of those she loved, Dorothy was able to recover her customary strength and optimism. "I think of my Brother who is taken from us," she at last reflected, "with tranquility and frequent joy unalterable. His exalted Nature has not perished—but Oh! for better—and we who remain on Earth shall have him with us, a perpetual presence."[80]

Dorothy's recovery came just in time for her to confront another emotional crisis. On 16 August 1806, Coleridge returned from Malta.[81] After debarking at Portsmouth following quarantine, rather than proceeding home to Keswick, he traveled instead to London, where he took up residence with the Lambs, who were then writing *Tales of Shakespear*. His refusal to meet or to communicate with his wife caused much concern to his friends—none more than Mary, who wrote to William, asking him to mediate. He "dare[s] not go home," William reported after contacting his friend, "he recoils so much from the thought of domesticating with Mrs. Coleridge, with whom, though on many accounts he much respects her, he is so miserable that he dare not encounter it."[82]

Finally, on September 16, a month after his return to England and after William offered to come to London and persuade him to come home, Coleridge at last contacted his wife. He wrote her that he would arrive home at Greta Hall on the 29th and intended to seek a formal separation (divorce being unavailable

at the time).[83] His friends were startled at his boldness. Having avoided taking
this step for over six years, his unexpected determination seemed to signify he
had finally regained his old fire. But when Dorothy met him on October 26, she
was horrified by his actual condition.[84] Since she had last seen him two years
earlier, Coleridge had grown very fat, had difficulty in walking, and could not
hold a conversation without wandering off on tangents. He was in a wretched
state, and Dorothy feared he would never have the physical and mental
perseverance to go forward with his decision.

Yet this was not so. As was the case with all substance abusers, Coleridge,
despite all the ills he had inflicted on his mind and body, remained convinced
that he still possessed the strength to cure himself at any time. Believing he
could achieve this end through breaking with his wife, he stood by his resolution;
and at first, he appeared to be correct.

Dorothy Wordsworth to Catherine Clarkson[85]
November 24, 1806

I have at last the comfort of writing to you with a settled hope that poor
Coleridge may be restored to himself and his friends. Lost he has been, oppressed
even to the death of all his noble faculties (at least for any profitable work either
in himself or for the good of others) but Heaven be praised, his weakness is
conquered (I trust it is) and all will be well. Last night Wm and I walked to the
post-office (two miles off) tempted through the miry roads by the possibility not
the hope of a letter; but a letter we found and I will give you his own word—I
dare not believe that he has written to you or that he will be able to write to any
body or fulfil any of the duties of friendship till he has left Keswick. He says
"We have *determined* to part absolutely and finally, Hartley and Derwent [his
sons] to be with me but to visit their Mother as they would do if at public
school."[86]

William and Mary, who now had two children, and Dorothy were spending
the winter of 1806-07 on a country estate in Coleorton, Leicestershire; and it was
here, on December 21 that Coleridge arrived from Keswick, having at last
separated from his wife:

Dorothy Wordsworth to Lady Beaumont
December 23, 1806

Coleridge and his son Hartley arrived on Sunday afternoon. My dear Lady
Beaumont, the pleasure of welcoming him to your house mingled with our joy,
and I think I never was more happy than when we had him an hour by the
fireside; for his looks were much more like his own old self, and, though we only
talked of common things, and of our Friends, we perceived that he was contented
in his mind and had settled his affairs at home to his satisfaction. He has been
tolerably well and chearful ever since: and has begun with his books.[87]

Traditionally, Sarah Fricker Coleridge has been portrayed as the partner solely responsible for the collapse of her marriage. She, so this interpretation goes, was a harsh, domineering, uncultured woman who possessed no appreciation for her husband's talents or compassion for his emotional weakness. As a loyal friend, Dorothy certainly wished to believe this argument at the time, and did all she could to win everyone around her to it. Yet this view is clearly too simplistic. Marriage to a genius is hard enough, but marriage to a genius who was also a drug addict must have been almost unendurable. With her husband frequently absent for months at a time, and in later years physically incapacitated as well, Mrs. Coleridge bore full responsibility for raising the children and managing the family's finances and received no acknowledgment for it. The hardly camouflaged dislike shown her by her husband's intimates was also a great strain. That she was embittered by these experiences is only natural. However, while Coleridge's partisans did much to criticize her actions in later years, his wife refused ever to retaliate by exposing his weaknesses.

The twelve months following the separation witnessed a surprising improvement in Coleridge's condition, and hence also in Dorothy's emotional peace. During most of this period her friend lived in London, where he delivered several very popular series of lectures at the Royal Academy on the works of Shakespeare and Milton. Dorothy did not approve of his becoming a public speaker, believing he was permitting himself to be put on display for the titillation of celebrity stalkers and scandal-sheet readers. Nonetheless, she was pleased at what she took for an indication of his renewed health and vitality. Free to devote time to her own interests, she travelled to the West Riding in Yorkshire during the summer of 1807 with her brother and Mary, their children, and Sara Hutchinson to visit the remains of the great twelfth-century Cistercian abbeys plundered by Henry VIII, a trip that later prompted William to write *The White Doe Of Rylstone* (1809-10). As restoration work on the sites would not commence until the second half of the century, these once-grand symbols of clerical power were in ruins when Dorothy visited them—their towers toppled, their battlements pulled down, their chapels roofless, and their windows broken. Dorothy found the occasion very stimulating; the natural environment combined with the remnants of passed glory, appealed much to her romantic nature:

Dorothy Wordsworth to Catherine Clarkson
July 19, 1807

About an hour after their departure, William and Mr. Marshall got upon horseback, and Mrs. Marshall, Mrs. Rawson, one of Mrs. Marshall's Sisters and I went in their carriage to Otley and up the Wharf as far as Bolton Abbey; I hope you have been there. The Abbey stands in the most beautiful valley that ever was seen; the Ruin is greatly inferior to Kirstall; but the situation infinitely more beautiful, a retired woody winding valley, with steep banks and rock scars, no manufactories—no horrible Forges and yet the Forge near Kirkstall has often a very grand effect. We spent a very pleasant day in the neighborhood of Bolton with our friends, and parted from them at six miles distant from Burnsall, the place where we were to lodge. We had a *delightful* walk to Burnsall, and there we were received at the little Inn with that true welcoming which you only meet with in lonely places; and we had an hour's very interesting conversation with the Landlord, a most intelligent man. Burnsall is a pretty village, by the side of the Wharf—now not a very large stream; the fields green, but wanting wood, and fenced with stone walls. From Burnsall we walked with a guide over bare hills to Gordale, and there we rested under the huge rock for several hours, and drank of its cold waters and ate our dinner.[88]

Unfortunately, this period of serenity was not to last forever. Early in the following year, 1808, not long before she and the rest of the Wordsworth family moved from Dove Cottage to a larger home nearby known as Allan Bank, Dorothy received word that Coleridge had relapsed.[89]

Dorothy Wordsworth to Catherine Clarkson
February 5, 1808

Poor Coleridge! The only good news we have heard of him is that his lectures have begun. We never hear anything but in [-] directly; and nothing has reached us but one distressing detail of illness after another; and I fear it will never be otherwise; for setting aside that he takes no care to guard against wet or cold, I have no doubt that he continues the practice of taking Opiates as much as ever. I wish you may have seen him—you will at least be able to tell us if he was in tolerable spirits.[90]

It was not long before Dorothy learned directly about the true condition of Coleridge's spirits. He began sending her and William paranoid notes accusing the Wordsworths of reading his correspondence with Sara Hutchinson and dictating her replies. William angrily replied that the charge was ridiculous and insisted that Sara, who after all was now thirty-four, would not have tolerated any interference in her personal relationships. He also rebuked Coleridge for ever doubting the lady who had long demonstrated her affection for him. The Wordsworths' anger was soon transformed to concern, however. In London, Coleridge visited Mary Lamb, who reported to Dorothy that though he refused to admit it, their friend was in an extremely disturbed mental condition and begged he be forgiven his irrational accusations. Perhaps after a rest in the country and some close attention he would get better. In September, therefore, Dorothy and William once more invited Coleridge to come and live with them in Grasmere.[91]

Under the supervision of the Wordsworths, Coleridge yet again appeared to throw off his addiction and win back his strength. The nineteenth century was the golden age of the literary periodical. Dozens existed in Britain alone, containing articles written by all the important authors of the era. Nearly every piece of fiction, scientific research, criticism, or history appeared in the pages of the periodicals before becoming available in book form. Such was the prestige and extensive readership of publications like the *Edinburgh Review* and *Blackwood's Magazine* that they frequently possessed the power to make or destroy an author's entire career. Coleridge knew their power from personal experience, and Dorothy and William judged it a sure sign of his mental and physical recovery when he announced to them in November his intention of launching a new periodical of his own. He entitled it *The Friend*. It was to be a weekly, containing essays on the literary, moral, and political events of the day. Eager for the project to be a success, Dorothy spent most of the remaining weeks of 1808 persuading both intimates and acquaintances to order subscriptions. She also got advertisements for *The Friend* placed in many local businesses and newspapers. Surely, she hoped, if the enterprise were successful, it would give Coleridge the energy finally to conquer his drug dependence.

The first issue of *The Friend* went on sale on 1 June 1809.[92] In the coming months, William would contribute three articles, *Letter to Mathetes,* Parts One and Two (14 December 1809 and 4 January 1810), and *Essay on Epitaphs* (1 February 1810).[93] As was customary during the nineteenth century, they were printed anonymously. All the others that appeared were entirely the work of Coleridge; he was not only the journal's owner and managing editor but also its primary literary contributor. He could not have done this, however, without the assistance of Sara Hutchinson. While she often spent extended periods of time at Grasmere, her permanent home still remained in Sockburn. Then, at the beginning of 1809, when she and Coleridge were traveling to Penrith to work out the final arrangements for the publication of the periodical, she at last made the decision to move permanently into Allan Bank. Once settled, she devoted herself completely to publishing her companion's work. Although Coleridge originally intended to operate the editorial side of *The Friend* entirely by himself, his fragile physical condition soon rendered this impossible. After only the third issue, he was too tired to continue alone. Sara Hutchinson promptly took on the job of his assistant; while all the articles save three were the work of Coleridge, all those he wrote after the third issue were dictated to, and edited by, Sara.

Faced by so many competitors, a totally new periodical's chances of surviving and winning a loyal audience appeared slim. And yet the root of *The Friend*'s failure lay not in a lack of readership, but rather in its owner's poor management. Though a great poet, Coleridge was not a businessman. In order to obtain as many subscribers as possible, he had promised not to collect the required fee until after he published the twentieth issue. The debt he immediately took on increased still further when, lacking cash, he could purchase the machinery he needed to print his journal only on credit. His strategy to make *The Friend* popular succeeded, but it also multiplied the owner's financial distress. The deathblow came when, after the publication of the twentieth issue at the start of 1810, the majority of subscribers refused to pay their bills. Since the law code of the day provided Coleridge with no means of compelling them to pay, he had to absorb the obligation himself. Somehow he scraped together enough resources to carry on for seven more issues, but finally, in February 1810, now in debt for over three hundred pounds, he admitted defeat and shut down his presses.[94]

The collapse of *The Friend* also dealt a fatal wound to the Lake District's literary triumvirate. Despondent over his journal's failure and aware that much of the responsibility lay with his own poor management, Coleridge yet again sought escape from his troubles in the placid forgetfulness of opium. Finally, Dorothy could take his self-destructive behavior no longer. Time and time again, she had convinced herself that Coleridge would conquer his addiction if given just a little more support; for years she had forgiven him his many impositions on her family, always casting the blame for his misdeeds on others, even herself. But now the limit of her endurance had been surpassed.

Dorothy Wordsworth to Catherine Clarkson
April 12, 1810

We have no hope for him—none that he will ever do anything more than he had already done. If he were not under our Roof, he would be just as much the slave of stimulants as ever, and his whole time and thoughts, (except when he is reading and he reads a great deal), are employed in deceiving himself, and seeking to deceive others. He will tell me that he has been writing, that he has written half a *Friend*; when I know that he has not written a single line. This Habit pervades all his words and actions; and you feel perpetually new hollowness and emptiness. I am loth to say this, and burn this letter, I entreat you. He lies in bed, always till after 12 o'clock, sometimes much later; and never walks out—Even the finest spring day does not tempt him to seek the fresh air; and this beautiful valley seems a blank to him.[95]

The paranoid illusions Coleridge had exhibited earlier now returned, but this time they were not directed against the Wordsworths. No one had labored harder and more faithfully with Coleridge on *The Friend* than Sara Hutchinson; but now he suddenly began to berate her ferociously for her supposed lack of loyalty, for her failing to do enough to save the journal. She was deeply wounded by his verbal abuse and started to become violently ill. Dorothy, who had herself developed a speech impediment from the tense situation, feared for Sara's safety and convinced her to leave. "He harassed and agitated her mind continually," Dorothy wrote Mrs. Clarkson, "and we saw that he was doing her health perpetual injury."[96] It was under these bitter circumstances that Coleridge's painful and ill-fated relationship with Sara Hutchinson came to an end.

It would be best, Dorothy thought, if Coleridge departed from the scene as well; but given his physical condition, this did not appear likely. Even after he returned to his home in neighboring Keswick during a momentary period of mental sobriety, he quickly became incapacitated again. It seemed that Dorothy and her brother were now fated to be his guardians forever. In October, however, the Wordsworths' old friend Basil Montagu, whose son Dorothy had tutored at Racedown Lodge and Alfoxden Park, proposed to relieve them of this responsibility. Montagu, who now lived in London, at No. 55 Frith Street, Soho, prided himself for his life of self-discipline.[97] He rose early every morning, exercised, never drank or overindulged at the dinner table, and devoted as much of his day as possible to his business affairs and to study. Unaware of Coleridge's opium addiction, he believed the poet's creative decline was due instead to laziness and lack of moral vigor. He therefore proposed to take him on and, by forcing him to follow his own robust lifestyle, reawaken his powers. Despite its spartan nature, Coleridge immediately accepted the proposal, perhaps as a means of getting back at the Wordsworths for their recent hostility. At this moment, William took Montagu aside and, with carefully selected words, discreetly revealed to him the actual nature of Coleridge's troubles.[98] Surprisingly, the disclosure did not at first appear to bother Montagu. He still insisted on taking Coleridge on, and a few days later the two departed for London.

William's disclosure provoked the friends' final break. In May of the following year, 1811, Dorothy learned, probably through Henry Crabb Robinson, that Montagu and Coleridge had quarreled. Despite his most determined efforts, Montagu was unable to perform a cure. His countless attempts to make Coleridge exercise, sleep less, and read uplifting books failed in the face of his patient's persistent lethargy. At last, feeling insulted at what he viewed as contempt for his goodwill, Montagu rashly blurted out to him that he understood the real reason for his behavior.[99] Coleridge was furious; he knew this knowledge could have been divulged by only one source. On October 28, as Dorothy and William were watching from their front window at Dove Cottage, Coleridge who for years had always paid them a visit upon returning from a trip, before going on to Keswick, now passed by without stopping.[100]

With this act, the famous fellowship of Coleridge and the Wordsworths tragically came to an end. Late in the following year, 1812, after the premature death of two of William's young children, Thomas and Catherine, a truce was established and relations were renewed. But these never advanced beyond the uncomfortable, formal level. The three continued to meet occasionally and always championed each other's works to the public; but, once broken, their old bond of affection, so influential on British literature, could never be restored.

Ironically, the rift with Coleridge took place just as the literary style he and the Wordsworths had advocated since the 1790s was about to win acceptance by Britain's critics and general reading public. When William first published his collected works in 1815, the event was greeted with approbation. Long neglected or underappreciated, the poetry of the Romantic Movement at last began to receive the respect it rightly deserved. Yet the influential role Dorothy played during this period would remain largely unrecognized for over one hundred and fifty years.

Dorothy's intimate relationship with her brother, retiring lifestyle, and most important, lack of published works, combined during the nineteenth century to create a public impression of someone who was a passive, unquestioning observer of other peoples' lives. While Coleridge wrote in 1797 of his friend's "ardent" and "impressive" soul, most contemporaries, unacquainted with her writings or literary influence, tended to favor the description of her made by Thomas De Quincey, who in his *Recollections of the Lakes and Lake Poets* spoke of how Dorothy's

maidenly condition, (for she had rejected all offers of marriage, out of pure sisterly regard to her brother and his children,) gave to her whole demeanor and to her conversation, an air of embarrassment and even of self-conflict that was sometimes distressing to witness.[101]

Though the twentieth-century publication of Dorothy's voluminous correspondence and assorted diaries quickly demonstrated the falsity of this patronizing image, it did not immediately inspire interest in her as a separate and distinct literary and historical figure. Until approximately twenty-five years ago, Dorothy's life and writing continued to be viewed by both academics and the general reading public as purely ancillary to her brother's. As stated earlier, the significance of the *Grasmere Journal* was still believed to lie solely in the information it provided on William. Few publications of the work ever appeared that did not include large extracts of his poetry and frequent footnotes detailing his actions. To the extent that Dorothy was studied separately, it was primarily by psychohistorians who felt they detected in her journal's references to William as "My Beloved," its constant statements of concern for his success and health, and finally her description of his wedding the possible existence of an incestuous relationship. It was not until the rise of the feminist movement in the 1970s and the rejection of the traditional entirely male-oriented theory of history that Dorothy's life began to be examined for its own importance. Only then was she recognized as a participant as well as a chronicler of her age.

It is incorrect, however, to attribute the long lack of appreciation for Dorothy's true historical importance entirely to the influence of unimaginative literary critics and conservative academic scholars; the cause lay also in Dorothy's own actions. Despite her many innovative ideas in the spheres of literature and sociology, she was in other ways a woman very much of her own time. Henry Crabb Robinson tried repeatedly to persuade her to publish her diaries, but she steadfastly refused. "I think journals except as far as one is interested in the travellers," Dorothy commented, ". . . very uninteresting. . . . I can hardly read [them] myself."[102] The poet Samuel Rogers urged her to publish her verse; and although she finally consented to having three pieces printed, they all appeared under the pseudonym "A Female Authoress"[103] in an appendix to William's collection of 1815—the same year as the appearance of Mary Lamb's early feminist article in the *Lady's British Magazine*. Unlike her friend and contemporary, Dorothy explained to Robinson, it was not her intention to be remembered primarily as a writer. No matter how good an author or social commentator she might be, her first duty as a woman, Dorothy insisted, was to be of assistance to her family and to do good works for the community. It was by her performance in these traditional feminine endeavors that her true worth would ultimately be measured.

It must be remembered that the *Grasmere Journal* was originally intended as simply a source of ideas for her brother's poetry. The ease with which she was received into Britain's predominately male literary circles did nothing to modify her conviction. Although artistic revolutionaries, men like William and Coleridge proved to be quite conventional in their views on relations between the sexes—acknowledging Dorothy's intellectual equality, yet at the same time doing little to encourage her to obtain a similar political and social status. Even the noble sister of *Tintern Abbey* is an essentially passive figure, an eager helpmate rather than an independent agent. She may be the source of inspiration, but it is her brother who puts her ideals into action. Living in an environment where those who most appreciated her intellect at the same time consigned her as a woman to a restricted lifestyle, Dorothy not unnaturally in the end accepted much of this theory herself. It was her desire to pursue a literary career while still conducting herself in a manner befitting a ''proper'' nineteenth-century British *lady* that eventually led Dorothy to her fateful decision not to publish and therefore to provide credibility to her society's long underestimation of her abilities.

After her break with Coleridge in 1811 and the Wordsworths' move to Rydal Mount in 1813, Dorothy's profession as a diarist temporarily came to an end. Although she continued her extensive correspondence with the other influential members of the British literary world, her main concern during the decade between 1812 and 1822 was the nurturing of her family. William and Mary had three remaining children: John, Dorothy, and William, Jr. Their education, along with that of the orphaned children of her brother Richard (who died in 1816), took up nearly all her time. Dorothy's account of the trip she took to France, Switzerland, and Italy with William and her sister-in-law in 1820, *Journal of a Tour on the Continent,* makes interesting reading, but unlike the *Alfoxden* and *Grasmere Journals* or *A Tour Made in Scotland*, it is essentially a travelogue containing none of the social commentary of the previous works. It was not until the autumn of 1822 that Dorothy truly returned to her old profession of social commentator with *Journal of My Second Tour in Scotland.*

Mary Wordsworth's sister, Joanna Hutchinson, had recently begun to exhibit symptoms of consumption, a disease that had claimed the life of another sister, Margaret, in 1796. Dorothy volunteered to escort her on a leisurely journey through Scotland, her first visit since 1803, in the hope that the cooler climate would improve Joanna's health. Though the journey ultimately failed to achieve this purpose, the diary that Dorothy kept during the months of September and October permitted her to write another intriguing eyewitness account of daily life in early nineteenth-century Scotland, as well as to describe the then highly unconventional experience of women traveling alone.

One of the first places the travelers visited was the mill town of New Lanark, south of Glasgow. Founded in 1800 by the utopian socialist Robert Owen, it was history's first successful cooperative community. In a period when the vast majority of industrial workers were little more than slaves, totally subject to the arbitrary will of their employers, the inhabitants of New Lanark were masters of their own destiny. Here, foremen and laborers were treated as equals; employees jointly owned the factories they worked in, producing for themselves the same garments they made for others. After salaries, all profits went to the construction of schools for the community's children and housing for its families. Workers were even supplied with an early form of health insurance. Traditional economists scoffed at Owen's theories, declaring that a business could never succeed in an egalitarian environment. Yet in spite of all the predictions of disaster, New Lanark not only survived but prospered. As it was a much talked-about experiment in social engineering, not surprisingly Dorothy decided to see the town for herself:

September 27, Wednesday:. . . Mr Owen's son shewed me the manufactory—the children looked chearful and healthy, and the young women, as far as I could judge, were modest in their deportment. It was a pretty sight when they came out of the Mill at dinner time, generally in companies of two or three, perhaps leaning on each other's arms and talking chearfully. Their dress and appearance I thought much superior to those of the women I have before seen employed in cotton mills.[104]

However, it was not the community's industry that most interested Dorothy but rather its nontraditional system of education, which she viewed with some sympathy, but also some misgiving. "Mr Owen himself arrived." She related:

I was writing a note for him on a desk at the end of one of his very large rooms, with benches across like a chapel, and at the other end a sort of pulpit from which moral, and sometimes *religious* discourses are delivered. The geography lesson was now to be exhibited, and it was surprizing to hear with what readiness boys from seven to ten years old gave the names of rivers with uncouth names, of distant seas and countries, at the pointing of a wand over a large map of the world placed on a frame near the head of the room, the class standing in a semi-circle before it. The room is hung round with materials for study—paintings of beasts and birds, fossils and flowers. The flowers (with all their parts according to botanical arrangement) are painted on a great length of canvas, which is unrolled for exhibition, at the same time winding up again from the bottom. The walls of another apartment are hung with symbolical representations of the origin, genealogies and out-spreading of nations and people, beginning at the source of a great central river, that sends out streams in all directions over a space of canvas, I am afraid to guess how many feet in length and breadth. What is the result of this upon some few individual minds I leave for others to imagine; and as, though the parents are at liberty to instruct their children in their own religion, it appears that religious duties (*as such*) are not enforced in Mr Owen's schools, one cannot but apprehend that numbers will grow up to slight and even despise what they see is not reverenced by so kind and virtuous a man, to whose care they are indebted for so many comforts.[105]

Owen offered to introduce Dorothy and Joanna to the radical Whig orator Lord Brougham, the arch-political rival of the Earl of Lonsdale, but they declined and instead went to seek a room for the night in nearby Old Lanark. None of the houses was numbered, however, and it was only after great difficulty that they eventually found the hotel they were seeking. The next day took them across the Clyde river and through large stretches of farmland, which had changed very little since the Wordsworths' first journey to the Highlands. This time though, the lonely and scattered huts Dorothy saw did not evoke the same melancholy feelings they did in 1803. She was more concerned now with personal safety. Most of the locals they met along the road looked askance at the two ladies; traveling without male escort, they must certainly be up to no good. Carriage drivers passed them by, refused to take them as far as they asked, or tried to cheat them on the fare. At last, at about midnight, they were offered shelter by a kindly couple who ran an inn. But just as they entered, they were confronted by a band of toughs, a not uncommon occurrence in rural Scotland. "The woman told them she had no whiskey, and that it was not a publick-house," Dorothy wrote. "But we are tired," the men replied,

[and] have come from Aberdeen, and to-day have travelled far, and you will let us sit by the fire till the Coach comes." She looked inquiringly in our faces, and asked in a low voice "Do you know anything of these men?" and, turning to them replied that there would probably be no places for them—these ladies were waiting for the Coach, and must be first served—it was a fine moonlight night, and only six miles to Moffat. The men had a rattling wild air and demeanor which would have completely upset us had they overtaken us on the road. They reminded me of the roughest of the Heidelberg Students. Each carried a knapsack, with a stout staff in hand, and leather caps on the head. You may judge that we were anxious that the house should be cleared of them, especially as we were convinced that it must have been one of these men whom Joanna had seen, and that they had hurried forward to overtake us; and we even *suspected*, from the tenor of their discourse, that they *had heard something* about us. They were surly and abusive when the landlord upheld his wife in refusing them stay: at length, however, they moved away grumbling, and the door was bolted against them, and we soon began to feel ourselves at ease and thankful for a shelter.[106]

Their hosts must have been accustomed to such incidents and were not overly concerned, but Dorothy and Joanna spent a restless night. "After the coach had passed," Dorothy remembered,

I had snatches of disturbed sleep, but poor Joanna was wakeful all night—and no wonder—for it was a strange situation into which we had imprudently brought ourselves; and the thought of the wild hills, between which we had travelled so far to this spot (the central point of the lonely road from Elvan-foot to Moffat) and that here we were completely in the power of people entirely unknown to us—these thoughts haunted her the night through.[107]

When she heard the innkeeper's brother walking down the hall at about two o'clock in the morning, Dorothy was seized with terror:

The outer door was opened from within, and the landlord's brother went out as I distinctly heard. He had moved very quietly, and my fears cannot be described for at that moment I was struck with the horrible thought that he had got out of bed to admit the two men who had come in after us in the evening—and, recollecting that both he and his brother, during the parley, had gone out with the men talking about their journey—I thought what if they then settled upon murdering us! Joanna and I lay trembling side by side—the door was again locked on the inside, and what was my comfort when I heard the crying of a child, as if disturbed by his uncle's getting into of bed.[108]

Dorothy was relieved when dawn finally came, and after a good morning meal she and her companion preceded on their journey. The toughs had moved on, and the two travelers were now able to spend the next few days contemplating the grace of the Highland countryside unperturbed:

October 1, Monday: At 8 o'clock departed—wide valley—plantations on the hills—junction of the rivers, Moffat and Annan. Another stream from a very pretty woody dell—Church on an eminence to the left—a beautiful walk up that dell. Leaving the Vale, travel over open country to Borland (12 miles)—cross a stream. Publick-house where we dined—valley pleasing—Gentleman's house and plantations—the Church on the hill surrounded by tall Ash trees.[109]

Descend toward Eskdale through farm yard of white house sheltered by fine trees, after a curious twisting road down the steep. The Esk a pretty Moorland stream. Lower down, a few neat houses—green fields—woody by the river side. Burial ground and white gravestones opposite. Often inquire the road never nearer—and darkness comes on. Surprized by the fine woods of Wester Hall.[110]

Unfortunately, the physical exertions the trip required eventually proved too much for Joanna. "Poor Joanna," Dorothy wrote on 2 October, "stiff and tired, and soon very sick."[111] She hired a carriage to transport her friend back to Edinburgh on October 6. The baths there did not revive her health, and on 11 October the two decided to return to Rydal Mount. "From Langholm," Dorothy wrote of the trip home, "we took the inside and saw little, but by glimpses, of the richer vale of the Esk—a little foggy near the water and very cold."[112]

My Second Tour in Scotland is not as lengthy or as famous today as Dorothy's earlier journals. Yet its interesting character sketches, social comments, and firsthand descriptions of what life was like for a woman in early nineteenth-century Britain, make it a not-insignificant addition to Dorothy's works. The interesting observations she makes about New Lanark and the Owenites also reveal that, as with other first-generation members of the Romantic movement, some of the radical beliefs of Dorothy's youth were beginning to give way to a more traditional, Victorian brand of liberalism. While she continued to possess great sympathy for the working class and continued to advocate political and social reforms that would improve their lives, she now looked with some suspicion upon those who proposed to achieve these goals by less than conventional, parliamentary methods.

After her return to the Lake District, Dorothy once more devoted most of her attention to her family: taking charge of the management of Rydal Mount, directing the education of the children, and using her influence to obtain positions for them when they were old enough to venture out on their own. As before, these activities provided her with little time to write except in response to her correspondence. In 1828, however, with the house running well and the younger Wordsworths started in life, she decided it would be permissible for her to take a brief respite from her labors. The vacation she took with Joanna and her brother Henry Hutchinson from late June to the middle of July finally gave Dorothy an opportunity to write another journal, *A Tour in the Isle of Man*. Most people today remember this fishing community in the Irish Sea only as the home of the tailless Manx cat. But in the pages of what would prove to be her final diary, Dorothy expands the reader's knowledge of the island's culture and people in a style that demonstrates that her gifts of observation and description were as sharp as in any of her previous works.

The eastern shore of the island, that facing the coast of England, offered a view that would excite the imagination of any romantic. "Tilted 'cross the harbour to the Island Castle," Dorothy recorded as she walked along the beach during the morning of Wednesday, July 9,

very grand and very wild, with cathedral tower, and extensive ruins, and tombstones of recent date, several of shipwrecked men. Our guide showed us the place where Fenella, as Sir Walter Scott tells us, was confined, and another dungeon where Lady Stanley was shut up for 15 years, and died there, and used to appear in the shape of a black dog, and a soldier who used to laugh at the story would speak to it and die raving mad. The Castle was built before artillery was used, and the walls are so thin, it is surprising it has stood so long. The grassy floor of [the] hill delightful to rest on through a summer's day, and view the ships and sea, and hear the dashing waves, here gentle, for the entrance to this narrow harbour is very rocky. Fine caves to the north, but it being high water, we could not get to them.[113]

The island's church and nearby cemetery caught Dorothy's eye as well. The scene was as fascinating in its way as anything she had come across hiking with William in Wales. The comingling of Christianity and paganism, she saw, stood as a vivid reminder of how the culture of the past always weighs heavily upon the thoughts and actions of the present. "The views of Ramsey Bay [are] delightful from the Head," Dorothy wrote:

—a fine green steep, on the edge of which stands the pretty chapel, with one bell outside, an antient pedestal curiously carved, Christ on the cross, the mother and infant Jesus, the Manx arms, and other devices; near it the square foundation [is] surrounded with [the] steps of another cross, on which is now placed a small sundial, the whole lately barbarously whitewashed, with the church and roof—a glaring contrast with the grey thatched cottages, and green trees, which partly embower the church. Numerous are the gravestones surrounding that neat and humble building: a sanctuary taken from the waste, where fern and heath grow round, and *over*grow the graves. I sate on the hill, wile Henry sought the Holy Well, visited once a year by the Manx men and women, where they leave their offering—a pin or any other trifle.[114]

However, the Isle of Man possessed more than dramatic vistas and thought-provoking cemeteries, it also had inhabitants. Although isolated and small in number, they and the events of their lives offered the observer many fine representations of the larger world across the sea. The arrival of the sister of a famous poet was considered a great occasion, and the Manx felt honored when Dorothy asked to be allowed to visit and interview them. On 11 July 1828, for instance, a Methodist missionary invited Dorothy to accompany him on his round of daily visits. Although the majority of the island's inhabitants were Calvinists—the descendants of French Huguenots who had sought refuge there from religious persecution in the seventeenth-century—in recent years the Methodists had been making inroads. As in England and Wales, the cheerfulness and optimism that characterized their faith was often very attractive to the impoverished members of the lower classes. For her part, Dorothy was not impressed. More than enthusiastic speeches, she wrote in her journal, were required to cure the injustices of the world. "We descended to Laxey," she recalled:

a village at the foot of a long glen headed by the Snaefell mountains. One pretty gentleman's cottage. Bridge and rocky bay, a few boats and bleaching ground. Tempted by the cleanliness of a poor hut to enter it with my companion, a young Methodist, who exclaimed to the poor inmate "How happy you are—here you have every thing—health and contentment." "Nay," says she, "I have very little. I have only what I get by spinning, and that is but so much the hank, and so much the pound." "Well, but there are good people to help you." "Good people are but scarce in this world. I do not get much in that way." "Well! but you have health and that is the best of earthly blessings." "It is a great blessing, but I have nothing else." Now there was no reason why the young Methodist should include that this poor woman had any unusual share of health. She had no appearance of it, and must have been over 50 years of age. She had never been married, had lived alone, and was one of 9 children, all now dead or dispersed. After all, my friend again exclaimed, "How sweet! here is everything that is needed for contentment," and so satisfied, parted with these words uttered in a soft piping tone, "Peace be with you, think upon Jesus!" Again replied the old woman, "that is the only thing, that is the best thing." I certainly saw but little except the extreme cleanliness of her poor hovel, and divided between her and an aged neighbour, who was keeping her company the few halfpence I had in my bag, which certainly seemed to give her more comfort than my friend's felicitations on her blessed condition.[115]

Most of the individuals Dorothy encountered, however, are described in a more positive manner. She found the Manx, especially the women, a very friendly people; and her journal illustrates the determination they showed to make a good life for themselves on the isolated rock that was their home:

Home to Mrs Brew's—walked on sands to small rocky caverns, and after dinner with Miss Trevett to Mrs Hoskins's deserted cottage—once a place of revelry, or rather of elegant festivity, for she was, they say, a very amiable woman. The spot is now desolate and the garden destroyed all but the gravel walks, yet many a flower still grows wild. It was since tenanted by a Mrs Stepney and her pretended husband, who lived concealed for 2 years, were at length discovered by agents of her real husband, and a divorce obtained. She is now married to her paramour who has retaken his own name and given it to her. The parties [were] all cousins, and as an alleviation of her guilt it is affirmed that she was in youth prevailed on by friends to marry the former. They are returned to a cottage near the old one, going to build, and every one will visit her as heretofore.[116]

Thence to Mrs Gubbins, the aging widow of the late Vicar General who died a few months ago at 83 years of age. She and her 3 daughters reside at a house belonging to Deemster Christian, a substantial dwelling rather genteel but all unfurbished, the avenue to the house winding, and the garden tangled and rank and dull. A very flourishing tulip tree and nothing wanting but pruning and neatness. The ladies themselves, however, very neat and lady-like, and intelligent in all Manx affairs and evidently much pleased with my approbation of their little Isle. Home by Mrs Duke's—still the same comfortable kindness, uncomfortable dirt and close smells, and pretty behaved, pretty curly-headed lasses, who repaid me for their sixpence with a hundred thanks.[117]

On 19 July 1828, after three weeks of entries, Dorothy's latest journal came to an end.[118] As was the case with her second trip to Scotland six years earlier, her tour of the Isle of Man was in part motivated by her hope that travel would help alleviate Joanna Hutchinson's consumption. Unfortunately, instead of improving her health, the long hours of travel required each day only increased her sister-in-law's spasms of short breath and weakness in the limbs. Finally, Dorothy decided she had no choice but to restore Joanna to the care of her family at Rydal Mount. Upon arriving home, Dorothy rested for a few days and put her papers back in order. But within a week she had once more resumed her duties as mistress of the house. She would never again take up her pen as a diarist.

In April 1829, Dorothy, now fifty-seven, travelled to the town of Whitwick, in Leicestershire. The previous autumn her nephew, John Wordsworth, graduated from Oxford but failed to obtain a fellowship at his college. The family's friend Sir George Beaumont then offered the young man an alternative source of income by naming him vicar of a church on his property. Though his father had rejected a similar offer from the Reverend Dr. Cookson in 1791, John did not foresee a poetic career in his future, and accepted. Although the appointment assured him a lifelong means of financial support, John quickly found existence in the damp, dirty colliery town of Whitwick bleak and depressing. His duties were monotonous, and he had no friends; the inhabitants were not particularly interested in religion, and as an outsider he was always looked upon with suspicion. Concerned for her nephew's welfare, Dorothy decided to pay him a visit in order to build up his spirits. Not long after her arrival, however, she suddenly suffered what was originally diagnosed as a bad case of influenza, but was probably the first of several strokes. Her condition quickly became worse, showing signs that she had actually experienced a stroke. Besides her general bodily weakness, Dorothy also developed swellings in her eyelids so large she could no longer see. For a few days, she also lost the ability to speak. The family was alarmed and, not judging Whitwick a place conducive to her recovery, had Dorothy moved first to Halifax and then to Sir George Beaumont's country estate at Coleorton Hall. By the end of the year the swellings had disappeared, and Dorothy was in good-enough health to be transported back to Rydal Mount.

Dorothy remained as active as she could, continuing to proofread William's poems for publication as she had done at Dove Cottage, staying abreast of all the latest literature, and taking an energetic part in dinner discussions. But no matter how much she pushed herself, she was unable to hide the fact that she was now an invalid, able to leave her wheelchair only on special occasions. In 1831, the mysterious illness that had first overtaken Dorothy at Whitwick returned. It flared up yet again in the spring of 1832, and this time the high temperature and difficulty breathing it caused almost killed her. As in earlier days, William remained always near her. "My Sister," he wrote a friend, "the only one I ever had, and who has lived with me for the last 35 years, is now in so weak and alarming [a] state of health that I could not quit home, except under absolute necessity."[119] Finally, in May 1835, after six years of bodily suffering, Dorothy experienced a mental collapse comparable to Mary Lamb's in 1833. Medicine during the period was still in its infancy, and no reliable written evidence about her condition has ever been discovered. However it is reasonable to assume that unlike her friend's lifelong psychological illness, the progressive physical decline that seized Dorothy in her late fifties was probably the result of Alzheimer's disease or arteriosclerosis.

Once William's eager partner in life, Dorothy was now reduced to a state in which she was completely dependent upon him, like a small child. Almost no sign remained in her of the vital spirit that inspired his thoughts at Tintern Abbey:

William Wordsworth to Henry Crabb Robinson
July 6, 1835

My sister's health of body seems to have suffered less than her mind. Her recollection is greatly impaired since the event. I mean her recollection of recent events. She complains of weakness and foolishness of mind which is sad to hear of—the bilious sickness and cough and expectoration which harassed her and weakened her so much are gone; but no doubt will return. . . . I fear you cannot read this Letter. I feel my hand-shaking. I have had so much agitation to-day, in attempting to quiet my poor Sister, and from being under the necessity of refusing her things that would be improper to her. She has a great craving for oatmeal porridge principal[ly] for the sake of the butter that she eats along with it and butter is sure to bring on a fit of bile sooner or later.[120]

Dorothy's mental collapse was followed within a month by the sudden death from rheumatic fever of Sara Hutchinson, who had survived her tormented lover, Coleridge, by one year.[121] Despite Dorothy's current state, William was sure his sister was yet capable of intimate emotions and believed she could never endure the loss of someone as important and influential in her life as Sara, unassisted. He therefore informed Dorothy only after first giving her a strong dose of opium. Even this measure did not remove all the shock the news brought, however. She grew very ill, losing much weight and becoming nearly paralyzed. William was sure the end was near.

Yet Dorothy did not die; she recovered and lived on for twenty years. The painful experiences of recent times were now almost totally lost to her. She dwelt only in the glorious past; she recognized the world around her, but only insofar as it evoked thoughts of days gone by.

William Wordsworth to Christopher Wordsworth
September 26, 1835

Her case at present is very strange to me; her judgement, her memory, and all her faculties are perfect as ever, with exception of what relates to her own illness, and passing occurrences. If I ask her opinion upon any point of Literature, she answers with all her former acuteness; if I read Milton, or any favorite Author, and pause, she goes on with the passage from memory; but she forgets instantly the circumstances of the day.[122]

William Wordsworth to Samuel Rogers
September 28, 1836

Our dear Sister is very well and generally very happy—but her Mind does not strengthen—tho her memory is now good, that is *partially*—And it is most strange, as you will think, when I tell you that sometimes she amuses herself by pouring out verses—as by inspiration—in a moment and seemingly without thought she will write down (and in as good a hand as ever she wrote) 6 or 8 very respectable lines—generally addressed to her attendants. . . . She reads the Newspapers, but an old one—read a doz times—pleases equally with a new one.[123]

Others wrote or remarked similarly about Dorothy's condition. Henry Crabb Robinson remembered that she was never a cause of trouble to her caretakers, being always in a good humor, never violent or obstructive. When dinner parties were held, he said, she was frequently allowed to sit at the table. Dorothy recognized him; although not precisely sure who he was, she understood he was a friend. She often recited her brother's poetry to him or sang the ballads of Sir Walter Scott. In 1845, Mary Wordsworth wrote Coleridge's daughter, Sara, telling her how Dorothy had recently described the day on which she first met her father bounding over the wall at Racedown Lodge, forty-eight years before. "My poor Sister," she commented, "has just been speaking of it to me with much feeling and tenderness."[124]

On 23 April 1850, William, now poet laureate, died at the age of eighty and was buried in Grasmere churchyard.[125] A memorial was later erected to him in Westminster Abbey, where it now stands not far from the one honoring Coleridge. Once ridiculed for his supposed lack of talent, his poetry dismissed as vulgar, William and his writings were now celebrated as one of the nation's great cultural treasures. As in the case of Mary Lamb, the extent to which Dorothy fully comprehended her brother's death can only be conjectured. However, in July, the posthumous publication of the *Preludes* provided William the chance to make his readers conscious of the great debt he owed her. Dorothy was, he told them, his primary adviser—the "sister of my soul" (*Preludes XIII*); she shared his passionate dedication to the natural world: "She was Nature's inmate" (*Prelude XI*); she was, in short, "the beloved woman. . ./" who "Maintained for me a saving intercourse/With my true self. . ." (*Prelude XI*).

Dorothy lived on quietly in her family's care for nearly five more years. She continued to experience periodic intervals of semirational thinking, even composing a few short letters. "I have had a good night so I think I will write," she informed her sister-in-law in her last surviving message, on 22 October 1853. "The weather was rough. I was in bed all day. I am well today. My love to [her attendants] Miss Fenwick and Miss Jane."[126] She died at last, peacefully, on 25 January 1855, at the age of eighty-three and was buried, as she had wished, beside her brother.[127] "Her restless Spirit I trust," wrote Mary, "is now among the blessed."[128]

A restless spirit, Dorothy indeed was. She was possessed of singular talents yet, unlike Mary Lamb, very much a person of her own time; her life, despite its many achievements, was also one of constant struggle, torn between a desire for intellectual self-expression and loyalty to harsh social convention. Her story is one of the sharpest and most compelling portrayals of the psychological conflict many women suffered in their quest for personal fulfillment in the British society of the nineteenth century.

NOTES: PART TWO

1. Samuel Taylor Coleridge, *Letters of Samuel Taylor Coleridge*, ed. Leslie Griggs (Oxford: Clarendon, 1956), vol. 1, 75.

2. Ernest de Selincourt, *Dorothy Wordsworth* (Oxford: Oxford University Press, 1933), 2.

3. Ibid., 5.

4. Ibid.

5. William and Dorothy Wordsworth, *The Letters of William and Dorothy Wordsworth*, 2d ed., ed. Ernest de Selincourt (Oxford: Clarendon, 1967), vol. 1, 8. Permission granted by Oxford University Press.

6. Selincourt, *Dorothy Wordsworth*, 10.

7. Mary Moorman, *William Wordsworth—A Biography, The Early Years, 1770-1803* (Oxford, Clarendon, 1965), 74.

8. William and Dorothy Wordsworth, *Letters*, 8.

9. Mary Wordsworth, *The Letters of Mary Wordsworth*, ed. Mary E. Burton (Oxford: Clarendon, 1958), xxi.

10. Selincourt, *Dorothy Wordsworth*, 19.

11. William and Dorothy Wordsworth, *Letters*, 26.

12. Ibid.

13. Ibid.

14. Selincourt, *Dorothy Wordsworth*, 25.

15. Ibid., 19.

16. Ibid.

17. William and Dorothy Wordsworth, *Letters*, 83.

18. Selincourt, *Dorothy Wordsworth*, 27.

19. Moorman, *William Wordsworth, The Early Years*, 74.

20. William and Dorothy Wordsworth, *Letters*, 88.

21. Ibid.

22. Selincourt, *Dorothy Wordsworth*, 57.

23. Frederika Beatty, *William Wordsworth of Dove Cottage* (New York: Bookman Associates, 1964), 10-11.

24. Ibid., 12.

25. Coleridge, *Letters*, 216.

26. William and Dorothy Wordsworth, *Letters*, 188.

27. Ibid.

28. Ibid.

29. Coleridge, *Letters*, 330.

30. William Wordsworth, *Memoirs* (Boston: Ticknor, Reed, and Fields, 1851), vol. 1, 101.

31. William and Dorothy Wordsworth, *Letters*, 190.

32. Wordsworth, *Memoirs*, 105-6.

33. Dorothy Wordsworth, *Alfoxden Journal: Journals of Dorothy Wordsworth*, ed. Ernest de Selincourt (New York: Macmillan, 1941), vol. 1, 3.

34. Ibid., 8.

35. Ibid., 13.

36. Ibid., 15.

37. Moorman, *William Wordsworth, The Early Years*, 402.

38. Richard Holmes, *Coleridge—Early Visions* (New York: Viking, 1990), 204.

39. Dorothy Wordsworth, *Hamburgh Journal: Journals of Dorothy Wordsworth*, ed. Ernest de Selincourt (New York: Macmillan, 1941), vol. 1, 34. *Kubla Khan* was not published until 1816.

40. Mary Wordsworth, *Letters*, xxiii.

41. Ibid., 176.

42. Selincourt, *Dorothy Wordsworth*, 58.

43. William and Dorothy Wordsworth, *Letters*, 108.

44. Dorothy Wordsworth, *The Grasmere Journal, Dorothy Wordsworth—Selections from the Journals*, ed. Paul Hamilton (New York: N.Y.U. Press, 1992), 19.

45. Ibid., 73.

46. Ibid., 28.

47. Ibid., 36.

48. Ibid., 107.

49. *Mary* and *Sara Points*, after the two Hutchinson sisters, were hills the Wordsworths often visited while strolling around Lake Grasmere.

50. Ibid., 24.

51. Ibid., 110.

52. William and Dorothy Wordsworth, *Letters*, 367.

53. Selincourt, *Dorothy Wordsworth*, 124.

54. Dorothy Wordsworth, *Grasmere Journal*, 57.

55. Ibid., 73.

56. Ibid., 79.

57. Ibid., 111.

58. Ibid., 39.

59. The Rev. Robert Jones, William Wordsworth's friend from St. John's College, Cambridge, with whom he had taken his trip to France in 1790-91. It was to Jones that he dedicated *Descriptive Sketches*.

60. Ibid., 42-43.

61. Ibid., 62-63.

62. Ibid., 71.

63. Ibid., 90. *Glow-Worm Rock* was another of the sites found on the Wordsworths' frequent walks around Lake Grasmere.

64. Ibid., 161.

65. Mary Wordsworth, *Letters*, xxiii.

66. Beatty, *William Wordsworth of Dove Cottage*, 124.

67. Dorothy Wordsworth, *Grasmere Journal*, 146.

68. Ibid., 148.

69. Ibid., 149.

70. Ibid.

71. Dorothy Wordsworth, *Journal of a Tour Made in Scotland: Journals of Dorothy Wordsworth*, ed. Ernest de Selincourt (New York: Macmillan, 1941), vol. 1, 198.

72. Ibid., 260.

73. Ibid., 244.

74. Ibid.

75. Ibid., 356.

76. William Heath, *Wordsworth and Coleridge—A Study of Their Literary Relations in 1801-02* (Oxford: Clarendon, 1970), 18.

77. Mary Moorman, *William Wordsworth—A Biography, The Later Years, 1803-50* (Oxford: Clarendon, 1965), 35.

78. Ibid.

79. Ibid., 44.

80. Ibid., 41-42.

81. Charles and Mary Lamb, *The Complete Letters of Charles and Mary Lamb*, ed. E. V. Lucas (London: Methuen, 1935), vol. 2, 20.

82. Ibid., 21.

83. Ibid.

84. William and Dorothy Wordsworth, *Letters*, vol. 2, 71.

85. Catherine Clarkson, wife of the famous abolitionist Thomas Clarkson and mutual friend of the Wordsworths and the Lambs. It was Mrs. Clarkson who accompanied Dorothy on 15 April 1802, when she saw the field of daffodils.

86. Ibid.

87. Ibid., 121. Lady Beaumont was the wife of Sir George Beaumont, owner of the house in which the Wordsworths were staying.

88. Ibid., 158.

89. Dove Cottage was being rented to Thomas De Quincey, who lived there intermittently until 1835.

90. Ibid., 192.

91. Ibid., 275.

92. Ibid., 231.

93. Ibid., 275.

94. Ibid.

95. Ibid., 400.

96. Ibid., 398.

97. Lamb, *Complete Letters*, vol. 2, 108.

98. Ibid., 399.

99. Ibid., 108.

100. Coleridge, *Letters*, vol. 3, 298.

101. Thomas De Quincey, *Recollections of the Lakes and the Lake Poets*, ed. David Wright (Harmondsworth: Penguin, 1970), 131-32.

102. William and Dorothy Wordsworth, *Letters*, vol. 1, 421.

103. Moorman, *William Wordsworth—The Later Years*, 278.

104. Dorothy Wordsworth, *My Second Tour in Scotland: The Journals of Dorothy Wordsworth*, ed. Ernest de Selincourt (New York: Macmillan, 1941), vol. 2, 388.

105. Ibid., 388-89.

106. Ibid., 391-92.

107. Ibid.

108. Ibid., 394.

109. Ibid., 395.

110. Ibid., 397.

111. Ibid.

112. Ibid.

113. Dorothy Wordsworth, *Tour in the Isle of Man: The Journals of Dorothy Wordsworth*, ed. Ernest de Selincourt (New York: Macmillan, 1941), vol. 2, 411.

114. Ibid., 413.

115. Ibid., 415-16.

116. Ibid., 414.

117. Ibid., 415-16.

118. Ibid., 189.

119. William and Dorothy Wordsworth, *Letters*, vol. 5, 520.

120. William and Dorothy Wordsworth, *Letters*, vol. 6, 78.

121. Ibid., 75.

122. Ibid., 96.

123. Ibid., 299-300.

124. William and Dorothy Wordsworth, *Letters*, vol. 7, 719-20.

125. Mary Wordsworth, *Letters*, 318.

126. William and Dorothy Wordsworth, *Letters*, 918.
127. Mary Wordsworth, *Letters*, 352.
128. Ibid.

Part Three

SARAH DISRAELI

Chapter Five

A Pure and Perfect Love

"We have returned to unspeakable sorrow," Benjamin Disraeli wrote to his friend Lady Frances Anne Castlereagh, Marchioness of Londonderry, on 12 December 1859, "to the bedside of my only sister, our nearest and dearest relative, who is soon, most unexpectedly, and suddenly, to be lost to us." "She was a person of great intelligence and charm," he continued, "one of those persons who are the soul of a house and the angelic spirit of a family."[1] Fate, he lamented, never permitted Sarah to attain the same distinguished position in Britain's intellectual community as Mary Lamb and Dorothy Wordsworth. Yet in her own circumscribed way, his beloved companion exercised just as much influence as they upon a more famous brother. If Sarah's life story lacked the great drama of these two other women, it was ultimately more representative than theirs of the struggle for self-expression facing the gifted but often overshadowed female child in nineteenth-century British society.

Sarah Disraeli, like Mary Lamb, was a native of London. She was born on 29 December 1802, at No. 6 King's Road (now No. 22 Theobald Street), about a fifteen-minute walk north of where the Lambs were then living in the Middle Temple.[2] This area, generally known today as Bloomsbury, could boast an almost equally important reputation as its neighbor in British history. The complex of centuries-old legal buildings abutting Sarah's house—Gray's Inn—once contained the living quarters of such part-time law students as Dr. Samuel Johnson, Oliver Goldsmith, Sir Philip Sidney, and Sir John Suckling. The front windows of Sarah's room looked out upon Gray's Inn Garden, one of London's most fashionable promenades and the inspiration for Sir Francis Bacon's famous essay *On Gardens*. Among its frequent strollers could be numbered Sir Walter Raleigh, Oliver Cromwell, Samuel Pepys, and Joseph Addison. Two catalpa trees, which stood at either end of the main walkway until at least the 1960s, were transplanted there by Raleigh from Virginia in the late 1590s. As debtors could not be arrested on the sabbath, the young Percy Bysshe Shelley was able to come out of hiding on Sundays for his romantic trysts here with Mary Wollstonecraft Godwin. At No. 1 Gray's Inn Square, on the southeast corner of the Gardens, stood the building where Sir Francis Bacon kept his legal chambers for fifty years and where he carried out most of his scientific experiments. Just to the right, across Gray's Inn Road, stood Gray's Hall. It was in this meetinghouse in 1594 that William Shakespeare's *Comedy of Errors* was first produced. Twenty-eight years earlier, in 1566, the Hall had witnessed the first performance of George Gascoigne's *The Supposes*, arguably the first dramatic comedy in English literature. Living amid such surroundings, young Sarah never spent a waking hour without being reminded of the great figures and events that molded her nation's history.

Unlike Mary Lamb, Sarah came from a comfortably upper-middle-class family, one that required no mentor like Samuel Salt to rise in the world. Also unlike Mary Lamb, and Dorothy Wordsworth for that matter, Sarah had a father who, rather than being a minor figure, exercised instead a major influence on her life. Isaac d'Israeli (he never followed his children in adopting the capital D) was a well-known man of letters—a friend of Lord Byron, Sir Walter Scott, Robert Southey, and Jeremy Bentham, as well as a frequent guest at the Lambs' on Wednesday evenings. He was born in 1766, in the East End neighborhood of Stoke Newington. Sarah's grandfather, the original Benjamin d'Israeli, had immigrated to England from Cento, in Italy, in 1748, becoming a successful ladies' hat merchant and in 1801 one of the founding members of the London Stock Exchange. Early in life, Isaac displayed an aptitude for writing, and although his father would have preferred his son to go into the family business, he eventually consented to let him pursue his calling. Success was not long in coming. In 1791, Isaac published *Curiosities of Literature*, a collection of biographical sketches, historical anecdotes, and literary essays. It proved to be the most popular nonfiction book of its time, eventually running into thirteen editions. Byron would later carry it with him into exile, describing the *Curiosities* as "a consolation and always a pleasure."[3] The royalties he received freed Isaac from any need ever to work again and also enabled him to move out of the ethnic East End and live among the fashionable set. Despite his friends' fears that this early success would give him a false sense of satisfaction and blunt his creative energies, Isaac continued his writing and over the years published, among other works, biographies of Charles I (1828-1830) and James I (1831). The former gained him an honorary doctorate at Oxford. Basing the book's conclusions upon the study of seventeenth-century government documents, many of which no longer exist, Isaac established himself as the first British historian to use primary sources. By the time his first child was born in 1802, Isaac had become one of the most famous and popular writers of his generation.

Unlike Isaac, Sarah's mother, Miriam (called Maria) Basevi, remains a shadowy figure. In the 1848 biography he wrote about their father, Sarah's brother does not even mention her. Like her husband's family, Miriam's was of Sephardic extraction, immigrating to Britain from Verona in the eighteenth century, and was also middle class. Isaac married her in 1801. She never exhibited any interest in her husband's intellectual endeavors, devoting herself instead entirely to the upkeep of her home. Besides Sarah, Miriam had four additional children, for none of whom does she appear to have had any particular affection, either. Nonetheless, despite her mother's lack of warmth, Sarah's associations with her seem to have always been polite.

As has been demonstrated, formal primary schooling for girls already existed at the beginning of the nineteenth century. However, like most daughters of the British middle and upper classes, Sarah was educated at home. Besides, her father enjoyed having her around—she made an excellent companion. Like his wife, Isaac had never been a very gregarious individual. A scholar before everything else, he much preferred researching his next book or discussing the latest specimens of Byron's poetry with his literary associates to fulfilling social obligations or making small talk in a crowded drawing room. Not a few of those introduced to him described Isaac as distant or even haughty. At the same time, though, they invariably commented that his relations with his daughter were conspicuous for their seemingly uncharacteristic warmth and intimacy.

No woman could have been a better homemaker than Miriam. She held sway as the absolute monarch of her little kingdom, removing from her husband the slightest need to concern himself with food, clothing, expenses, or any other aspect of his domestic life. Nevertheless, Isaac frequently found himself dissatisfied. Miriam's total lack of interest in his studies could be very exasperating. Though he was able to relieve some of his craving for intellectually stimulating conversation by having lunch with Sir Walter Scott or with the publisher John Murray, they were quite busy men and not always available; Mary Lamb's literary gatherings were a treat, but they too occurred only on Wednesday evenings. Luckily, Isaac's daughter was never far away, and it was to her that her father progressively turned for fellowship.

Early on, Sarah demonstrated a keen intelligence, an aptitude for book learning and a mastery of the high art of conversation. Anyone who met her could tell she would grow up to be a woman of considerable accomplishment. While most other girls and boys of her age were playing games, she enjoyed talking with her father about what her tender years could understand of the affairs of the world. Sarah was also able to put up with her father's recurrent grumpiness and did not appear to require major shows of affection from him. In short, for a man with Isaac's reserved personality, she proved to be the perfect person to serve as his protégée and later his private secretary. In his final years, however, Isaac's declining health and increasing demands for attention would transform this rewarding comradeship into an oppressive obligation. In the meantime, however, the young Sarah, as she grew from childhood into young womanhood, found her connection with her father a rewarding experience. Besides acquiring a taste for serious scholarship long before others of her age—a fascination with the works of Shakespeare, Pope, Dryden, and Milton—she was also furnished the rare opportunity of conversing with many of the great intellectual and artistic figures of the age. By remaining at home to serve as her father's aide-de-camp, Sarah ironically was provided a far more rewarding education than she could ever have hoped to receive at even the most prestigious girls' primary school of the period.

On 21 December 1804, just before Sarah reached her second birthday, she was presented with a brother, Benjamin.[4] She was to have three others: Naphtali, who was born in 1807 and died in infancy; Raphael (called Ralph), who was born in 1809; and Jacob, (called James) who was born in 1813. But it was Benjamin with whom her relations would be closest. So near to him in age, Sarah never went through the common ordeal for first children of feeling dethroned. Neither did she and her brother experience sibling rivalry. Rather, they possessed much of the powerful emotional connection common to twins. Details about these first years, as for most other aspects of the future prime minister's early life, are sketchy. A great romantic, Benjamin later did all he could to embellish the particulars of his ancestry and the events of his childhood. For a long time after his death in 1881, for example, it was commonly believed that he and Sarah were the heirs to a family of ancient aristocratic lineage and were born in a mansion in the exclusive West End London neighborhood of Belgravia. This naturally has persuaded many historians automatically to view stories concerning his private life with skepticism. In this case, however, their lifelong correspondence, Sarah's frequent appearances in her brother's writings, and the corroboration of such intimates as Sir Philip Rose, Benjamin's private secretary of thirty years, and his friend Baroness Charlotte de Rothschild, cast away any question as to the existence of Benjamin's special devotion to Sarah. "My letters are shorter than Napoleon's," he once scribbled off hurriedly to her during a busy day in 1833, "but I love you better than he did Josephine."[5]

"I loved my father dearly and deeply," relates the narrator of Benjamin's 1832 novel, Contarini Fleming, "but I seldom saw him. He was buried in the depths of affairs. A hurried kiss and a passing smile were the fleeting gifts of his affection."[6] "My step-mother" he continues, "swayed by my father, and perhaps a well-regulated mind, was vigilant in not violating the etiquette of maternal duty."[7] Though the fictional father is a politician and diplomat rather than a scholar, and his wife is not the narrator's natural mother, the reader cannot fail to perceive the autobiographical nature of this work. Letters clearly demonstrate that Benjamin was on good terms with his father; they show he greatly respected him and always sought his approval. Yet they also reveal that Isaac never responded to his son's affection by giving him the kind of intimacy he showed his daughter. He expected male children to take care of themselves. While Benjamin came to accept this situation as an adult, it must have been very troubling for him as a child. His mother was no more forthcoming in her sentiments. Not only was she aloof in her relations with him, but she probably did not even appreciate his abilities—once describing her eldest son to John

Murray as "clever, but no prodigy."[8] Growing up with parents who were too involved with their own preoccupations to care much for his emotional needs, the young Benjamin turned logically to his older sister and was rewarded. In the closing paragraph of his last completed novel, *Endymion* (1881), the hero and his sister, Myra, meet alone in the room where they were raised. Myra tells him:

What I came for, was to see our old nursery, where we lived so long together, and so fondly! . . . All I have desired, all I have dreamed, have come to pass. Darling beloved of my soul, by all our sorrows, by all our joys, in this scene of our childhood and bygone days let me give you my last embrace.[9]

To interpret from this quote, however, that Sarah considered her role in her brother's life as simply that of sympathetic onlooker or that she possessed no aspirations of her own would be a mistake; her concern for him was motivated by more than a strong filial attachment. As a woman in nineteenth-century Britain, Sarah was destined to experience a life filled with many disappointments. Everyone who met her commented that she was highly intelligent and talented. Her father frequently employed her to sound out his latest literary theories and appointed her the guardian of his papers. As rewarding as these little pieces of societal recognition might be, over time they only served to make Sarah more conscious of the greater opportunities that were closed to her. No matter how intelligent she might be, a world that denied her the right to vote, to own property, to obtain a higher education, or to practice a profession would never permit her completely to take advantage of the abilities she was given. Though it is true that Mary Lamb and Dorothy Wordsworth were confronted with many of these same handicaps, their careers as writers, their involvement as active participants in an important literary movement, and most especially, their freedom from economic dependence on their parents allowed them to achieve a measure of autonomy that was denied most other women of the time. Although still subject to many social restrictions and emotional conflicts, their energetic lifestyles enabled them to be at least in some degree the arbiters of their own destinies. Confined instead to the home, Sarah was never in a position to play the role of famous hostess or social commentator; and her closeness to her father, while the source of great intellectual stimulation in childhood, became the primary obstacle to her independence as an adult. Living the circumscribed existence of a middle-class Victorian lady, Sarah's preoccupation with her brother and his career would become, as the years passed, a method of vicariously satisfying her own frustrated hopes and ambitions. She would live not merely for him, but through him. Benjamin was keenly aware of this. When he was named prime minister for the first time, in the spring of 1868, nine years after Sarah's death, Sir Philip Rose remarked to him nostalgically, "If only your sister had been alive to witness your triumph, what happiness it would have given her." "Ah Sa, poor Sa?" Her brother replied reflectively, "We've lost our audience."[10]

On 28 August 1817, during the same year the Lambs moved out of the Temple, Sarah and her eldest brother were baptized as members of the Church of England by the Rev. John Thimbleby, rector of St. Andrew's, Holborn.[11] This event, which took place in the same church where Mary Lamb had served as a bridesmaid for her friend Sarah Stoddart in 1810, when she married William Hazlitt, possessed historical significance that went unperceived at the time. Initially, it represented the culmination of Isaac's four-year dispute with the Sephardic synagogue of Bevis Marks. As the first member of his family to receive a western secular education and have a career that enabled him to assimilate into British gentile society, Isaac had become steadily estranged from his Jewish heritage. As a student, he early developed an admiration for Voltaire and the other thinkers of the Enlightenment, which quickly fostered in him a skepticism and distrust for organized religion. His success as a writer made him new friends like Lord Byron and Sir Walter Scott—people he considered far more interesting to be with and appreciative of his work than his East End relatives with their foreign accents and lack of schooling. Isaac also saw how Jews were excluded by law from Parliament, the civil service, and higher education, as well as by tradition from professions like medicine and the bar. He remembered that although Oxford was prepared to award him an honorary degree for his biography of Charles I, it would never have accepted him as a student. This ambivalence toward his heritage was eventually transformed into outright hostility. Jews, he declared, were bound to fallacious and counterproductive rituals "cutting them off from the great family of Mankind and perpetuating their sorrow and shame."[12]

For a long time Isaac kept his opinions to himself. Then in 1813, for reasons that are still not clear, he was appointed parnas of his family's synagogue—a position roughly equivalent to that of warden in an Anglican church. The Sephardic synagogue of Bevis Marks, just to the north of Duke's Place, Aldgate, was, and still remains, the oldest existing Jewish house of worship in Britain. The present Wren-style building was constructed between 1699 and 1701 as a replacement for an earlier building erected in the 1650s, soon after Oliver Cromwell invited the Jews to return to England after their more than three hundred-and-fifty-year exile. Normally, selection to such a leadership post in the community would have been considered a tremendous honor. Isaac, however, was not interested. He declined, explaining that his secular lifestyle and general indifference to Jewish traditions made him a poor choice for the position. During the nineteenth century, such an open expression of disloyalty to one's religious leaders was viewed as totally unacceptable. The rabbi and elders fined Isaac forty pounds (quite a large sum for the time). He refused to pay, declaring they had no legal jurisdiction over him. The dispute simmered on for several years without resolution, probably because Isaac did not wish to trouble his elderly and devout father. But finally, in 1816, after his father died, Isaac formally broke with the synagogue.

Originally, Isaac had no intention of having his children baptized; his dislike for one religion was not fostered by any particular admiration for another. Eventually, though, his friend and fellow researcher from the British Museum, Sharon Turner, a well-known scholar of Icelandic and Anglo-Saxon history, convinced Isaac that they must go through with the ritual. The gentile majority, Turner warned, would never fully accept his children—provide Sarah with a good husband and her brothers with profitable careers—unless they first made a public renunciation of Judaism. This was not an uncommon argument during the nineteenth century; it was also made to the fathers of Felix Mendelssohn, Karl Marx, Heinrich Heine, and the great Russian pianist, Anton Rubinstein—Klesmer, in George Eliot's *Daniel Deronda*. Isaac at last agreed. The fact that his two eldest children were baptized a month after the two younger boys, Ralph and James, has led some to believe that they must have resisted and finally had to be pressured into denying their ancient heritage. As appealing as this conjecture may be, no evidence exists to back it up. Perhaps Sarah and Benjamin were unwell or the rector was unavailable. The rabbi of Bevis Marks immediately declared that the baptisms were invalid, and to this day the synagogue has never officially accepted the Disraeli children's departure from the Jewish religion.

Their conversion to Christianity affected Isaac's children in different ways. At the time, the younger sons, Ralph and James, were eight and four. Since neither was to exhibit much curiosity about his Jewish ancestry in later years, they both were probably too young in 1817 to remember much about what they had lost. Their older brother, Benjamin, however, was twelve, clearly mature enough to understand the consequences of the act that had been performed on him. His later desire to reestablish the severed bond with his heritage would become one of the dominant features of his adult life, doing much to influence his literary career, his political aspirations, and even his foreign policy as prime minister. Sarah, who was fourteen, undoubtedly realized the significance of her baptism as well; yet her concern for her Jewishness was not to prove as visible a force in her life. From her letters, the reader gathers that she was not a terribly spiritual individual to begin with. At the same time, however, her letters also demonstrate that she was always very sympathetic to her eldest brother's metaphysical yearnings. He let the world understand how grateful he was for this special sensitivity; it would be to Sarah that Benjamin dedicated his 1833 novel about Jewish history, *The Wondrous Tale of Alroy*; and it would be a character modeled after Sarah who played a major part in Benjamin's proto-Zionist work, *Tancred* (1847).

In 1821, while Charles Lamb's *Elia* essays were appearing in the *London Magazine*, Sarah, now nineteen, became engaged to William Meredith, a student at Brasenose College, Oxford. One year older than she, he and his parents, who lived at Nottingham Place, within walking distance northeast of Bloomsbury, were long-time friends of the Disraeli family. A serious, academic-minded young man, everyone who met him predicted Meredith had a fine career ahead of him.

He was, in fact, to become a fellow of his college and a member of the Royal Academy before the age of thirty, one of the youngest men ever to attain such an honor. He appeared to be the perfect husband for his bookish future bride. Meredith was also a close companion of Benjamin. At the time of his sister's engagement, Benjamin and her fiancé were coauthoring a satiric blank-verse play set in sixteenth-century Oxford, *Rumpel Stilts Kin.* It was not a remarkable piece of writing, and only two copies survive. Yet as Benjamin's first sally into the literary profession, it was a harbinger of many things to come. Sarah was taking part in the project, too, providing the illustrations. While both Mary Lamb and Dorothy Wordsworth had rejected the possibility of matrimony, Sarah, for her part, thought differently. If the first two feared that marriage in the nineteenth century would inevitably render them, as women, subject to the arbitrary will of a domineering husband, Sarah was sure that her case would be otherwise. The proposal she had received came from an enlightened man whose feelings for her, she knew, were motivated purely by respect and affection.

Contrary to Sharon Turner's assurances, baptism did not provide the Disraeli children with automatic acceptance into the bosom of British gentile society. On being informed of Sarah's engagement, the Merediths' uncle, on whom the family was financially dependent, pronounced from his seat in Worcestershire that he would never condone a relative of his marrying a Jew, even a baptized one. His nephew could go forward with his plans if he were foolish enough, but he and his parents should then not anticipate any further monetary support. Defiance of the family patriarch would result in the end of William's promising career at Oxford. This declaration immediately brought Sarah's wedding preparations to a halt; she would not ask her fiancé to abandon his family and academic future for her. However, his uncle's threat did not make William sever his relationship with Sarah, as many expected. Rather, he reaffirmed his determination to marry her eventually. Certainly, he promised her, his uncle would relent in the end. After all, he had no other heirs. If he wished to continue the family line, he would eventually be forced to agree to their wedding. In the meantime, the two would stay close friends. Alas, this was all they were fated to be.

During the summer of 1824, while the outcome of the controversy was still uncertain, Isaac decided to lead Benjamin and William Meredith on an abbreviated version of the Grand Tour. For six weeks, the two young men were guided through the famous cities of Flanders, the Netherlands, and western Germany, being introduced to historical sites and works of art they had until now known about only from books. Sarah was left at home, an event that was to become all too common; Isaac wanted her to keep his papers in order. Benjamin must have sensed his sister's feeling of disappointment and wished to make up for it. From every city he traveled through, he wrote back long letters attempting to supply her with a very detailed and entertaining image of what Sarah was missing:

Benjamin Disraeli to Sarah Disraeli
August 2, 1824
(Ghent)

We arrived in Ghent after a pleasant passage of three hours at three. I was greatly surprised by the place which I had imagined would be Bruges on a larger scale. Its character however is perfectly different. There seems to be a great deal of business going on, or at least the numerous canals and the river Scheldt by which it is intersected, and which are tolerably well filled with shipping have that appearance. We of course visited Mr. Schamp's collection, the university, cathedral etc., and of course we always thought each thing more wonderful than the other. We were exceedingly delighted and tired to death. We left Ghent this morning after having attended a high mass in the cathedral.[13]

Benjamin Disraeli to Sarah Disraeli
August 14, 1824
(Cologne)

We are in a city in which there are so many churches to lionize, that I am afraid I shall never get out of it. . . . We found a collection of paintings etc., . . . and a most original possessor of them. He talked in a loud voice, and a most swaggering manner about himself and his wealth. He informed us that he had been a colonel of cavalry; and that he was the richest person in the world, and the possessor of the most rare curiosities. He opened a cameo of jewels and cameos . . . and exhibited a profusion of Van Dykes and Rubens.[14]

Benjamin Disraeli to Sarah Disraeli
August 23, 1824
(Heidelberg)

The opera is one of the best in Germany. We went on Thursday night to Cherubini's *Medea*. The house was crammed full. The boxes were private as in London, save two in the center for strangers. We were much amused. . . . The casino is: an institution similar to our crack London clubs, and not inferior to them in style and splendor. There we read all the English newspapers and billiardized.[15]

It would be interesting to know exactly what Sarah said to Benjamin about his letters when he returned to London in September. Although no record is available, she must have told her brother she was pleased. Benjamin's account to her of his 1824 continental tour was to mark the beginning of a correspondence he continued with his sister for thirty-five years. Initiated as a simple travel narrative, the letters were to expand into discussions of such wide-ranging topics as politics, literature, religion, and journalism. Most of the letters Sarah wrote in reply do not survive. Although fortunately not the case with Mary Lamb and Dorothy Wordsworth, it was common practice in Britain during the nineteenth century for families to destroy the personal papers of a recently deceased female relative, lest the revelation of their contents somehow injure her name. In Sarah's case, the deed was probably committed by her brother Ralph, who edited the first publications of Benjamin's letters. *Home Letters* (1881), for instance, that purports to contain Benjamin's correspondence with his sister during his voyage to the East from 1830 to 1831, actually contains only his missives. Those of Sarah's letters that did escape the flames, however, clearly demonstrate that she shared with Benjamin an equally profound interest in social, political, and cultural topics. Their correspondence, more than anything else, illustrates the depth of the friendship that existed between sister and brother.

In the spring of 1830, the Merediths' uncle displayed evidence of finally yielding. In what was to become a nineteenth-century British tradition, he wrote his nephew announcing that if William agreed to go on a trip for a year and returned still determined to marry Sarah, he would grant his consent to the match. William immediately took his uncle up on the challenge and decided to accompany Benjamin on the voyage he was preparing to make through the Mediterranean and the Middle East.

In 1830, Benjamin was recovering from a mysterious illness. For two years he had been plagued by violent headaches, a weakness in his limbs so severe it frequently left him bedridden, and even periods of blindness. The physical cause for this disorder has never been determined. It may instead have been mental in origin, perhaps a nervous breakdown brought on by the strain of his recent experiences as a journalist, writer, and speculator. In 1825, at the age of only twenty-one, Benjamin, already exhibiting the bold and persuasive personality that would later lead him to political power, had convinced the publisher John Murray to take him on as his junior partner in his attempt to challenge *The Times* as London's principle newspaper. *The Representative*, as Benjamin christened the new organ, proved a failure; unable to capture a significant readership, it folded after only six months of operation. Murray, whose poor management of the newspaper was chiefly responsible for the debacle, rashly and publicly cast the entire blame on his young colleague.

In the following year, 1826, Benjamin retaliated with his first novel, *Vivian Grey*. A social satire, it lampooned Murray as an incompetent buffoon with delusions of grandeur. *Vivian Grey* proved quite popular and greatly embarrassed the publisher. Though the book was printed anonymously, Murray eventually discovered the author's identity and openly attacked him in his other journals. At almost the same time, a South American gold-mining company in which Benjamin rashly had invested nearly all his savings, collapsed, leaving him several thousand pounds in debt and ushering in a lifelong struggle with creditors.

The unsettling experiences of Benjamin's introduction to the public arena, rather than any real medical condition, may very well have been the cause of his recent ailment. A great admirer of Byron, Benjamin remembered how, after suffering similar emotional trials in his youth, the immortal poet sought consolation in a voyage to the East. Benjamin had just completed his second full-length novel, *The Young Duke*; borrowing five hundred pounds from the publisher John Colbourn on the strength of the book's future sales, he set out on his odyssey aboard the Royal Steamer *HMS Shannon* from Falmouth on 28 May 1830, William accompanying him.

As the Merediths' uncle demanded, Sarah remained at home in London. However, this did not prevent her from keeping in continuous contact with the travelers by letter. Before departing, Benjamin supplied his sister with his itinerary and the locations of the various British naval bases and consulates to which she could direct her mail. Sarah wrote many letters to her brother, keeping him closely informed about all the latest events taking place back in England. When his ship arrived at Gibraltar, for instance, Benjamin found a missive announcing that the degenerate and reactionary old George IV had finally died. During his youth, as an ambitious Prince of Wales, he courted the supporters of suffrage reform, but once safely ensconced as Regent in 1810, he promptly betrayed his former allies and transferred his support to the most diehard opponents of political change. His replacement by his more malleable brother, the Duke of Clarence, now William IV, wrote Sarah, assured that some measure of reform would at last be instituted.

In another of Sarah's news bulletins, she reported the results of the general election that followed the new king's ascension, a contest that resulted in the victory of Lord Charles Grey and the Whigs returning to power for the first time in two generations. Sarah appears to have been conscious of Benjamin's political ambitions since at least as early as 1830. She looked forward to his success and hoped that these recent developments had brought this day closer. Therefore, while she enjoyed her brother's amusing descriptions of playing squash in the British naval officers' club on Malta and of his invitation to wild Turkish feasts in Albania and his accounts of the stunning sites of Greece, she at the same time worried that he was not conducting himself in the serious manner expected of a future member of the House of Commons. Writing to Benjamin in Corfu, she expressed her concerns for him in an admonishing, almost motherly fashion:

Sarah Disraeli to Benjamin Disraeli
December 4, 1830

You have been too gay and dissipated among your Maltese heroes and I flatter myself that a little hard biscuit and salt water and good naval discipline has superseded the vinous propensities of your friends. . . . Goodbye dear Ben. May God bless and preserve you for us and for the world.[16]

Yet not all Sarah's correspondence was so sober. Besides public affairs, she also kept Benjamin informed about literary events in Britain, especially the public response in early 1831 to his new novel, *The Young Duke*, another story of society and political intrigue:

Sarah Disraeli to Benjamin Disraeli
April 4, 1831

As for *The Young Duke*, it is excellent—most excellent. There is not a dull half-page, not a half-line. Your story is unparalleled, for though it ends in a marriage which one can tell without peeping it grows more exciting as it winds toward its close.[17]

"Wherever we go," Sarah wrote glowingly in another dispatch, "*The Young Duke* is before us, and its praises for ever resounding. The book is reviewed in all weekly and sunday papers—all with excessive praises."[18]

Just as he had vividly described for Sarah the great cities of northern Europe in 1824, so Benjamin in 1830 and 1831 painted for his homebound sister exciting pictures of the fabled sites of the Middle East:

Benjamin Disraeli to Sarah Disraeli
March 1831
(Jerusalem)

In the wild, strong ravines of these shaggy rocks, we were ascending the whole day; at length after crossing a vast hill, the Holy City . . . I was thunderstruck. I saw before me apparently a gorgeous city. Nothing can be conceived more wild and terrible and barren than the surrounding scenery; dark, strong and severe . . . the ground is thrown about in such undulations that the mind is full of the sublime. Except Athens, I never saw anything more essentially striking; no city except that, whose site was so preeminently impressive.[19]

Benjamin Disraeli to Sarah Disraeli
June 20, 1831
(Cairo)

The banks of the river studded with villages of mud, but all clustered in palm groves; beautiful moonlight on the Nile, incredibly charming, and the palms of the light really magical. Grand Cairo a large town of dingy houses of unbaked brick, looking terribly dilapidated, but swarming with population rich in costume. Visited the pyramids and ascended the Great one.[20]

Sarah was gladdened to once again receive such fascinating descriptions of countries she had never seen. "I cannot," she wrote back, "sufficiently recommend your letters. They are in every respect charming—very lively and witty, and full exactly of the stuff I want . . . you might rival Lady Mary [Wortley Montagu] herself."[21]

As the months of their separation increased, not all of Sarah's letters were so optimistic. Amid her preoccupation with Benjamin's political success and literary fame, she started to worry about his physical well-being; grave rumors were creeping back to her in London about the outbreak of a plague in the lands in which he and William were currently traveling. Setting aside her earlier interests, she wrote, "We should be more satisfied could we hear that you & William are well for in these days of universal plague we know not what we fear, and fancy all sorts of evils."[22]

Sarah's forbodings of coming disasters proved justified, but it was not her brother who would become their victim. Relations between the two sightseers had recently cooled. Greatly attracted to the powerful sexuality of the Islamic world—hidden behind latticed windows or long robes, but never far from sight—Benjamin, like Gustave Flaubert on a similar trip twenty years later, began to spend long periods of time during his party's journey through the Ottoman Empire in brothels. In later years, his political opponents would use his youthful activities in order to claim he had contracted venereal disease. The reserved and studious William became increasingly dissatisfied with his companion's adventures. Bitter arguments ensued. In the spring of 1831, while traveling through Syria, the two finally separated, Benjamin going on to Alexandria and Cairo alone. When William finally arrived in Egypt in June, he proceeded up the Nile with a different party. "Meredith now in Thebes," Benjamin wrote to Sarah. "I have no communication with him."[23] Not long after posting this letter, he received news that William had contracted a fever. The malady quickly revealed itself to be smallpox. He was rushed back to Alexandria, but in a land totally lacking in modern medical treatment, there was no hope for a recovery. After great suffering, William died on July 19. Ironically, at almost the same time back in England, his uncle, who had undergone a change of heart, was formally announcing his consent to his nephew's marriage with Sarah.

Despite their recent differences, Benjamin was sincerely saddened by the death of his long-time friend. But most of all, he thought of how Sarah would feel. He transmitted the news of the tragedy secretly to Isaac. "For your eyes alone," he wrote in bold letters on the top of his dispatch. For several days, Isaac held back the information; but, aware that Sarah was expecting William to return to England in only a few months time anyway, he knew his daughter could not be forever shielded from the terrible knowledge. She wept bitterly at the news. For ten years, she and her fiancé had been kept apart by the forces of prejudice; now, when their union seemed at last at hand, she discovered she would be separated from him forever, by death.

Benjamin wanted to console Sarah, but at first found it beyond his power. "I cannot trust myself to write to her," he confessed to William's sister Georgiana Meredith, while "her sweet and virtuous soul struggles under this overwhelming affliction."[24] Sir Philip Rose later described the profound emotions the future prime minister felt for his sister during this dark time for her: "I believe he never entirely got over his deep sense of suffering at the crushing disappointment of her early hopes, and, amid the many stirring incidents of his eventful life, the deathbed of Cairo was not seldom recalled."[25]

The death of William Meredith proved to be the pivotal event in Sarah's adult life. Twenty-eight years old and still not married, she was by the standards of the nineteenth century an "old maid." The perception that she was somehow damaged goods, combined with British society's general antipathy toward persons of Jewish ancestry, assured that she now had practically no hope of ever finding a husband. Without the monetary support marriage provided, Sarah would never be independent of her father. This sad milestone also proved to be critical in determining the breadth of Sarah's future relationship with her eldest brother. Her own feelings were clear; already her letters of 1830 and 1831 disclose the deep interest and concern she had for Benjamin's future. In them, she clearly reveals her hope to attain emotional and intellectual fulfillment through his political and literary successes.

Benjamin's own correspondence up to this time, however, was not yet as confidential and self-revealing. Until now, his letters to Sarah had been primarily amusing travel narratives. Since his earliest childhood, Benjamin had looked to his sister for companionship and understanding. He knew she loved him more than anyone else. Yet until the summer of 1831, he always regarded their intimacy as something that must at some time come to an end. Benjamin was mindful that he should not become too dependent upon her; eventually, Sarah would marry and be with him no longer. Now, with William's death, all that had changed. Aware that her fiancé's death meant that Sarah would be at his side forever, the dimensions of Benjamin's association with her, as the new tone of his letters demonstrates, became more comprehensive. He started to consider her not simply as an adoring sibling but as a trusted aide. The most important role Sarah was to perform in her brother's life had begun.

"Yes my beloved!" Benjamin finally wrote Sarah before leaving Egypt,

be my genius, my solace, my companion, my joy! We will never part, and if I cannot be to you all of our lost friend, at least we will feel that life can never be a blank while illumined by the pure and perfect love of a sister and brother.[26]

Chapter Six

Witness to History

Sarah remained in mourning for William Meredith for several months. After losing not only her one chance for romantic love but also her one prospect for a life in which she might gain fulfillment through her own actions, she at first showed little inclination to continue with her existence. Then, toward the end of the year, she abruptly cast off her sadness and with a new determination turned her attention again to the affairs of the world. She found renewed joy in the presence of her brother. She discovered that his voyage to the East had not only restored his physical health but also inspired in him a powerful urge to win a name for himself in history. Having visited the domains of ancient emperors, kings, and patriarchs, having contemplated their past glory, Benjamin became filled with the desire that his own name and deeds be equally remembered and honored by future generations. Would he achieve his fame in politics or literature or as the champion of a noble cause? At the moment, Benjamin was not sure. Sarah did not know either; but whichever it was, she would be there with him.

Throughout his journey, Sarah had kept Benjamin closely informed about domestic politics. His months in the East corresponded with the new Whig government's introduction of the Great Reform Bill. Although the first draft had been thrown out by the reactionary House of Lords, the public clamor for a major expansion of the right to vote had become so great by the winter of 1831 that many people feared a violent revolution if it was not granted soon. As he watched the stormy birth of a new age in British history, Benjamin decided that the time might now be propitious for a career in Parliament.

The Whigs and Tories who had controlled the Parliament Benjamin wished to enter since the Glorious Revolution of 1688 bore little resemblance to modern political parties. Rather, they were loose alliances of semi-independent factions. Responsible before 1832 to only four percent of the male population, neither group could honestly claim to speak for a nationwide following. Lacking a campaign treasury, a central party apparatus, and parliamentary whips, prime ministers and their counterparts in the opposition had only the force of their own personality to maintain the loyalty of their subordinates. Backbench insurrections were not infrequent, sometimes even succeeding in overthrowing the leadership. It would be as the spokesman for one such victorious rebellion in 1846 that Benjamin began his rise to power. Although the pre-Reform Bill Tories are generally regarded today as the defenders of the status quo and the Whigs as champions of some measure of social change, constant internal dissension prevented either body from developing into what would be seen now as a truly "conservative" or "liberal" party.

Benjamin looked upon both the Whigs and Tories with contempt. The former he saw as representing the interests of the ruthless new plutocracy spawned from the Industrial Revolution—the bankers and businessowners who gained their fortunes by exploiting the labor of the landless working class. The latter he dismissed as the self-consumed and prejudiced advocates of the propertied aristocracy, men devoted to maintaining social hierarchy and little else. Neither the Whigs nor the Tories, he argued to Sarah, displayed any concern for improving the lives of average British citizens. People of goodwill, Benjamin was convinced, must therefore look to a new party. He first came to this decision as a teenager while studying in Isaac's library after he left school, in 1819. He developed his ideas further over the next few years and first presented them to the public during his brief involvement with *The Representative* in 1825 and in his first novel, *Vivian Grey*, in 1826. To these political beliefs he added his romantic temperament, his innate desire to be a hero. Basically, Benjamin wished to create a popularly based and socially progressive conservative party. Founded on the principles of family, religion, civic responsibility, and intellectual tolerance, such a party, he was convinced, would be far more successful in establishing a truly just and united society than those dedicated merely to the interests of capitalists or landholders. Before he could realize this grand design, however, Benjamin understood he would need to acquire political influence, which could be obtained only by first winning the sponsorship of one of the two groups he so disliked and planned to eventually supplant. Many today may find some of his tactics hypocritical, but he felt they were necessary for an outsider like him to climb the greasy pole of British politics.

The late-twentieth-century reader might question why Sarah, who as a woman was naturally forbidden to vote, became as interested in politics as her brother. Even with her emotional concern for Benjamin's career, one may ask, why did she still not feel a degree of resentment, or at least apathy, toward the institutions that decided her future without requesting her consent? But it must be understood that during a period when the vast majority of men were equally excluded from the political system, female suffrage, for Sarah, was probably not yet a primary issue. It would not be until 1867, eight years after her death, that John Stuart Mill would propose the first bill in the House of Commons giving women the vote. She would not have viewed herself as singled out for discrimination. Also, witnessing how other disenfranchised groups like tradesmen, farmers, laborers, and shopkeepers actively involved themselves in the public arena, Sarah would not have considered her own inability to vote as grounds to refrain from having her voice heard. For most of Britain's population during the nineteenth century, whatever their sex, social and economic improvement was possible only through supporting others with more privileges than they.

Because party endorsements during the nineteenth century were obtained as much through social connections as through the ability to garner votes, Benjamin began his quest for office by first procuring access to the exclusive townhouses of Grosvenor Square. He achieved this through the help of his new friend, Edward Bulwer (later Lord Bulwer-Lytton), the historical novelist and author of such vastly popular books as *Rienzi*—later turned into an opera by Richard Wagner—and *The Last Days of Pompeii*, a book that even today still shapes the popular conception of ancient Rome. Although he enjoyed playing the dandy and social rebel (he had defied his mother's marriage plans for him and now lived openly with his scandalous Irish mistress), Bulwer was also a high luminary of élite society. As Whig MP for St. Ives, he used his connections to introduce the ambitious newcomer to his brother, Henry Bulwer, the ambassador to Paris, and to the powerful Whig foreign minister, Lord Palmerston. Besides these male notables, Bulwer also presented Benjamin to several prominent hostesses. As the unquestioned arbiters of taste, it was often they and not their husbands or lovers who possessed the keys to the political kingdom. Among these figures were Lady Marguerite Gardiner, Countess of Blessington, leader of the literary salon at Gore House; and the Hon. Mrs. Frederick Norton, mistress of the Whig Home secretary, Lord Melbourne. A third, a Tory hostess, was the Hon. Mrs. Wyndham Lewis, whom Benjamin first encountered while dining at Bulwer's home on 1 April 1832. He did not care much for her. "The little flirt and prattle" he reported to Sarah, would not let him alone all evening. She was: "indeed gifted with a vocabulary I should think unequaled and which I can convey no idea. She told me that she liked silent, melancholy men. I answered that I had no doubt of it."[27] He was later to confess that his initial opinion of the lady was made too hastily.

After evaluating his recent experiences, Benjamin decided that his best chance for success lay with the Tories. Demoralized by their defeat in the last general election and fearful of the consequences of coming reform, the Tories, he believed, would be more anxious to recruit new supporters than the victorious Whigs. To prove that a middle-class intellectual of Jewish ancestry could be trusted by the party of wine cellars and fox hunts, Benjamin understood he would temporarily have to champion some very reactionary policies. It was in an effort to do this that he wrote a booklet entitled *England and France: or, A Cure for Ministerial Gallomania.*

Based on purported French government documents, supplied to the author by an adventurer who went under the name of Moritz von Haber, *Gallomania* bitterly criticized the constitutional monarchy of King Louis Philippe, established after the July Revolution of 1830. It claimed that the modest suffrage extension passed under the new regime would inevitably propel the nation into violent class warfare and perhaps even another reign of terror. Clearly, Britain could look forward to the same catastrophe if she followed France's reformist example. As a warning, the work was dedicated to the Whig prime minister, Lord Grey.

The tenderhearted Sarah was extremely upset when her brother showed her the manuscript of *Gallomania*. Like him, she believed that only a new, socially progressive conservative party with a mass popular following could transform Industrial Revolution Britain into a peaceful and just society. She believed, too, that only Benjamin possessed the vision to be its creator and leader. But *Gallomania*, she feared, with its condemnation of all social and political reform threatened to jeopardize his chance of achieving this aim. Her brother's booklet might win the blessing of the entrenched aristocracy, but it would only alienate the disenfranchised members of the middle and lower classes—those upon whom Benjamin's success ultimately depended. If he really wished to attain respect and notoriety with his pen, Sarah insisted, Benjamin should stop wasting his talents with political tracts and write a comprehensive history of England. She knew he could do it, and she was ready to assist him with the research. "What do you think of Hallam announcing a History of British Literature," she prodded her brother in a letter. "It is announced in the gossip [section] of the last *Athenaeum*, but without any bookseller mentioned. If he be now only commencing, it will be sometime before he comes thundering upon us. . . ."[28] Benjamin told Sarah not to be worried; every new politician had to write a piece like *Gallomania*, it was a test of his mettle, a rite of passage. Besides, it was printed anonymously, and against the insistence of some Tory leaders he had refused to make his criticisms of the Whigs personal. Finally, once he had established himself, he would follow Sarah's advice and write something of which she would be proud.

Believing he had now demonstrated his loyalty, Benjamin waited with anticipation for a Tory seat to fall vacant. Under the prereform election rules, a candidate for Parliament had to be worth at least six hundred pounds to stand for a county seat, and three hundred for a borough seat. His unpaid bills still mounting—now not only from bad business investments but even more from stylish tailors—Benjamin lacked the required funds. But thanks to some of the Grosvenor Square ladies, he was able to borrow what he needed. Yet when an open seat did at last become available, in the borough of High Wycombe, in Buckinghamshire, during the spring of 1832, the Tories had still not given Benjamin their party's official endorsement. What was more, the open seat was situated not in a Tory stronghold, but rather in a county controlled by the Whigs. Benjamin pondered for a moment and then decided he could not let the opportunity pass him by. Whigs and Tories, Tories and Whigs—there was not really that much to distinguish between them anyway. His primary objective, after all, was to get elected.

High Wycombe, a prosperous garment and furniture manufacturing community of approximately six thousand, had the special advantage of also being his family's own parliamentary seat. In 1829, the Disraelis moved out of London and rented a large Tudor period country house near the village of Bradenham, within the jurisdiction of High Wycombe. Here, only a day's coach ride south of the capital, Isaac could fulfil his new yearning to be a country gentleman and still be close enough to his Bloomsbury friends to visit them when he wished. He also found it amusing that as resident of the Bradenham house, he, a Jew, had the privilege of selecting the village's Anglican curate. Benjamin hoped that his position as a local inhabitant would enhance his chances of victory.[29]

The Great Reform Bill would finally become law on 7 June 1832. Expanding the suffrage from four to thirty-three percent of the male population and opening the doors of Parliament to the middle class, it, more than any other single piece of legislation, inaugurated democracy in Britain. As its provisions were not to go into effect until the next general election however, the present contest at High Wycombe would still be fought under the old rules. According to them, suffrage was restricted to the members of the Corporation—in medieval times, the House of Burghers—a body made up of the community's forty most prosperous landholders and merchants. Proud, exclusive, and accustomed to getting its way, this élite was yet not blind to reality. It understood that recent events left it no choice but to accept the coming reform. This present by-election in fact became necessary when the Corporation forced the resignation of the standing Whig MP, Sir John Dashwood King, after he refused to vote for the suffrage extension. Rather than be represented by an old, discredited opponent of change, High Wycombe's élite was searching for someone who could operate successfully within the new political order and assure the Corporation's de facto dominance of the community even after it lost its monopoly over the vote. It was to this assembly that Benjamin came courting.

Sarah was less than sure of her brother's chances. *Gallomania* had just appeared and had received glowing compliments from antireformist circles. Its printing also coincided with the outbreak of rumors that the Whig government was going to be replaced, rumors that caused a brief panic on the London Exchange. Despite the fact that *Gallomania* was published anonymously, suspicion was rife in the area that Benjamin, already known to have significant Tory connections, was the author of this reactionary volume. If this were ever confirmed, Sarah was sure her brother would never win in the Whig Corporation:

Sarah Disraeli to Benjamin Disraeli
May 11 or 12, 1832
(Bradenham)

You can imagine the astonishment and consternation of old and young Wycombe. Screwing up their courage to the sticking point, some to have their throats cut, some to cut. Parker, as white as a sheet, says, "we have gone too far." Huffan [a local Whig militant] came over yesterday morning. I do not exactly know the purpose of his visit [,] whether to find out what you were going to do, or for us to convey to you his feelings. . . . He felt that you were going to betray him by proving yourself a Tory after he has for so many months sworn to all Wycombe that you were not one. . . . What will happen? I should be sorry to give up the plan of regenerating and turning them all unconsciously into Tories [conservatives].[30]

"I too, have read the *Gallomania*," she continued, "and I long to see you that you may read me many riddles. The principle one is, how you will reconcile your constituents to your politics."[31]

As it happened, no firm evidence of Benjamin's authorship was ever uncovered. Suspicion was even diverted in the direction of the Tory party leadership. "We are delighted," wrote Sarah, "that Croker[32] has seen the proofs, now no responsibility can be with you."[33] As the critical day approached, even though some members of the Corporation continued to have their doubts about Benjamin, it appeared as if the majority were prepared to vote for him. A new age, they reasoned, called for a new face. Benjamin had never expected his public career to move forward so quickly. If he was not going to transform the Tories into a new party, he would transform the Whigs.

Unfortunately, on the eve of the election, a new candidate, Col. Charles Grey, suddenly arrived. He was a poor public speaker and offered no innovative political ideas, but as the prime minister's son he could guarantee the Corporation a great deal more influence in London than could Benjamin. Also, no one suspected him of pamphleteering for the other party. When the ballots were cast on June 28, the result was Grey 23, Disraeli 12.[34]

Benjamin was disappointed, but he did not have long to wait to try again. Having passed suffrage reform, the Whig government called a new general election for December 17. Still waiting to obtain the Tories' public endorsement and having been defeated as a Whig, Benjamin ran this time as a Radical, or progressive independent. "I am neither a Whig nor a Tory," he declared to the crowd. "My politics can be described in one word, and that word is England."[35] With a broader electorate, he did much better. But it was not enough. Even after the new reform, suffrage was quite restricted; and the working class, to whom Benjamin's message was chiefly directed, was still unable to give him its help. In the following year, 1833, he stood unsuccessfully for High Wycombe yet a third time. Running for another open seat, at Marylebone, in London in 1834, Benjamin was rejected a fourth time. Concluding at last that he could never hope to win without party backing, he decided to renew his contacts with his acquaintances at Grosvenor Square.

Success in the political arena temporarily stalled, Benjamin turned his attention back to literature. He had, after all, promised Sarah when he completed *Gallomania* that his next effort would be on a respectable topic. In 1833, he published *The Wondrous Tale of Alroy*. Though it proved to be his least successful novel commercially, it was to be of great historical importance. "My works are the embodiment of my feelings," Benjamin wrote in his diary in 1833. "In *Vivian Grey* I portrayed my active and real ambition. In *Alroy*, my ideal ambition."[36] Not only did he wish his writing to bring him before the public eye, he also wanted it to win support for a noble cause.

Baptized as he had been near the age for his bar mitzvah, Benjamin had been old enough not to forget the faith into which he was born. But growing up in a household where interest in Judaism was constantly scorned, he was given no opportunity to examine it freely; he knew only that the other members of his community considered him an intruder. His travels to the East in 1830 and 1831 finally gave him a chance to investigate his background. Freed at last from the close intellectual supervision of his anti-religious father, Benjamin was fascinated by such great symbols of Jewish history and culture as Granada, Jerusalem, and Alexandria. He felt an instant attraction to the heritage from which he had been divided. He recorded his feelings in his next novel. *Alroy* tells the passionate story of a young Jewish leader who, for a brief time during the Middle Ages, is able to reestablish an independent state in Palestine. Though generally judged by critics as melodramatic, Benjamin's work must nonetheless be remembered today as one of the earliest testaments of modern Zionism.

Benjamin dedicated his novel to Sarah: "For all the beautiful impressions of love you have poured out to me."[37] Throughout his life, she had given him her emotional and intellectual support. It was time he formally thanked her.

"Sweet sister," the main character declares in *Alroy*,

as I wandered on the mountains of Zion, behold! a gazelle came bounding o'er the hills! It perceived me, it started back, it gazed at me with trembling surprise. Ah! fear not! fair creature, I fondly exclaimed, fear not, and flee not away! I too have a gazelle in a distant land; not less beautiful in her airy form, than thine, and her dark eyes not less tremulously bright.

Trust in a brother's love, the purest sympathy of our fallen state. "If I can recall the gleam to thy pensive cheek, not in vain I strike my lonely lyre, or throw these laurels at thy fair feet."[38]

Sarah was deeply moved. "My darling brother," she wrote upon reading these words,

what can I say for all the beautiful expressions of love you have poured out to me. I who am nothing, so utterly unworthy of belonging to you. Yet I am indeed proud of your love and tenderness, for which all mine is but a poor return.[39]

Alroy would be only the first instance in which Benjamin took up the cause of Jewish political emancipation and statehood with his pen. It would also be only the first time he associated Sarah with this crusade.

In order to be closer to the society figures who might assist him in capturing a seat in Parliament, Benjamin moved at the start of 1833 to London, renting a set of furnished rooms on Duke Street. In the autumn, however, he came back to Bradenham for a few months vacation. To help pass the time, he and Sarah decided to compose a piece of fiction together, she writing the first eighteen chapters and he the second. The pseudonyms sister and brother adopted—*Cherry* and *Fair Star*—were the names of the principal characters in a recently revived 1822 Covent Garden melodrama by John Fawcett, entitled *The Children of Cyprus*. No evidence exists however that either actually saw it.

"Our honeymoon being over," Cherry (Sarah) writes in the preface, "we have amused ourselves during the autumn by writing a novel. All we hope is that the public will deem our literary union as felicitous as we find our personal one."[40]

A Year at Hartlebury, which was published the following March, was basically a fictional account of the elections of 1832. The topography of the borough of Fanchester corresponds to that of High Wycombe; and the large country house, Bohun Hall, where much of the action takes place, is clearly Bradenham Manor. The book also contains some interesting revelations about Sarah's opinion of her brother and her views on politics.

The story begins on the eve of the general election made necessary by the passage of the Great Reform Bill, "that great and misconceived event," writes Sarah, "which already its enemies have ceased to dread, and its friends have begun to abuse."[41] Considering it in the light of her brother's recent setbacks and the fact that two-thirds of the male population still remained disenfranchised, Sarah now viewed the Reform Act not as a forward-looking piece of legislation but rather as a cynical effort to reinforce the established power structure—as a sop to progressives. Despite all the talk of change, fictional Fanchester, like historical High Wycombe, is still controlled by landed Tories of mediocre talent, and Whig "swindlers."[42]

Prospects for true political reform and an end to the old élite's continued domination are improved radically when the novel's hero suddenly returns from abroad and declares his candidacy. "Aubrey Bohun combined a fine political temperament," writes Sarah,

with a great love of action. That combination is rare. He was a man of genius. But with great powers he possessed what does not always fall to the lot of their possessors—a great destiny. . . . If a theory hitherto erroneous had induced him to waste his youth in what some woud style unprofitable and unsatisfactory pleasure . . . fortune was his lot in life, that at this moment with energy unsubdued though matured, a career was at his command in which he might redeem those years.[43]

While his ever-mounting debts, garish clothing, hypochondria, and blatant social climbing had convinced many who met him that Benjamin was nothing but a dandy and opportunist, Sarah never doubted that her brother was born to greatness. It was simply taking him longer than other such figures to prove it. Now, like Aubrey Bohun, he would make his qualities known.

The Whigs, the most powerful wing of the Fanchester oligarchy, instantly perceive the threat Bohun poses to their continued dominance and successfully engineer his defeat in the year's first election. Not discouraged, he decides to stand again, this time as an independent, forming a populist alliance with men of goodwill disaffected from both of the major parties. "Bohun—The Friend of People" is his battle cry.[44] Defying the odds, he wins by one vote and goes on to Parliament as a spokesman of reform.

After this rousing climax, the second half of *A Year at Hartlebury* mysteriously takes the reader off in a very different and disappointing direction. Bohun, "The Friend of the People," now reveals himself to be a cad. He becomes a seducer, a blackmailer, and a bigamist. In the end, he is stabbed to death while waiting for a secret rendezvous with a tavern keeper's wife. Apparently, by the end of 1833, Benjamin no longer had much time to devote to the joint project. He was now involved in London society again and was also busy composing a yet another pro-Tory political tract, *The Revolutionary Epick*. Wanting to complete *Hartlebury* quickly, he dashed off its conclusion without much thought as to how it would compare with the story's opening half.

Saunders and Otley, the firm that printed the book and actually selected the title, gave Benjamin an advance of ten pounds, all of which he passed on to Sarah. He was angered at the piddling amount, feeling it insulting to his sister. He demanded that it be doubled, and the publishers finally complied. But for Sarah, who was not planning to become a professional author, money was not an important issue. "I intended to write to you today," she related to Benjamin, "to assure you that one of the parties concerned would consider ten pounds an ample renumeration."[45] Being able to assist her brother in a literary enterprise and having her name remembered with his in one of the fields she was sure would gain Benjamin fame was quite enough reward for her. Unfortunately, Sarah's involvement in Benjamin's writing career would not be recognized until long after her death. In spite of generally favorable reviews, Saunders and Otley did not feel sales of *A Year at Hartlebury* were sufficient to warrant a second edition. It would not be until 1979 that the identities of *Cherry* and *Fair Star* were discovered.

As it turned out, Sarah did more than act simply as Benjamin's assistant; she also presented him with ideas he later introduced into his own works. In 1833, at the same time she was collaborating with her brother on *A Year at Hartlebury*, Sarah was also composing a piece of her own, a question-and-answer book on the Old Testament for Christian schoolchildren. Though never very religious, Sarah was nonetheless conscious of her Jewish heritage; she was angered at seeing it constantly demeaned and libeled by an ignorant gentile society, one whose only perception of Judaism came from bigoted popular stereotypes. As religious instruction played such a significant role in nineteenth-century British education, the best means of countering spiritual intolerance, Sarah believed, was in the schools. She therefore decided to write a book that would enable the members of Britain's younger generation to reject the prejudices implanted in them by their elders and to appreciate the great historical and cultural debt their society owed to its Jewish forebears. Benjamin was most impressed by what he called his sister's catechism. He wrote to the publishers, praising the author and her manuscript:

Benjamin Disraeli to Messrs. Rivington
June 20, 1833
(London)

[Clearly] the fair author shows that the New Testament is always first put into the hands of children, and that the difficulty of explaining many parts of this from their ignorance of preceding scriptures occasioned the present work, which has been found to produce the best effect. If it is learned while the children are reading the NT it will assist their comprehension by explaining the history of the peculiar people of God, and the connection of the prophesies from the time of Abraham to their completion in the coming of our savior.[46]

Unfortunately, the publishers were not interested. A pedagogical work on a nontraditional religious topic, written by an unknown female author, did not look to them like a major moneymaker. Sadly, Sarah put her work aside. Her brother, however, did not forget it. Sarah's endeavors to combat anti-Semitism by writing books promoting popular interest in Jewish history and culture were to play a large part in the creation of Benjamin's two most famous novels, *Coningsby* (1844) and *Tancred* (1847). They were to be the inspiration for his best-remembered fictional creation, the scholar and financier Sidonia.

In 1835, Benjamin stood for Parliament in the county of Taunton in Somersetshire and was defeated in this fifth attempt. But even though success continued to elude him, he was now convinced his fortune was about to improve. On this occasion, when he went to the hustings to concede he did so no longer as an outsider, but instead as an official party candidate.

A year earlier, thanks to the good offices of his friend and periodic lover, the hostess Lady Henrietta Sykes, Benjamin was introduced to the Tory leader Baron Lyndhurst. Son of the American colonial painter John Singleton Copley, Lyndhurst had served three times as lord chancellor and was a powerful figure in his party. Whatever he thought of Benjamin's Jewish background and his social climbing is not recorded. As an agnostic, notorious rake and progenitor of many famous scandals, he probably felt he was not in a position to make a judgment. What interested him was Benjamin's intelligence, charm, and determination to win. The Tories needed such people, he reasoned; they needed to be seen as more than merely the representatives of the high aristocracy. Lyndhurst's and his party's support came at a price, of course. Benjamin was required to cease all future communications with the Whigs, publish a long series of pro-Tory pamphlets, and publicly condemn the Irish nationalist leader Daniel O'Connell—someone with whom he had heretofore been prepared to ally himself. What he said to Sarah about these arrangements is not known. If he ever discussed them with her, he probably told her they were vulgar but necessary.

Once he was elected in the next contest, he could be his own man.

On 20 June 1837, William IV, the last in the long series of unpopular Hanoverian kings, died at Windsor Castle. As a show of favor, Lyndhurst, who was a member of the Royal Privy Council, invited Benjamin to accompany him to Kensington Palace that night to appear at the first meeting presided over by the King's successor, his seventeen-year-old niece, Victoria. Among the other attendants were Melbourne, now prime minister, the Duke of Wellington, Palmerston, Peel, and Russell. Benjamin was most impressed though by the little Queen; only five feet tall, barely more than a child, she already possessed the grace and presence of a true British monarch. "She read her address well," Benjamin wrote Sarah, "and was perfectly composed though alone in the council chamber and attended by no women."[47]

The accession of a new monarch was traditionally followed by the adjournment of Parliament and the holding of a general election. Now assured of the full backing of Lord Lyndhurst and the Tory party, Benjamin believed that victory, so long elusive, was at last within his grasp. Or was it? Even in the early nineteenth century, political campaigns were expensive. A candidate was expected to offer a free tumbler of rum to everyone who agreed to vote for him; he also needed to hire a brass band, a gang of toughs, and a crowd paid to cheer his speeches and jeer those of his opponents. Constantly pursued by creditors, Benjamin had no way of paying for these himself. He might have Tory sponsorship, but the party did not yet have a treasury to finance his efforts. Luckily, when Benjamin had almost despaired, an old acquaintance came to his assistance.

Mrs. Wyndham Lewis had not lost her attraction to the "silent, dark and melancholy" gentleman she first met at Edward Bulwer's house on 1 April 1832. It is also clear that despite the initial poor impression she had made, Benjamin had quickly revised his opinion of her. A letter survives that he sent her only four days later. Containing a few comments on Sir Walter Scott's novel *Robert of Paris*, it is signed with the name of one of the romantic characters, Raymond of Toulouse. "The first note I ever received from dear Dizzy,"[48] Mrs. Wyndham Lewis later wrote across the top. As the general election of 1837 approached, the two had been sending each other little communiqués periodically for five years. One Benjamin received was addressed to a "true knight." It was now high time that their discreet relationship be expanded. Benjamin contacted Mrs. Wyndham Lewis and asked if she could give him some assistance. She soon replied, saying that she had convinced her husband to take him on as his running mate in the two-seat borough of Maidstone in Kent.

Although he and Benjamin had never been introduced, Wyndham Lewis MP, a prosperous Welsh mineowner and regional Tory leader, had been hearing about him from his wife for many years. When the two men finally came face to face in early July, Lewis was satisfied these praises were based on fact. But there was not much time to waste; after a little socializing, the two candidates quickly departed to launch their campaign. Benjamin was supremely confident now. To his creed of family, religion, civic responsibility, and intellectual tolerance, he now added abolition of the 1834 Poor Law—that odious act, immortalized by Dickens, which condemned indigents to the workhouse. The proverbial cries of ''Shylock'' and ''Rag-Man'' that used to irritate him so, he now either ignored or answered with blithe contempt. Everyone who heard Benjamin at the hustings said he delivered the best address of his career. This time when the votes were counted, it was someone else who had to make the concession speech. With Isaac needing a proofreader for his new manuscript and her mother too ill at the moment to keep house, Sarah was unable to be present at her brother's triumph; but Benjamin made sure that she was the first to learn the glorious tidings:

Benjamin Disraeli to Sarah Disraeli
July 27, 1837
(Maidstone)

11 PM

Dearest,
Lewis 707, Disraeli 616, Thompson 412. The constituency is almost exhausted.
In haste,
Dizzy[49]

Writing that same night to her own brother, Major John Viney Evans, Mrs. Wyndham Lewis declared, ''Mark what I prophesy, Mr. Disraeli will in a very few years be one of the greatest men of his day.''[50]

Sarah was filled with happiness. The one for whom she was his ''solace,'' his ''Companion,'' and his ''Joy,'' was now about to step into history. Yet the pleasure she experienced on learning of Benjamin's victory was also to be a pleasure she would never quite experience again.

On 15 November 1837, Benjamin took his seat in Parliament. He found himself in a cramped and very crowded hall. Three years earlier, medieval Westminster Palace, the site of British government for centuries, the place that once resounded with the words of Sir Thomas More, Oliver Cromwell, Sir Robert Walpole, Charles James Fox, and the Pitts, burned to the ground. Sir Charles Barry's great neo-Gothic edifice would not be completed until 1860, and until that time the Commons were forced to double up with the Lords in the Court of Requests.

Just as he had earlier written to Sarah about the cities of northern Europe and described for her the marvels of the Middle East, so Benjamin now kept her closely informed about his political career:

Benjamin Disraeli to Sarah Disraeli
November 15, 1837

My Dearest, I took my seat this morning. I went down to the House with Wyndham at two, and found it very full, the members standing in groups and talking. About three, there was a cry of "order, order," and "all to their seats," (myself on the second bench behind Sir Robert Peel) and a messenger summons the Commons.[51]

On December 5, Benjamin was called upon to cast his first vote. For a man who would become so associated with the cause of Zionism, it was perhaps fitting that this vote should concern the Jew. Currently, only Anglicans, Roman Catholics, and members of major nonconformist denominations like Presbyterians were permitted to sit in Parliament. The Melbourne government now presented a bill expanding this list to include Moravians and Quakers. At the last moment, it also decided to include the Jews. As much as the author of *Alroy* would have liked to support the motion, Benjamin knew very well that in the social climate of 1837 there was absolutely no chance of its succeeding. Even if the bill somehow managed to get by the Commons, it would immediately be thrown out by the Lords. For Benjamin to remedy the situation, he would first need to gain influence; in order to do so, he had temporarily to follow his party line. He therefore opposed the bill. "Nobody looked at me," he wrote to Sarah, "and I was not in the least uncomfortable, but voted with the utmost sangfroid."[52] As he had expected, the bill was defeated. The vote was 172 to 156.[53]

Two days later, on December 7, Benjamin rose to deliver his maiden speech.[54] Such orations have commonly been regarded as a portent of the speaker's political future and, to produce the maximum effect, are often directed against an already-established figure. In this way, Lloyd George employed his first speech to criticize Joseph Chamberlain and was in turn the target of the opening remarks of Sir Winston Churchill and Aneurin Bevan. If there was any truth to this tradition, Benjamin's future looked very bleak indeed. He chose as the subject of his address the recent by-elections in Ireland and accused the Nationalist leader Daniel O'Connell of ballot-stuffing. It was a disaster. The speech was filled with melodramatic phrases, poetic quotes, and allusions to totally unrelated topics. The listeners immediately responded with a torrent of jeers, shouts, and lewd epithets, the most vicious coming from the Irish seats; even Benjamin's own colleagues could not restrain themselves from joining in. Despite his great embarrassment, however, Benjamin did not allow himself to be intimidated. He struggled on to complete his speech, closing with the prophetic words, "I sit down now, but the time will come when you shall hear me."[55]

Benjamin described the whole bitter episode to Sarah. Lest she be too upset, though, in the same letter he also included what happened to him next. On the following day, Edward Bulwer invited him to dinner at the Athenaeum Club and there introduced him to the Irish MP, Richard Sheil. The second-in-command to O'Connell, Sheil had been one of Benjamin's most violent tormentors. But now that the battle was over, he offered him some warm words of encouragement. As a noted orator himself, the Irishman told Benjamin that, in spite of that opening failure, he could tell that Benjamin actually had a great talent as a public speaker. The trouble with his recent oration lay not in its substance or delivery, but rather in its timing. "Put away your genius for a session," Sheil advised Benjamin. "Be dull."[56] If Benjamin really wanted respect from his audience, he should first establish himself in their eyes as an expert on weighty subjects—facts, figures, statistics. Concern for such items was nearly always seen by listeners as a sign of high intelligence. Once he achieved this, Benjamin could speak in as grandiose a manner as he wished. Following Sheil's suggestions, Benjamin dedicated his next speech to the revision of British copyright law and the following speech to the Corn Laws (not yet a controversial issue). Finally, after several more such learned discourses, he returned to the question of Ireland, speaking once again in his natural oratorical style. This time, the House did hear him.

Sarah learned the news from her younger brother, James, who was then visiting London:

Sarah Disraeli to Benjamin Disraeli
March 17, 1838
(Bradenham)

We were gratified for your long dispatch. Jem told us enough to make us desire to hear what you felt. Now that four hundred have heard you, I seem to care for nothing. It was James's debut in the House, so that we did not know how much to trust him. He describes the rush into the House as prodigious when you began to speak, and then the profound silence, and then all the cheers. He heard many people speak to you, rejoicing in your speech and your reception; and once before you spoke Castlereagh rushed in, saying "Has Disraeli been up?" It seemed by his account of all the sensation produced that you were quite as great a man at Westminster as at Aylesbury.[57]

Only a few days after Benjamin's first parliamentary triumph, an even more important event in his life occurred, an event that also profoundly influenced his relationship with Sarah. Wyndham Lewis, Benjamin's political mentor, suddenly suffered a fatal stroke. Reports had already been circulating that Lewis's wife and his political protégé were more than simply casual friends. To silence such rumors, Mrs. Wyndham Lewis went into mourning and told Benjamin that they must temporarily halt their private contacts. For several months, they observed a ceremonious distance from one another, meeting only when in the presence of other social acquaintances. By the autumn, however, they decided they had fulfilled all their societal obligations and could safely reinstitute their earlier intimacy. Benjamin promptly began to invite his friend for prolonged calls to the Disraeli family home at Bradenham.

The first extended contacts between the two most important women in Benjamin's life appear to have been amicable. In recounting her first visit to Bradenham in September 1838, Mrs. Wyndham Lewis told her brother Major Evans of her admiration for Sarah's intellectual gifts and her selfless devotion to her brother's career. For her part, Sarah found her new acquaintance a charming and entertaining lady. If Benjamin's relationship with her had not progressed beyond this point, the two women might have become good friends; but this was not to be.

By the time of Mrs. Wyndham Lewis's trip to Bradenham, Benjamin was clearly courting her. By the end of the year, many even spoke of the possibility of the two marrying. A brief crisis erupted when some of Mrs. Wyndham Lewis's older friends who were hostile to the match attempted to prevent it. In February 1839, they accused the debt-troubled Benjamin of being an adventurer who was actually only looking for a rich wife. Benjamin's vigorous denials, however, eventually won the day, and relations between the lovers were repaired. On 28 August 1839, they were married at St. George's Church, Hanover Square.[58] Lyndhurst was given the honor of being best man.

Neither Isaac or Maria was healthy enough to attend the ceremony. As their attendant, Sarah was compelled to remain at Bradenham as well. She dispatched Benjamin and his new wife a letter apologizing for her inability to come to the wedding and extending them her best wishes for the future. Behind this outward demonstration of goodwill, however, Sarah was deeply saddened. Into the happy and rewarding comradeship she possessed with her brother had now intruded a stranger, one who might very well destroy it.

Like Dorothy Wordsworth, Sarah never doubted her brother might marry someday. Like her, too, she did not at first believe marriage would threaten her special relationship with him. In nineteenth-century British society, after all, it was the duty of all eldest sons of the middle and upper classes to preserve the family name. At the end of 1838, Sarah had even gone so far as to prepare a list of potential spouses for Benjamin's consideration. Among them was Ellen Meredith, a sister of Sarah's own late fiancé. All the candidates were highly intelligent, sophisticated, and ladylike. As longtime intimates of Sarah, they were well aware of her feelings for her brother and, she believed, would offer no objection to her playing an equal role with them in caring for Benjamin and managing his glorious future. Benjamin's sudden decision to marry Mrs. Wyndham Lewis instead upset all these elaborate plans and filled Sarah with foreboding. Intriguing at first glance, yet shallow on closer examination, her sister-in-law was precisely the kind of woman Sarah was convinced Benjamin should avoid.

First, there was the matter of age. At forty-six, the new Mary Anne Disraeli was twelve years her husband's senior. Such a significant difference, Sarah feared, could only bode ill for a secure and rewarding partnership. Having already failed to bear any children during her twenty-four-year marriage with Wyndham Lewis, it was highly doubtful that she would produce an heir now. Second, with her lack of formal education and her constant preoccupation with parties, fashion, and society gossip, Mary Anne, Sarah was convinced, was incapable of ever becoming the intellectual helpmate Benjamin needed. Finally, as a famous political hostess, a woman accustomed to getting her own way in relationships, Mary Anne would be too proud ever to allow Sarah to maintain her close tie with Benjamin.

Sarah was too influenced by her emotions to render an accurate estimation of Mary Anne's character. Her sister-in-law was, in fact, no less devoted to Benjamin and concerned with his place in history than herself. While lacking Sarah's education and intellectual sophistication, Mary Anne nevertheless shared her shrewd, natural mental aptitude. A bond servant of fashion, a flirt, Mary Anne might be, but it was also she who had been one of Benjamin's earliest champions, discerning his genius when he was being scorned by Melbourne, Peel, and Palmerston. In the twenty-three years of their marriage, until Mary Anne's death from cancer in 1872, she would play an invaluable role as her husband's confidante, adviser, and protector, taking on duties and responsibilities that greatly aided his rise to power. "She was," Benjamin reminisced after her death, "the perfect wife." Having already demonstrated her devotion to her husband, Mary Anne bitterly resented Sarah's continued suspicions of her. She interpreted Sarah's present efforts to maintain her influence over Benjamin's affairs as an assault on her own rightful position as his wife.

Benjamin loved them both and refused to choose between them. With Sarah, he possessed a bond of emotional and intellectual solidarity dating back to childhood; with Mary Anne, he held a romantic attachment and a debt for much of his career. He tried to dispense his affection evenly. Alas, a conflict was inevitable. For the next twenty years, Sarah and Mary Anne would be locked in a bitter struggle for possession of the man they both so dearly loved. By 1845, Mary Anne would be banished from Bradenham, and Sarah would find the doors of her brother's London home at No. 93 Park Lane closed to her. When staying at one residence, Benjamin communicated with his wife or sister at the other only through the secret assistance of some third party. The emotional strain damaged the health of all involved. Soon, the members of the Disraeli family and all their friends were compelled to declare openly their loyalty to one or the other of Benjamin's two ladies. The battle only ended with Sarah's untimely death in 1859. Who was to blame for this tragic rift, Sarah or Mary Anne? Neither. Rather, it was the fault of a society that refused so many women the ability to attain mental and emotional satisfaction through their own achievements. Both highly intelligent, Sarah and Mary Anne were permitted to obtain fulfillment only through the parts they played in another man's life.

With Benjamin residing primarily in London with Mary Anne, there was now no excuse for Sarah not to devote more time than ever to assisting her father with his literary undertakings. With his eyesight quickly failing him, Isaac now depended on his daughter to be not simply his sounding board but also his editor, secretary, proofreader, and researcher—none of these tasks accompanied by any monetary reward. When his next collection of essays, *Amenities of Literature* was published in 1840, Isaac, perhaps with a slight feeling of guilt, decided to acknowledge publicly his obligation. "Amid this partial darkness," he wrote in the dedication,

I am not left without a distant hope of a present consolation; and to *Her* who has so often lent me the light of her eyes, the intelligence of her voice, and the careful work of her hand, the author must ever owe the "debt immense" of paternal gratitude.[59]

How much these words succeeded in lifting Sarah's spirits during the dark months after her brother's marriage is debatable. She always appreciated these periodic little recognitions of her services, but by 1840 she must have yearned for more in her existence. Now thirty-seven, having exceeded more than half the life expectancy for the majority of women during the mid-nineteenth century, Sarah had yet to make a name for herself, to win the respect of those outside a secluded circle of intimates. As a child she had studied the classics, modern languages, European literature, and world history and been praised for her accomplishments by such figures as Scott and Bentham. As an adult, however, she had been denied the freedom of movement and the peace of mind to make use of any of her gifts. The person chiefly responsible for this sad situation was of course her father, and no amount of book dedications could alter what he had done. By his constant demands for assistance and his refusal to give his daughter any degree of financial independence, he had reduced Sarah to the status of glorified nursemaid. All her attention was devoted to his advancement. While the prospect of being Isaac's protégée excited her as a child, by her middle age the role had become oppressive. Because so many of Sarah's letters were destroyed after her death, it is impossible to say for certain whether or not she ever voiced her feelings to others; yet, her brother appears to have clearly detected her despondency. As Benjamin had done so many times before, he tried to cheer his sister up by writing entertaining letters, supplying her first this time with information on the latest society scandals:

Benjamin Disraeli to Sarah Disraeli
August 21, 1840
London (Carlton Club)

Lord Walpole is the favorite against the field for Miss Burdett—but my theory is she will not marry—none of these heiress ever have—to wit: Baroness Wenman, Baroness Bassett, Miss Lawrence, Miss Tylney are our exceptions. I do not think of encouraging any one. "The cool of the evening," as Sydney Smith has dubbed Monckton Milnes, is however full of confidence.[60]

Benjamin Disraeli to Sarah Disraeli
September 18, 1840
(London)

I write merely to say I am alive. Nothing can be more dead than London [in the summer]—and nothing but Walpole and his hopes and fears keeps us alive. I cannot myself entertain a doubt he will be successful. Miss Coutts is out of town but only on the border of the Thames near Kensington. The comedy is most amusing and better than any Spanish play I know—but Walpole is really in love—at least he says so.[61]

As always, Sarah found her brother's social adventures amusing, but his political career remained her greatest concern. To his light, chatty letters, she replied with detailed reports about Benjamin's constituency—providing him with accounts of the local voters' reactions to the positions he had taken in Parliament and offering him suggestions for how he could best address their concerns. In the following year, 1841, Melbourne's Whig government fell and a new general election was called. When Benjamin was first elected to Parliament from Maidstone in 1837, he had been so upon the coattails of Wyndham Lewis. Now that he was making a reputation for himself, he wished to run for a seat where he could stand on the strength of his own name. For a moment, he contemplated making yet another try for High Wycombe, but Sarah convinced him that after three defeats any real chance of success there was gone. He reluctantly agreed; following some negotiations with local leaders, he was selected to represent his party at Shrewsbury in Somersetshire.

Sarah involved herself deeply in the contest, not simply supplying advice by letter, as in the past, but now performing her part in the field as a campaign worker. Observing that the constituency included a large population of newly enfranchised Nonconformists—non-Anglican Protestants—she personally contacted several of the most prominent and influential Methodist parsons and persuaded them to endorse her brother. She also mailed out dozens of requests for support to the county's industrialists and landowners. While all bearing Benjamin's name, these early examples of direct-mail electioneering were actually written by his sister. Among other issues, the leaflets proclaimed the candidate's (and Sarah's own) strong support for domestic agriculture, full employment, and local control of education and reasserted his long opposition to the 1834 Poor Law. Reflecting on his victory in a letter to his mother, Benjamin wrote that Sarah's efforts in his behalf had been "a very great service indeed."[62] Faced with her continued inability to establish a life of her own, emotional and intellectual accomplishment remained attainable for Sarah only through helping her brother.

Nationally, Peel and the Tories captured a majority of some ninety-three seats; as a rising new talent, Benjamin looked forward confidently to being picked for a place in the new cabinet. In September, Peel announced his selections: Lord Aberdeen was named foreign minister; Henry Goulbourn received the Exchequer; Lord Lyndhurst returned once more as chancellor; Sir James Graham was chosen for the Home Office; Lord Stanley got the colonies; the Duke of Wellington entered as minister without portfolio. Lord Ripon was made president of the Board of Trade, and the thirty-two-year-old William Ewart Gladstone attained his first cabinet level appointment as Vice President. As for Disraeli, no room was available.

Although several days behind, Sarah followed developments in London as closely as she could in her Bradenham newspaper. In one of her infrequent letters to Mary Anne, she tried to remain optimistic: "I suffer much for you and Dis' disappointment but we must not despair. After all, it is not half so bad as losing an election. We have, I hope, a long future before us, and changes may occur every day." But as days passed and the shape of the new government became clearer to her, Sarah's evaluation of the situation was less enthusiastic: "Our *Examiner* has missed this morning, so that we do not know the latest appointments; but up to the latest, except for Gladstone, there is not one single untitled or unaristocratic individual."[63]

Peel's rejection is traditionally attributed to the prime minister's prudishness and cultural snobbery. As a "Gentleman Jew," a lady's man, and a social climber, Benjamin, so the argument goes, was viewed as unfit to be in the company of the staid, pheasant-shooting, Public School Tory leadership. While these factors certainly played some part in Peel's decision, the full explanation is more complicated. Benjamin, Peel and his allies reasoned, could not be trusted. A critic of the class system since the time of *Vivian Grey*, an advocate of mass participatory democracy since his earliest days in active politics at High Wycombe, Benjamin could never be depended upon as a champion of the party of the landlords and peers. It was well known by now that *Gallomania* and the other right-wing pamphlets he had written at Lyndhurst's request were no more than cynical efforts to ingratiate himself with party leaders; they were merely a disguise for their author's real beliefs. Rather than a sincere Tory, he was the party's enemy within.

Benjamin's detractors were largely correct, of course. It had always been his ultimate objective to overthrow them and to reconstruct the party according to his own guidelines. But instead of beating it back, his enemies' action only served to precipitate this final confrontation. Originally, Benjamin did not intend to make his challenge to the current leadership until he had first penetrated its ranks. But with his plans discovered and Peel appearing after the general election of 1841 firmly in command of the party for many years to come, Benjamin believed he had no alternative but to launch his attack now, and to do so from the outside.

If the Tory party, Benjamin declared, continued on its present course of advancing only the interests of the landed aristocracy and the great industrialists, it was heading for inevitable extinction. Before 1832, when all governmental power was monopolized by the richest four percent of the male population, this exclusivist strategy was viable. But given the great political and social transformations now underway—suffrage extension, the spread of education, the growth of urban employment, and so on—this policy was now obsolete. The Whigs, their leadership no less elitist than that of their rivals, already understood this, and were currently making great efforts to expand their voting base. To assure his party's success in this new democratic century, Benjamin called upon the Tories to form an alliance with the working class. Nothing could be more natural, he argued. One, the symbol of Parliament, Oxford, and the Church of

England; the other, exemplifying the industrious farmer, the diligent craftsman, the unsung hero of the Empire; together, they represented all that made the nation great. "A union between the Conservative Party and the radical masses," he wrote Sarah, "offers the only means by which we can preserve the Empire. . . . Their interests are identical; united they form the nation; and their division has only permitted a miserable minority, under the precious name of the people, to spoil all the rights of property and person."[64] Along with fellow reformist MPs, Lord John Manners, Sir George Smythe, and Alexander Baillie-Cochrane, Benjamin founded a group called *Young England*; its object was to win the Tory rank and file over to Benjamin's beliefs and eventually to challenge Peel for mastery of the party.

The most famous and most effective illustration of Benjamin's political and social beliefs is found in the trilogy of novels he wrote during this period. The first, *Coningsby—or The New Generation* (1844), is perhaps the best known today. Setting his story in the late 1820s and early 1830s, on the eve of the Great Reform Bill, the author employed the novel form to rally the British public's support for his reformist program. Through the adventures of the youthful and idealistic nobleman Harry Coningsby and his like-minded friends (all modeled on the members of *Young England*), the reader is introduced to the principles of government job creation and business regulation, a socially conscious Church of England, and the establishment of multiclass political parties. These doctrines, says the author, will assure that the "the character of England should be an assemblage of great qualities."[65] The book was Benjamin's first great popular success; with sales eventually amounting to over fifty thousand copies, with translations in French and German, it was by the standards of the nineteenth century a massive best-seller. *Coningsby* remains in print today. "I stop one minute," Sarah wrote her brother ecstatically from Bradenham, "to tell you that we are fascinated and delighted beyond expression. . . . Papa says the man who has made the finest speech of the session has written the best book that ever was written."[66]

Benjamin told her about the equally enthusiastic reaction of London society:

Lord Ponsonby is so "enchanted with [the character] Sidonia" that we are to dine together at the Lionels (Rothschilds) on Sunday. . . . Twice on our way to Longmann's in Paternoster Row we were congratulated. Once by [the famous socialite] Tom Jones, who almost embraced M.A.; which she returned though she denied it. He (Jones) was not surprised to find in Paternoster Row "the most successful author of the day."[67]

Coningsby soon started to appear in bookstores in the United States, where it outdistanced the sales of such popular British writers as Alfred, Lord Tennyson and John Henry Newman. "The fame of 'D'" and "the influence of Young England," Sarah proclaimed, "is all powerful."[68]

Sybil—or The Two Nations (1845), the second segment of the trilogy, was also a best-seller and also remains in print. It continues Benjamin's plea for a

Tory-worker alliance, this time through the romantic story of a Chartist's daughter who falls in love with the son of a peer. The popularity of his books convinced Benjamin that there was a sizable constituency for the political ideas they advocated.

The years during which he wrote his trilogy also correspond to the period of Benjamin's apotheosis as Britain's greatest spokesman for Jewish political emancipation. Unlike his first literary venture in the cause, *The Wondrous Tale of Alroy* (1833), his present works were set in contemporary times and, rather than simply sentimental tales, were direct attempts to influence the politics of his day. Whereas the Jewish hero of the earlier novel is a purely fictional creation, the brilliant and mysterious Sidonia of *Coningsby* and the final part of the trilogy, *Tancred* (1847), would have been easily recognizable to the reader of the time as a combination of the author and his friend, the great financier Baron Lionel Nathan de Rothschild. By portraying Jewish society in as realistic a way as possible, by demonstrating its contributions to British gentile society, the author hoped to gather popular support for Jewish aspirations. His strategy owed much to his sister. It was Sarah, after all, who first had expounded this approach to the issue in her abortive school textbook in 1833. Benjamin praised her theory at the time, and he showed his debt to her again by giving a character modeled on Sarah an important role in the final part of his new work.

The primary Jewish character in Benjamin's trilogy, the principal figure through whom he speaks, is Sidonia, Harry Coningsby's most respected adviser. An academic, diplomat, international financier, and philosopher, a speaker of all languages, living and dead, he may appear rather melodramatic to today's reader. But for a British reading audience accustomed to Jewish characters only as ragmen, usurers, and obsequious innkeepers, this completely new type of individual would have been impressive, someone whose beliefs warranted respect. Sidonia's description of his ancestry serves as a means of informing readers about the *Talmud* and the *Kaballah*, as well as the many other important contributions Jews made to ancient, medieval, and Renaissance culture. A discussion between Harry and Sidonia on contemporary affairs is used to draw readers' attention to the influence Jews currently exercise in theater, poetry, and music. Finally, Sidonia declares that Judaism with its principles of intellectual achievement, duty to the community, and social activism is the manifestation of what he describes as multiclass Tory democracy! How many converts to the cause of Jewish political emancipation these arguments won is hard to say. Probably not a great many. But that in the end was not important. The great commercial success of Benjamin's novel assured that the issue would now be a permanent part of public debate. It could never be ignored again. On reading *Coningsby*, Sarah must have reflected back on her baptism in 1817. She and her brother had never actually forsaken their heritage, she was now told. The one they transferred their allegiance to that day, the Church of England—that symbol of British historical and cultural tradition—was simply another form of their own.

One of the great intellectual questions of the nineteenth century was, how could the Church of England be reformed? Despite its mediocre leadership, slavish attachment to outmoded doctrine, and failure to involve itself in current political and social issues, many people, including Benjamin, believed the institution had the potential to be a great power for social progress. Just as *Coningsby* had been written to enlighten its gentile audience about the history of the Jews and to demonstrate their culture's important influence on modern British politics, so *Tancred—or The New Crusade*, Benjamin's favorite novel, was designed to show its Christian readers how their somnolent national church could reestablish its moral authority and recover its intellectual vigor by recognizing its historic roots. In the story, the idealistic Tancred de Montacute is filled with a deep spiritual yearning, but he discovers that the Church of England and the "mitred nullities" who govern it lack the ability to resolve the questions that trouble him. At the suggestion of Sidonia, he goes to seek the answers in the Middle East. What these answers are, the author never really makes clear; but Tancred's adventures—among them his visit to a monastery that performs its services in Hebrew—allow him to present his case that Christianity is an outgrowth of Judaism. He uses them as evidence that respect for Judaism and adoption of many of its ancient religious practices and communitarian social beliefs offers the only effective means of reviving the Anglican church.

Benjamin dedicated *Tancred* to Sarah. He also portrayed her in it as one of the novel's most vivid characters, Eva, the Maiden of Bethany. Adopting the same stimulating manner as his sister, the author makes Eva speak to us, not in vague symbolic terms, but plainly and directly. Benjamin gives her the honor of delivering his book's most famous condemnation of anti-Semitism and its boldest interpretation of Christianity's debt to Judaism. "Pray," Eva (Sarah) inquires of Tancred on their first meeting, "are you of those Franks who worship a Jewess; or of those others who revile her, break her images, and blaspheme her pictures?"[69] To the hero's assertion that Christ was born to expiate man's sins, Eva (Sarah) declares boldly, "Suppose the Jews had not prevailed with the Romans to crucify Jesus, what would have become of the Atonement?" To his assertion that the Crucifixion was preordained, Eva (Sarah) retorts:

Ah! Pre-ordained by the Creator of the world for countless ages! Where then was the inexpiatable crime of those who fulfilled the beneficent intention? The holy race supplied the victim and the emulators. Persecute us! Why if you believe what you profess you should kneel to us. You raise statues to the hero who saves the country, we have saved the human race, and you persecute us for doing it.[70]

An intelligent and talented woman destined by her society to an existence of dignified obscurity, Sarah must have gained great happiness and satisfaction upon seeing Benjamin choose her again, in his writings, as the representative to the world of his great ideas.

Unfortunately, *Tancred* was fated to appear almost simultaneously with

Charlotte Brontë's *Jane Eyre*. Although political novels like Benjamin's trilogy had long been fashionable, by 1847 the reading public was clearly in search of a more emotionally satisfying style of literature. Forced to compete with the romantic saga of the orphaned governess and the stormy Mr. Rochester, *Tancred* had nowhere near the same commercial success as Benjamin's previous two novels, selling at most only half as many copies as *Coningsby* and *Sybil*. This, however, did not diminish the novel's historical importance. No author in the nineteenth century had ever gone so far to enunciate Christianity's debt to Judaism and to demand it make a recompense. Through his writings, Benjamin did much to create the intellectual and political climate necessary for the British power structure's eventual acceptance of the principles of Theodor Herzl's *Der Judenstaat*.

The conclusion of Benjamin's literary trilogy coincided with the defeat of the Tory government and the final breakup of the original eighteenth-century conservative parliamentary alliance over the contentious issue of free trade. At this moment, Benjamin made the strategic decision to champion the minority, anti-Peel, anti-Gladstone Protectionist faction. The great landed aristocrats who made up this group certainly had no liking for the upstart "Gentleman Jew." Yet at the same time they had to admit that none of their own number came anywhere near him in ability. Reluctantly, they appointed him their leader in the House of Commons and their public spokesman. The rise of the living Sidonia to the top of the "greasy pole" of nineteenth-century British politics had now begun.

The publication of the final segment of Benjamin's trilogy also coincided with the dissolution of Sarah's little world at Bradenham. On 12 April 1847, her mother died.[71] Miriam was seventy-one. She had exhibited no recent symptoms of poor health and appears to have died of a sudden and unexpected stroke or heart attack. Sarah cannot have felt much sorrow. Ever the diligent homemaker, her mother demonstrated no more interest in her daughter as an adult than she had as a child. Sarah evidently did not believe Benjamin would be very upset either. She did not bother to deliver the news to him for several weeks. When she finally did inform him, however, she was able to add to the message that one of their mother's last statements was a belated approval of Benjamin's career. "Mama," she wrote him, "at last confesses that she never before thought Dis was equal to Mr. Pitt."[72]

Isaac survived his wife by only eight months. Now completely blind and unable to devote his time to any intellectual pursuits, he declined rapidly. Soon after the new year, he contracted influenza and died, on 19 January 1848.[73] Although he remained a fervent opponent of organized religion to the end of his life, no nondenominational cemeteries existed at this time, and there was no option but to bury him next to his wife in the nearby Anglican churchyard. There is no written record of how Sarah reacted to her father's death, but she must have been saddened. Isaac had been a difficult father—demanding of his daughter's time and energy, parsimonious in his displays of affection. Yet despite how much he exploited her for his own purposes, he was the first to recognize and nurture Sarah's intellectual abilities.

Isaac left his children an estate of approximately eleven thousand pounds—not a fortune, but a very respectable sum at a time when a servant could expect to earn an annual salary of no more than thirty pounds. Sarah and Benjamin were each bequeathed a third, and their younger brothers, James and Ralph, a sixth.[74] What remained went to the family's aged servant, Tita—Lord Byron's former valet—whom Benjamin had first employed during his trip to the Continent with William Meredith in 1824. Benjamin also received his father's twenty-five-thousand-book library. Many of these volumes, ironically on Jewish subjects—among them a medieval Spanish edition of *The Song of Solomon* in Ladino, Menasseh Ben Israel's 1699 *The Term of Life* in Hebrew, and the 1771 *Transactions of the Parisian Sanhedrin*—were quite valuable; and Benjamin had them transported to Hughenden Hall, where he and Mary Anne now lived, several miles away. The remainder were auctioned off in London at Sotheby's and fetched about four hundred pounds.

Sarah was prepared to stay on at Bradenham, at last the mistress of her own home. Unfortunately, the lease on the property expired with Isaac's death, and she had to go elsewhere. Benjamin would have invited her to live with him, but Sarah's difficult relations with Mary Anne made this impossible. Ralph was living a lighthearted bachelor's life in London and was not anxious to put his sister up; and James, a proverbial malcontent, was never pleasant company. Sarah therefore moved briefly to Hastings, before finally settling alone into a suite of furnished rooms at No. 3 Ailsa Park Villas, Twickenham. Now a part of the Greater London metropolitan area, it was then a quiet semirural village. Formerly the dwelling place of Alexander Pope, it was also situated not far from Horace Walpole's Strawberry Hill, the most famous example of British neo-Gothic architecture. Once adjusted to her new surroundings, Sarah undertook the task of editing a new, posthumous edition of Isaac's most popular work, *Curiosities of Literature*, which appeared in 1849. In this, the siblings' final literary co-project, Benjamin wrote the book's introduction.

Whatever her own place of residence, Benjamin's political career remained, as always, his sister's primary concern. After her work on their father's book was completed, Sarah decided to renew the job she had performed in 1841 as her brother's local political agent. In this capacity, she undertook a tour of the constituencies in and around the Worcestershire area, despatching Benjamin detailed reports on how the regional notables answered her many enquiries about his actions in Parliament. Since the battle over the abrogation of the Corn Laws in 1845-46, consumer prices had proven to be a powerful political issue. Sarah was keenly aware of this fact. Along with her reports on the opinions of the county gentry, she sent her brother equally detailed records of the rise and fall of the area's food prices. Wheat, oats, barley, beef, pork, potatoes—no product escaped her attention; it can only be imagined how many long hours of investigation this took her. In the present age, she reasoned correctly, a change in the value of such commodities might have as much influence on the outcome of the next general election as the passage of a long sought-after piece of legislation in Parliament.

On 20 February 1852, Lord Russell's Whig government was defeated. The Queen called upon the gouty Edward Stanley, fourteenth Earl of Derby, the leader of the Protectionist Tories in the House of Lords, to form a minority coalition. Derby was one of those High Tory peers most responsible for keeping Benjamin out of Peel's cabinet in 1841. "If that scum has any part in it," he is reputed to have warned Peel, "I resign." Eleven years later, however, with most of his former colleagues in opposition, Derby believed he now had no alternative but to appoint that same "scum" as his Chancellor of the Exchequer.

Sarah, now fifty, was overjoyed upon hearing the news. In only five years, Benjamin had risen from scorned backbencher to the position of second highest-leader in the land; now he would finally be appreciated for the brilliant qualities his sister had perceived first, so long ago. Sarah was also amused at the level of prestige and influence she personally had suddenly acquired among the citizens of Twickenham:

Sarah Disraeli to Mrs. Benjamin Disraeli
February 26, 1852
(Twickenham)

I had to grant perpetual audiences yesterday to people who wanted something. First came my little postman to ask me to put him on the town district; he did not ask me for my interest, but requested at once to transfer him. I noticed he spoke with a very tremulous voice, which impressed me strongly with a sense of my extraordinary power. Then came a friend of mine who wanted the Chancellor of the Exchequer to read a pamphlet he had written on the currency. Then a letter from a lady who wants a place for her husband.

Tell dear Dis I left the Board of the Inland Revenue in a state of great flutter; all speculating on the new master. Mr. Pressly, one of the mainstays—Dis knows him—and heard that he had grown much of late.[75]

Benjamin's main responsibility in his new office was to present a budget. Given the condition of his personal finances, many of his colleagues suspected he was not up to the task. Yet when it came to public funds, Benjamin proved quite imaginative. His most important act was to convince his associates to abandon the issue that had brought them to office. "One thing is certain," Sarah had advised her brother in 1851, during her journey through Worcestershire, "and this is that whomever puts himself at this moment courageously at the head of the Protectionists must be PM two years hence."[76] Benjamin was not so confident. Contrary to dire predictions, consumer prices had declined, not risen, after the abrogation of the Corn Laws; and increased foreign trade had helped to strengthen, not to weaken, the British economy. If the Protectionists now went forward with their pledge to restore high tariffs, Benjamin warned, they would be interpreted as the enemies of the working man, and be doomed to perpetual minority status. Protectionism, he declared, was not only dead, it was damned! Reluctantly, Derby and the others consented, but on condition they did not have to make a public renunciation of their previous stand. This was a historic moment, one that Benjamin had looked forward to since his days as an adolescent reading in his father's library. By at last persuading the High Tories to relinquish voluntarily their traditional opposition to free trade, Benjamin had made the first move in transforming them from an elitist eighteenth-century landowners' league into a modern conservative party that spoke for the interests of all the classes.

Unfortunately, the time was not yet ripe for Benjamin to witness the full realization of his ambition. The rise to power in France of Napoleon III sparked off a war scare in Britain, and the Derby Coalition felt pressured to raise defense spending, especially to strengthen fortifications along the Channel. To find the needed revenue after he had already promised to continue free trade and to lower the sales tax, Benjamin was obliged to add to his budget proposal an increase in property assessments. This recommendation was greeted immediately with intense opposition in the House of Commons. Despite Benjamin's strong speech in support of his policy, his coalition simply did not command the necessary votes to pass it, and the budget was defeated. The next morning the cabinet resigned, and the Queen sent for Lord Aberdeen, leader of the other segment of the fractured Tories, to form a new coalition with the Whigs.[77] Benjamin went back into opposition, disappointed but not discouraged; the skill he had shown as a member of a beleaguered minority government, convinced him that in a more favorable political climate he would clearly be able to make the nation finally accept his ideas.

The year 1852 represented a crucial turning point in Sarah's life. While it brought her great pleasure as the period in which her brother first ascended to cabinet office, it also marked the beginning of the end of the most intimate part of their relationship. Now that Benjamin was firmly established as a national figure—a major power in the House of Commons, as well as Chancellor of the Exchequer for a second time in 1858-59—he had progressively less time to correspond with his foremost admirer and supporter. Instead of long discussions about parliamentary colleagues and national issues, his letters to his sister became shorter and were more often restricted to amusing society anecdotes. Benjamin's new status in the public arena also obliged him to serve as the host of a growing number of banquets, both in London and at Hughenden Hall. Among the guests were many of the most important figures in the land, not only politicians but also novelists, poets, painters, and academics. However, in spite of her occasional letters to Mary Anne, Sarah's relations with her sister-in-law remained embittered, and she was never invited to any of these functions. Only once, in 1853, did the Benjamin Disraelis come together to see Sarah at her home at Twickenham. When she was visiting relatives during the holiday season, Sarah now stayed with Ralph or James. What her reaction was to this new state of affairs is difficult to say, as no written comments by her on the subject have survived. Probably, she reluctantly agreed that, with all Benjamin's new responsibilities, a decline in their intimacy was inevitable. After all, she may have reasoned, this might be the price she had to pay for his acquiring the greatness she always wanted for him. Sarah's willingness in 1853 to serve as editor of the first complete collection of Benjamin's writings certainly does not testify to any loss of affection or admiration for him. Of one volume of this work, Benjamin's biography of his late political ally, *Lord George Bentinck*, Sarah remarked that never before was "a memorial so exalting" ever "raised by the hand of friendship."[78]

Unlike so many Victorian men and women who constantly filled their letters and journals with detailed reports on their aches and pains, Sarah seldom, if ever, mentioned the subject of her health in her correspondence. As a result, historians can only speculate as to what caused the steady physical decline that set in upon her suddenly at the beginning of the spring of 1859. As both of her parents also experienced a similar rapid deterioration in health before falling victim to an apparent stroke or heart attack, Sarah probably suffered from the same affliction. The unusually hot and humid weather of that summer bothered her a great deal, making her very weak and leading her to cancel a trip she had planned to London. The cooler temperature of the autumn brought no improvement in her condition. When she visited her brother at Hughenden Hall in September, Benjamin described her as being extremely "delicate." She did not leave Twickenham again, and as winter approached it became clear to her family that she was dying. At the beginning of December, she suffered what was most likely a stroke and became semiparalyzed. On December 12, the day Benjamin wrote his mournful letter to the Marchioness of Londonderry, Sarah was on her deathbed. She died five days later, on December 17. She was fifty-seven.

Benjamin was grief-stricken; unlike Charles Lamb and William Wordsworth, each of whom died before his sister, he was left behind to feel the pain of her loss. As his primary adviser, companion, and comforter, as the maternal figure who was ever ready to offer him an unconditional and unquestioning love, Sarah was viewed by her brother as much more than simply another mortal human being. "She was the harbor of refuge in all the storms of my life," he wrote Ralph mournfully, "& I hoped she would have closed my eyes."[79] Fate, however, had determined otherwise. While he was to go on to greatness, to serve two terms as prime minister and to become the very manifestation of the nineteenth-century *Pax Britannica*, Benjamin would never find anyone to replace Sarah in his affections. He met many fascinating women over these years, but in none could he find Sarah's same gentle and idealistic spirit. He would never again possess a soulmate. "You know the blessing of a sister," he once reflected to his cabinet colleague Lord John Manners. "Alas! Mine was an only one—my first and ever faithful friend."[80]

Yet Sarah was meant to be more than her brother's "faithful friend," more than "the angelic spirit of the family." Her life was not simply one of tarnished hopes but also a tragedy characteristic of so many intelligent women in nineteenth-century British society. With her chance for a marriage of love and partnership lost by the early death of William Meredith, with her continued financial dependence on a dominating father, and with her lack of a constructive outlet for her abilities, Sarah could obtain fulfillment only vicariously, through her brother. Benjamin's political and literary triumphs brought her much of the emotional and intellectual satisfaction she sought. But inevitably, the higher he rose, the more these same achievements isolated her from him, leaving Sarah in the end as only a distant spectator.

Through their success in winning a measure of equality within a male-dominated society and their attainment of a renown that made them more than simply famous men's female siblings, Mary Lamb and Dorothy Wordsworth are usually considered today as much more important figures than Sarah Disraeli. But her life, even with its many bitter disappointments, possesses a special historical significance all its own. It is perhaps the finest and most eloquent memorial to that far greater proportion of British women, with talents equal to those of the Hostess of the Middle Temple and the Lady of Grasmere, who unlike them were never allowed to flourish and whose gifts will probably never be remembered.

NOTES: PART THREE

1. Benjamin Disraeli, *Letters from Benjamin Disraeli to Frances Anne, Marchioness of Londonderry* (London: Macmillan, 1938), 164.

2. J. F. Monypenny and G. E. Buckle, *The Life of Benjamin Disraeli* (London: Macmillan, 1910-20), vol. 1, 22.

3. George Gordon, Lord Byron, *Byron: A Self-Portrait*, ed. Peter Quennell (Oxford: Oxford University Press, 1990), 702.

4. Monypenny and Buckle, *Life of Disraeli*, 18.

5. Wilfred Meynell, *Benjamin Disraeli—An Unconventional Biography* (London: Hutchinson, 1903), 211.

6. Benjamin Disraeli, *Contarini Fleming* (London: Murray, 1832), ch. 2.

7. Ibid., ch. 1.

8. Monypenny and Buckle, *Life of Disraeli*, 76.

9. Benjamin Disraeli, *Endymion* (London: Murray, 1881), ch. 101

10. Monypenny and Buckle, *Life of Disraeli*, 180.

11. Ibid., 23.

12. J. A. Froude, *Lord Beaconsfield* (London: Sampson Low, 1890), 13.

13. Benjamin Disraeli, *Letters*, eds. J .A .W. Gunn, J. Matthewson, D. M. Shurman, and M. G. Wiebe (Toronto: University of Toronto Press, 1982-93), vol. 1, 11-12.

14. Ibid.

15. Ibid., 15.

16. Robert Blake, *Disraeli's Grand Tour* (New York: Oxford, 1982), 121.

17. Monypenny and Buckle, *Life of Disraeli*, 133-34.

18. Ibid.

19. Disraeli, *Letters*, 186-87.

20. Benjamin Disraeli, *Home Letters*, ed. Ralph Disraeli (London: Murray, 1881), 132-33.

21. Disraeli, *Letters*, 196. Mary Wortley Montagu (1689-1762), noted letter-writer, diarist, patron of the arts, and travel writer. Sarah was probably thinking of Lady Montagu's famous journey in 1718, when she went alone to Constantinople and visited the Sultan's harem.

22. Stanley Weintraub, *Disraeli—A Biography* (New York: Dutton, 1993), 111.

23. Disraeli, *Home Letters*, 123-24.

24. Monypenny and Buckle, *Life of Disraeli*, 179.

25. Ibid., 179-80.

26. Disraeli, *Letters*, 201.

27. Ibid., 187.

28. Disraeli, *Letters*, vol. 2, 128. Henry Hallam (1777-1859), journalist and scholar, best known today for his pro-Whig accounts of British history. He did not in fact complete the work of which Sarah had just learned.

29. In Great Britain, members of Parliament are not required to live in their constituencies.

30. Disraeli, *Letters*, vol. 1, 188.

31. Monypenny and Buckle, *Life of Disraeli*, vol. 1, 210-11.

32. John Wilson Croker (1780-1857), journalist, historian, and reactionary Tory leader. A strong opponent of all suffrage reform, he is perhaps best remembered today as the author of the *Quarterly Review* article attacking Keats's *Endymion* (1818).

33. Disraeli, *Letters*, vol. 1, 255.

34. Ibid., 291.

35. Monypenny and Buckle, *Life of Disraeli*, vol. 1, 218.

36. Disraeli, *Letters*, vol. 1, 447.

37. Weintraub, *Disraeli*, 143.

38. Disraeli, *Letters*, vol. 1, 339.

39. Ibid.

40. Benjamin and Sarah Disraeli, *A Year at Hartlebury* (Toronto: University of Toronto, 1979), Preface.

41. Ibid., ch. 14.

42. Ibid., ch. 2.

43. Ibid., ch. 14.

44. Ibid.

45. Ibid., Appendix 1.

46. Disraeli, *Letters*, vol. 1, 365.

47. Disraeli, *Letters*, vol. 2, 272.

48. Disraeli, *Letters*, vol. 1, 258.

49. André Maurois, *Disraeli, A Picture of the Victorian Age* (New York: Appleton, 1928), 113.

50. Ibid., 111. In the general election, the Whigs held on to power, although with a reduced majority.

51. Disraeli, *Letters*, vol. 2, 312.

52. Ibid., 227.

53. Ibid., 324.

54. *Hansard's Parliamentary Debates*, 39, 1837, cols. 802-07.

55. Ibid.

56. Disraeli, *Letters*, vol. 2, 330.

57. Monypenny and Buckle, *Life of Disraeli*, vol. 2, 32.

58. St. George's, Hanover Square, constructed between 1713 and 1724, has been the scene of several fashionable and historical weddings. Besides that of the Disraelis in 1839, it was also the site of the weddings of Sir William Hamilton and Emma Hart in 1791; Percy Bysshe Shelley and Harriet Westbrook in 1814 (confirming an earlier Scottish one in 1811); Theodore Roosevelt and Edith Carow in 1886; and Herbert Asquith and Margaret "Margot" Tennant in 1894.

59. Meynell, *Benjamin Disraeli*, 213.

60. Disraeli, *Letters*, vol. 3, 290.

61. Ibid., 295.

62. Ibid., 346.

63. Monypenny and Buckle, *Life of Disraeli*, vol. 2, 122.

64. Disraeli, *Letters*, vol. 2, 272.

65. Benjamin Disraeli, *Coningsby* (London: Colburn, 1844) Book, 4, ch. 13.

66. Monypenny and Buckle, *Life of Disraeli*, vol. 2, 318.

67. Ibid., 225.

68. Disraeli, *Letters*, vol. 4, 197.

69. Benjamin Disraeli, (London: Colburn, 1847), *Tancred*, Book 3, ch. 14.

70. Ibid., Book 3, ch. 7.

71. Monypenny and Buckle, *Life of Disraeli*, vol. 3, 142.

72. Ibid.

73. Ibid., 145.

74. James Ogden, *Isaac d'Israeli* (Oxford: Clarendon Press, 1969), 189.

75. Monypenny and Buckle, *Life of Disraeli*, vol. 3, 347.

76. Ibid., 210-11.

77. Still much attached to fine clothing, Benjamin refused to hand over the Chancellor of the Exchequer's traditional robes of state to his successor, Gladstone—yet another example of the two men's long emotional, as well as political, rivalry. The garments can still be found today at Hughenden Hall.

78. Ibid., 330.

79. Weintraub, *Disraeli*, 301.

80. Monypenny and Buckle, *Life of Disraeli*, vol. 4, 268.

Selected Bibliography

LITERARY WORKS

Disraeli, Benjamin. *Bradenham Edition of Novels and Tales*, Edited by Philip
 Guedalla, 12 vols. New York: Alfred A. Knopf, 1926-27.
Disraeli, Benjamin and Sarah. *A Year at Hartlebury*, Edited by J. Matthews, Toronto:
 University of Toronto Press, 1983.
Lamb, Charles. *The Life, Letters, and Writings of Charles Lamb*, Edited by Percy
 Fitzgerald. Vol. 1. London: Constable, 1875.
———. *The Essays of Elia*, Edited by E. V. Lucas, London: Methuen,1902.
Lamb, Charles and Mary. *The Works of Charles and Mary Lamb*, Edited by E. V.
 Lucas, 5 vols. London: Methuen, 1904.
Wordsworth, Dorothy. *Journals of Dorothy Wordsworth*, Edited by Ernest de
 Selincourt, 2 vols. New York: Macmillan, 1941.
———. *Dorothy Wordsworth—Selections from the Journals*, Edited by Paul Hamilton,
 New York: New York University Press, 1992.
Wordsworth, William. *The Poetical Works of William Wordsworth*, Edited by Ernest
 de Selincourt and Helen Darbishire, 5 vols. Oxford: Clarendon, 1940-49.

LETTERS

Byron, George Gordon, Lord. *Byron: A Self-Portrait*, Edited by Peter Quennell,
 Oxford: Oxford University Press, 1990.
Coleridge, Samuel Taylor. *Collected Letters of Samuel Taylor Coleridge*, Edited by
 Leslie Griggs, 5 vols. Oxford: Clarendon, 1956.
Disraeli, Benjamin. *Home Letters*, Edited by Ralph Disraeli, London: Murray, 1885.
———. *Letters*, Edited by J. A. W. Gunn, J. Matthewson, M. M. Shurman, and M. G.
 Wiebe, 5 vols. Toronto: Toronto University Press, 1982-92.

————. *Letters from Benjamin Disraeli to Frances Anne, Marchioness of Londonderry*, London: Macmillan, 1938.

Lamb, Charles and Mary. *The Complete Letters of Charles and Mary Lamb*, Edited by E. V. Lucas, 3 vols. London: Methuen, 1935.

————.*The Letters of Charles and Lamb*, Edited by Edwin Marrs, Jr. 3 vols. Ithaca: Cornell, 1978.

Shelley, Mary Wollstonecraft. *The Letters of Mary Wollstonecraft Shelley*, Edited by B. Barrett, Vol. 1, Baltimore: Johns Hopkins University Press, 1980.

Wordsworth, John. *The Letters of John Wordsworth*, Edited by Carl H. Ketchum, Ithaca: Cornell University Press, 1969.

Wordsworth, Mary. *The Letters of Mary Wordsworth*, Edited by Mary E. Burton, Oxford: Clarendon, 1958.

Wordsworth, William and Dorothy. *The Letters of William and Dorothy Wordsworth*, 2nd ed. Edited by Ernest de Selincourt, 7 vols, Oxford: Clarendon, 1967-88.

MEMOIRS

Cornwall, Barry (Bryan Waller Procter). *Charles Lamb: A Memoir* London: Moxon, 1876.

De Quincey, Thomas. *Recollections of the Lakes and the Lake Poets*, Edited by David Wright, Harmondsworth: Penguin, 1970.

Robinson, Henry Crabb. *Diary, Reminiscences, and Correspondence of Henry Crabb Robinson*, Edited by T.S. Sadler, 3 vols. London: Macmillan, 1872.

Talfourd, Sir Thomas Noon. *Memoirs of Charles Lamb*, London: Gibbings, 1892.

Wordsworth, William. *Memoirs*, 2 vols. Boston: Ticknor, Reed, and Fields, 1851.

NEWSPAPERS AND PERIODICALS

Blackwood's Magazine
Friend, The
Hansard's Parliamentary Debates
Lady's British Magazine
London Morning Chronicle

SECONDARY SOURCES

Aaron, Jane. *A Double Singleness*, Oxford: Clarendon, 1991.

Ainger, Alfred. *Charles Lamb*, New York: Harpers, 1902.

Anthony, Katherine. *The Lambs, A Story of Pre-Victorian England*, New York: Alfred. A. Knopf, 1945.

Beatty, Frederika. *William Wordsworth of Dove Cottage*, New York: Bookman Associates, 1964.

Blake, Robert. *Disraeli*, London: St. Martin's Press, 1966.

————. *Disraeli's Grand Tour*, New York: Oxford, 1982.

Blunden, Edmund. *Charles Lamb and His Contemporaries*, Cambridge: Cambridge University Press, 1933.

Courtney, Winifred F. *Young Charles Lamb*, New York: New York University Press, 1982.

Elwin, Malcolm. *Landor*, London: MacDonald, 1958.

Froude, J. A. *Lord Beaconsfield*, London: Sampson Low, 1890.

Hazlitt, William Carew. *The Lambs*, London: Matthews, 1897.

Heath, William, *Wordsworth and Coleridge—A Study of Their Literary Relations in 1801-02*, Oxford: Clarendon, 1970.

Hine, Reginald L. *Charles Lamb and His Hertfordshire*, New York: Dent, 1949.

Holmes, Richard. *Coleridge—Early Visions*, New York: Viking, 1990.

Howe, Will D. *Charles Lamb and His Friends*, Indianapolis: Bobbs-Merrill, 1944.

Jerman, Bernard. *The Young Disraeli*, Princeton: Princeton University Press, 1960.

Lucas, E. V. *The Life of Chrles Lamb*, 2 vols. New York: Putnam's, 1905.

Maurois, André. *Disraeli, A Portrait of the Victorian Age*, New York: Appleton, 1928.

Meynell, Wilfrid. *Benjamin Disraeli—An Unconventional Biography*, London: Hutchinson, 1903.

Monypenny, J. F. and Buckle, G. E. *The Life of Benjamin Disraeli*, 6 vols. London: Macmillan, 1910-20.

Moorman, Mary. *William Wordsworth*, 2 vols. Oxford: Clarendon, 1966.

Ogden, James. *Isaac d'Israeli*, Oxford: Clarendon Press, 1969.

Ross, Ernest C. *The Ordeal of Bridget Elia*, Norman: University of Oklahoma Press, 1940.

Selincourt, Ernest de. *Dorothy Wordsworth*, Oxford: Clarendon, 1965.

Woolf, Virginia. *A Room of One's Own*, London: Hogarth Press, 1929.

Index

About the Author

MICHAEL POLOWETZKY was born in London and currently lives in New York. His most recent book, *Jerusalem Recovered* (Praeger, 1995), analyzes the role of British Victorian intellectuals in the creation of modern Zionism.

ISBN 0-275-95716-0

HARDCOVER BAR CODE